VOTE FIRST OR DIE

The New Hampshire Primary:
America's Discerning, Magnificent, *and*
Absurd Road *to the* White House

SCOTT CONROY

PublicAffairs
New York

Copyright © 2017 by Scott Conroy
Published by PublicAffairs™, an imprint of Perseus Books, LLC,
a subsidiary of Hachette Book Group, Inc.
All rights reserved.

Printed in the United States of America.

PublicAffairs books are available at special discounts for bulk purchases in
the U.S. by corporations, institutions, and other organizations. For more
information, please contact the Special Markets Department at Perseus
Books, 2300 Chestnut Street, Suite 200, Philadelphia, PA 19103, call
(800) 810-4145, ext. 5000, or e-mail special.markets@perseusbooks.com.

Book Design by Jack Lenzo

Library of Congress Cataloging-in-Publication Data
Names: Conroy, Scott, author.
Title: Vote first or die : the New Hampshire primary : America's discerning,
    magnificent, and absurd road to the White House / Scott Conroy.
Description: 1 | New York : PublicAffairs, 2017. | Includes bibliographical refer-
    ences and index.
Identifiers: LCCN 2016046367 (print) | LCCN 2016054865 (ebook) | ISBN
    9781610395816 (hardback) | ISBN 9781610395823 (ebook)
Subjects: LCSH: Primaries—New Hampshire. | BISAC: POLITICAL
    SCIENCE / Political Process / Elections. | HISTORY / United States /
    State & Local / New England (CT, MA, ME, NH, RI, VT). |
    POLITICAL SCIENCE / Civics & Citizenship.
Classification: LCC JK2075.N42 C66 2017 (print) | LCC JK2075.N42 (ebook) |
    DDC 324.2742/0154—dc23
LC record available at https://lccn.loc.gov/2016046367

First Edition
10 9 8 7 6 5 4 3 2 1

For my wife, Jo, who made New Hampshire important

CONTENTS

CHAPTER 1

A S A POLITICAL REPORTER who abhors the cynical nature of modern presidential campaigns, I've at times considered a career change. Maybe I'd find myself surrounded by less duplicitous characters, I've sometimes thought, if I joined the bank-robbing trade. Or perhaps I could work in a more civilized environment, if I were to become a poisonous-snake wrangler. So why then did I decide to immerse myself even further in the largely distasteful world of presidential politics by writing a book about it in the summer of 2014? In short, it's because I've long thought of New Hampshire as a small but essential island of virtue and discernment adrift in the vast sea of contemptibility that consumes our public life every four years.

The inaugural New Hampshire presidential primary took place in 1916, and the state has held the nation's first such contest every four years since 1920. But that historically singular role is only part of the reason that New Hampshire is special. New Hampshirites engage in politics with the all-encompassing zeal that residents of other states dedicate to football or church. One reason for this passion is that a tremendously high percentage of New Hampshire's citizens are themselves elected officials. Composed of 424 members, the General Court of New Hampshire is the largest state legislature in the country. With about 3,000 New Hampshire residents for every legislator, the equivalent level of participation in California would require a statehouse of 12,780 lawmakers in Sacramento. New Hampshire legislators are paid a hundred bucks a year and receive no perks of any apparent psychological or material value. Suffice it to say, they don't do it for the recognition. And when presidential primary season rolls around, the grip that the campaign maintains over this tiny state is impossible to escape, even for those who might prefer to do so. The people of New Hampshire know how important their votes are, and they act accordingly.

But isn't it that way in Iowa, too? Why not write about the Hawkeye State—the real kickoff to the presidential election? Since 1972, the Iowa caucuses have been first on the calendar, beating New Hampshire to the punch every time. Without Iowa, there would have been no President Barack Obama, and the state has its own quirky political culture—one that's well worth exploring. On a personal level, I love Iowa. The Iowa State Fair is perhaps the only place on earth where fried butter on a stick is considered a reasonable lunch option, and if the people there were any nicer, you'd wonder if the tap water was laced with ecstasy. But as far as the political culture goes, Iowa is just not the same as New Hampshire.

There's a reason New Hampshire tends to garner equal time, more or less, from the candidates and the media in the lead-up to the voting every four years, even though the nation's first primary falls *after* the Iowa caucuses. The perception, earned over many decades, is that New Hampshire is the sober adult in the room left to clean up the mess that the unruly children of Iowa often make. Although it's an oversimplification, like many stereotypes this one is founded in some truth. For one thing, the process in Iowa is intentionally exclusive, as the caucuses can take a couple of hours out of a voter's day. The process in Iowa is also far more susceptible to shenanigans. In

2012, I sat inside a Republican caucus site outside of Des Moines and watched a little old lady shuffle from caucus-goer to caucus-goer, collecting crinkled up pieces of scrap paper and dropping them into a bucket. These were what passed for secure ballots, and though I didn't see her lose any of them, it didn't strike me as a particularly error-proof method of conducting a presidential election. And if you care at all about the sanctity of the secret ballot, you don't even want to hear about how the Iowa Democrats do it. Participants in the Democratic caucuses have to announce their votes publicly by standing in a designated area where they try to cajole supporters of other candidates to join them. Then, caucus-goers whose preferred candidate doesn't receive at least 15 percent of their precinct's vote are shit out of luck—barred entirely from having their support for their candidate of choice recorded. Once that little bit of disenfranchisement is complete, the backers of the candidates who did meet the so-called viability threshold resume their temporary roles of unscrupulous flea-market vendors, trying to convince the loser-backers to come over to their side. It's madness. Compelling madness for political reporters, no doubt, but madness nonetheless.

New Hampshire conducts its primary in a more straightforward way: campaigns cut a check to the state for a thousand bucks and then Democrats vote in one primary, Republicans in another, and independents can choose to participate in either one. The polls close, the votes are tallied, and the results are announced. It's a streamlined process that makes sense. The difference between New Hampshire and Iowa is like the difference between an Olympic wrestling match and a World Wrestling Entertainment fight.

In 2016, more than 358,000 people participated in the Iowa caucuses, including a record-shattering 186,932 Republicans. But amid this unusually robust turnout, that still meant that only about 17 percent of Iowa's more than 2 million registered voters bothered to show up on Caucus Day. In New Hampshire, by contrast, 542,433 people cast ballots in the 2016 primary—the highest number ever, and an overall turnout rate of 52.4 percent of its voting-eligible population. No other state saw a majority of qualified voters participate in its primary or caucus in 2016, with the average turnout around the country at about 30 percent. Yet again, New Hampshire's level of participation was higher than in any other state, all without such conveniences as early voting or vote-by-mail that residents elsewhere enjoy.

There's an earnestness that permeates the political culture in New Hampshire that is unlike what exists in Iowa or, for that matter, in South Carolina or Nevada—the other so-called carve-out states whose residents get to vote for president before anyone else, according to the rules of the Republican National Committee (RNC) and the Democratic National Committee (DNC). All of the carve-out states employ a permanent class of "operatives" from both parties, who do their best business in the run-up to each presidential year. The result is a nice little racket, in which a few people who are widely deemed to possess valuable local political knowledge make a whole lot of money. But in New Hampshire, it's a racket with a soul. Sure, there are some Granite State grifters who pose as knowledgeable consultants but are just looking for an opportunity to buy a summer home, thanks to the generosity of candidates who overestimate their value. But the good ones tend to lend their services to the person they think would be the best president, rather than the one they can most easily play for a sucker.

In 1988, New Hampshire governor John H. Sununu summed up the pervading attitude in the Granite State, which has since proven inaccurate several times over: "The people of Iowa pick corn; the people of New Hampshire pick presidents." That was indeed true between 1952 and 1988—a period when no one was elected president without first winning the New Hampshire primary. But even though every president elected since then had *lost* the New Hampshire primary on the way to winning the White House, New Hampshire's singular mystique largely remained intact when I set out to write this book. The New Hampshire primary has long epitomized how presidential elections *should* work—local, immersive, and discerning. Throughout its history, no other state has provided the level of up-close engagement that New Hampshire voters have long demanded and in turn received from the candidates. In Michigan, White House hopefuls do photo-ops at auto plants. In Florida, they hold massive rallies at retirement facilities. In New Hampshire, relatively little is staged—at least not traditionally. This is a state where candidates have almost always had to spend most of their time having real conversations and actually learning from voters.

Still, given its recent track record in failing to "pick presidents," I wanted to ascertain whether New Hampshire's stellar reputation really was so deserved. Was the primary still a smart way to begin the process of picking a president in earnest? And perhaps just as important, was it ever? I sought to find answers to these questions by embarking on a personal journey across the state over the year and a half leading up to the 2016 New Hampshire primary.

As much as the people and tools of the trade have changed over the decades, the fundamental nature of running a presidential campaign in New Hampshire has remained largely the same. The anecdotes I've chosen to feature come in part from secondary sources, but they rely most heavily on the interviews that I conducted with a couple of dozen people who were on the front lines of past New Hampshire campaigns and were generous enough to share their recollections with me. Throughout the narrative, I've included a hodgepodge of some of the most memorable moments from the 1972 campaign onward. Some of the scenes I've chosen to highlight are historically significant in their own right. Others are less momentous on their face than they are instructive of the essence of the New Hampshire primary itself and the people who have lived it. Comprehensive histories of the primary have been written, and so have academic studies. This book is neither.

In conducting research and experiencing the 2016 campaign in New Hampshire firsthand, I was continually surprised and often moved by the extent to which the primary has remained a singular force of participatory democracy in its purest form. That it has remained so in spite of its many inherent flaws—which were perhaps more pronounced during its 2016 iteration than at any other time in its history—is an achievement worthy of exploration and reflection, especially during a time when so many other facets of the American political system seem to have malfunctioned so thoroughly.

To be frank, I embarked on this project harboring a distinct pro–New Hampshire bias. During my reporting on the 2008 and 2012 campaigns, I'd already found that there is nothing in American politics that quite matches the sentimental feeling you get when driving along a dark, winding New Hampshire road in the dead of winter and pulling up to a candlelit, eighteenth-century meetinghouse where thirty people are waiting inside to hear from someone who wants to be their president. Maybe they've gathered to listen intently to an obscure former governor from a far-flung state, someone who entered the race with dreams of Air Force One but spent the previous night on an uncomfortable mattress at a motel in Franconia. Still, it's not the candidates who make New Hampshire unique. It's the people of the state who turn out for these kinds of events before anyone else is really paying attention and who conduct the process like the important high-level job interview it should be. Put it this way: For the most part, I've found that Iowa caucus-goers tend to ask candidates questions. New Hampshire primary voters, on the other hand, demand answers.

As much as that image of the old New England meetinghouse and its earnest inhabitants struck a chord with me, I liked to think that I could tell the difference between quaint and antiquated. I didn't want to end up making the case for New Hampshire based solely on nostalgia. This is a state where 94 percent of the population is white, and the largest city is home to only 110,000 people. To question why such a particular place should hold such outsized sway over an increasingly diverse and urbanized country was reasonable. Accumulated experience and tradition are important, but so are such concepts as fairness and the need to adjust to modernity. New Hampshire would have to prove to me that it deserved to keep the vital role that it had maintained over the previous century.

CHAPTER 2

G RANITE STATERS TEND TO be a nostalgic bunch. They'll tell you all about the lucky hat that they wore when New Hampshire native Carlton Fisk hit his foul-pole-straddling home run to win Game Six of the 1975 World Series. They'll show you the scar they have on their left knee from when they wiped out that time at Waterville Valley after skiing off that wicked-big mogul. And they'll recall every detail about the time they were buying a pack of cigs at the Exxon Tiger Mart and ran into Steve Forbes or sat next to Bill Bradley down at Joey's Diner. "Wicked-nice guy, that Gary Hart."

Because it was the New Hampshire primary's centennial anniversary, the lead-up to 2016 was a notably nostalgic one for this especially nostalgic state. But amid all of the celebratory panels, banquets, and C-Span retrospectives, one reality that typically went unmentioned was that nobody much cared about the primary during its first thirty-two years of existence. And for another two decades after that, until 1968, it was only occasionally and modestly relevant—a factor in determining the two major political parties' nominees only to the extent that the candidates themselves chose to make it one. Indeed, for a majority of the primary's history, that process was largely determined by the proverbial smoke-filled rooms, in which party leaders drank a few gins and settled on which prominent-chinned white Protestant man they were going to put up to lead the country next.

That inconvenient historical reality notwithstanding, the birth of the New Hampshire primary was indeed a momentous occurrence, given the influence that the event ultimately achieved. It was rooted in the prevailing early twentieth-century Progressive Era inclination to reform the presidential nominating process, giving a little less sway to the distinguished and corrupt gentlemen in charge and slightly more power to actual voters. In conjunction with the fight for women's suffrage around the country, there was at the time a significant expansion of the primary system within the states, allowing voters the opportunity to elect delegates to the national party conventions. But reforms that granted voters the ability to have a more direct role in choosing their parties' nominees for president—rather than merely the delegates who selected them—were still almost a half century away.

New Hampshire acquired its singular status in presidential politics almost entirely by accident. In 1913, Representative Stephen Bullock, a poultry farmer from the Cheshire County town of Richmond—tucked into New Hampshire's southwest corner—drafted a bill that the legislature in Concord subsequently passed, which established a statewide primary for the next presidential election in 1916. Again, the idea was not to allow voters to choose their nominees directly. It was, instead, merely an act to give the people of the state a direct role in selecting the *delegates* to the national conventions. In the lead-up to the 2016 race a century later, Bullock's desk sat prominently in the office of New Hampshire secretary of state Bill Gardner, who had recently obtained it. Gardner—a New Hampshire institution in his own right—is a man who studies the history of the primary with the level of detail that an NFL scout employs to analyze game tape. He ensured that every presidential candidate who filed for the 2016 primary did so at Bullock's desk.

After Bullock's legislation became law, the New Hampshire presidential primary was originally set to be held in May of that year, but in 1915, a different state legislator—one who, like many of his Yankee colleagues, had a knack for pinching pennies—offered a separate bill to move the presidential primary up to the second Tuesday in March. This date would coincide helpfully with New Hampshire's long-established "town meeting day," in which members of local communities set local government policy. It was a way to save money on administrative costs, not an attempt to hopscotch other states. Surprising no one with even a passing familiarity with the state's deep-seated tightfistedness, that bill passed easily. Still, New Hampshire didn't go first in the 1916 presidential primaries. Instead, it followed Indiana by a week and held its primary on the same day as Minnesota's contest. Four years later, in the 1920 election, New Hampshire had the first slot on the primary calendar all to itself and has enjoyed it every four years since.

Through the 1948 election, however, few people noticed. They had no reason to pay any particular attention. It wasn't until 1949 that the New Hampshire state legislature finally passed a law whereby presidential candidates' names were placed on the ballot directly in a separate presidential preference poll. It amounted to little more than a political beauty contest, but one that had an immediate and intensely significant psychological impact.

The first New Hampshire presidential primary campaign of real consequence took place in 1952. That year, first-term Tennessee senator Estes Kefauver took on President Harry S. Truman for the Democratic nomination. With the new presidential preference poll in place, Kefauver decided to try to persuade rank-and-file New Hampshire Democrats to vote for him and against the incumbent. It wasn't an easy task, especially because there was no blueprint for how to do such a thing. So Kefauver winged it. When he made his first campaign trip to New Hampshire, the Democratic challenger approached people at random on the street, asking for their votes, one by one. Previously, such a practice would have been considered gauche, and it was still highly unusual.

Truman never even set foot in the state before the 1952 primary. Kefauver, on the other hand, was working hard for each vote. Sort of. By the standards of modern campaigning, he wasn't exactly grinding it out, and the locally popular image of him pounding the pavement for extended periods is largely a myth. Kefauver made a grand total of two trips to New Hampshire before the primary. His rather minimal exertions, however, did make an impact when it came to generating free media. Truman's political team, meanwhile, didn't mobilize until the last week and a half of the primary campaign.

As the president dallied, Kefauver showed off a hint of the showmanship that would presage some of the more theatrical performances of candidates in later decades. His signature accessory was a coonskin cap, which he wore while traveling around to campaign events, sometimes by dogsled. It was pure shtick. The man was a Yale-educated lawyer trying to present himself as a maple-syrup-swilling Davy Crockett. But the act worked. Kefauver defeated Truman by eleven points—an astounding whack at a sitting president from voters of his own party.

In spite of the new preference poll, however, the primaries still held relatively little sway over who ultimately became the nominee at the convention. As such, his New Hampshire defeat wasn't necessarily a fatal blow to Truman—far from it. It was, however, a psychological walloping, and the president had gotten the message. Less than three weeks after the shocking primary results, Truman announced that he would not seek a second full term in the White House. Although the question of whether he had already largely settled on bowing out of the 1952 campaign remains a matter of some dispute, what's certain is that from that point forward, the New Hampshire primary acquired the slightly sinister reputation as a potential graveyard for the ambitions of lackluster presidential front-runners.

Over the next couple of decades, the event ascended in the national political power structure, but until 1968, competing in the

New Hampshire primary remained optional for most presidential candidates and little more than an opportunity to gain some attention for others. Typically, the primary remained more of a sideshow than a central component of the election drama, as it was in 1960 when John F. Kennedy won 85 percent of the New Hampshire Democratic primary vote in a year when none of his major opponents even competed in the state.

It wasn't until eight years later that the New Hampshire primary began to solidify its reputation as the inflamed appendix of presidential front-runners, who time and again dismissed its rumblings at their own peril. When he entered the Democratic primary race in November 1967 to challenge incumbent president Lyndon Johnson, Minnesota senator Eugene McCarthy did not circle New Hampshire on his initial list of primary targets. Eventually though, the anti-Vietnam upstart challenger came around to the view that if he wanted to show the country that he was serious about taking on LBJ's highly organized, heavily funded political machine, he'd have to start at the beginning of the nominating calendar and deliver an early and unexpected punch to the incumbent's gut, just as Estes Kefauver had done sixteen years earlier.

McCarthy's greatest advantage was his core of young, passionate supporters who were energized by the candidate's call for a US troop withdrawal in the escalating Vietnam War. Legions of out-of-state students flowed into New Hampshire to volunteer on his behalf—a wave of new-generation enthusiasm that became even more visible following the pivotal Tet Offensive that launched on January 30 and eventually proved to mark a turning point against the American public's support for the war. The influx of youthful energy behind McCarthy's campaign did not particularly rub off on the candidate himself, as the staid Minnesotan remained cool and serene on the stump. In his appearance and demeanor, this was not the mad-as-hell man of the people seemingly called for by the times. But his base of supporters adjusted to fit the appearance and temperament of their candidate. Many of the hippies who were on his side went "clean for Eugene," shaving off their facial hair, going easy on the tie-dye, and turning down the volume on their Jimi Hendrix records to more effectively present their case to the older squares who composed a sizable majority of the New Hampshire electorate.

In spite of the president's growing unpopularity within the Democratic base and the rapidly growing unease over the war, LBJ might still have dealt a significant blow to the rising furor had he made a concerted effort to compete in New Hampshire against his somewhat colorless challenger. Instead, the president declined to have his name placed on the ballot and instructed his supporters to wage a low-voltage write-in campaign. This was still a time when playing it cool and preserving a sense of detached dignity remained the principal political consideration for an incumbent president.

While their candidate remained officially on the sidelines, Johnson's supporters engaged in some old-fashioned fear-mongering. They took out newspaper ads urging New Hampshire voters to "support our fighting men" and warning them, "We know the Communists are watching the New Hampshire primary to see if we at home have the same determination as our soldiers in Vietnam." Meanwhile, the president never set foot in the state to campaign himself, and his minions' half-measures on his behalf proved unpersuasive for a majority of Democratic voters in the state.

When the votes were tallied, Johnson did beat McCarthy—48 percent to 41 percent—but his unexpectedly narrow, single-digit margin of victory made international headlines and torpedoed the president's air of inevitability. It was the first—but not the last— time a candidate would lose New Hampshire even though he technically won. The night of the count, New York senator Robert F. Kennedy—another antiwar Democrat—called to congratulate McCarthy on his much stronger than expected showing. No longer harboring any doubts that Johnson could be defeated after his disappointing New Hampshire showing, Kennedy jumped into the race four days later. LBJ dropped out two weeks after that. In the last Democratic nominating fight before Iowa jumped the line to hold the nation's first Democratic caucuses in 1972, New Hampshire's impact on the 1968 presidential primaries was singular. By knocking off a sitting president, the New Hampshire primary's image as a giant-slayer was cast, and with good reason, as the next four decades would contain similarly stunning episodes.

CHAPTER 3

I N THE LEAD-UP TO the 1984 primary, *Boston Globe* columnist
Mike Barnicle embarked on a personal crusade against New
Hampshire. His grievances were familiar. Barnicle thought it
ridiculous that one small state enjoyed such a privileged status on
the presidential primary calendar. But it was the manner in which he
made his case that resonated. Although the word *troll* was still decades from entering the common lexicon, Barnicle—a distinguished
man of letters from urbane Massachusetts—set out to do as much
damage as he could to the rubes to the north. As social commentary,
Barnicle's columns had the sophistication and subtlety of an uppercut
to the chin. His first anti–Granite State column carried the headline
"Truly a State to Laugh At" and included the knee-slapping observation that New Hampshire residents "take two hours to watch '60
Minutes' on television." In Barnicle's telling, New Hampshire was
"the igloo capital of the world" with "more pine cones than people"
and "a truck stop, not a state," whose "public people have the social
conscience of a subway rail."

He went on like this for years. My German-born aunt, who had been a Bedford, New Hampshire, resident for decades, threatened to cancel her subscription to the *Globe* after Barnicle published his 1994 piece "Vermont vs. New Hampshire." In that column, Barnicle had observed that in contrast to the untainted and altruistic citizens of Vermont, New Hampshire was home to thousands of former Massachusetts residents who "moved in out of pure selfishness, to avoid taxes or doing anything that might help a neighbor." In a column published shortly before the 1996 primary, Barnicle suggested that Michael Jackson would be at home in New Hampshire "because he is both white and slow." He made predictions about the primary's future, too. "Unfortunately, it's more than likely this will be the last time New Hampshire will play an inflated role in presidential elections on the flimsy grounds that it holds the nation's first primary," Barnicle wrote. "By the year 2000, everyone will be inter-active as well as on line and voters will select candidates in a national primary at half-time of the Rose Bowl." Barnicle didn't survive long enough at the *Globe* to see his prediction about the New Hampshire primary's demise fail to come true. In 1998, he resigned amid charges that he had plagiarized lines from George Carlin in one column and made up characters in another. Suffice it to say, few tears were shed in New Hampshire when Barnicle exited. It wasn't that Barnicle had it *all* wrong. Although New Hampshire offers plenty of great hiking, skiing, and good restaurants, it was also the place where J. D. Salinger decamped when he decided that twentieth-century civilization just wasn't for him. For most of the country, this image of the state as an ideal hiding place for government-loathing curmudgeons and weird, mountain-dwelling hermits persists. Where, after all, did meth kingpin Walter White go when he needed to move off the grid in the last season of *Breaking Bad*? New Hampshire. They'd never be able to find him there!

Although it offers no shortage of far-flung outposts where people can live in isolation, New Hampshire is also the twenty-first most densely populated state in the union. Granted, there is still no state income or sales tax, and yes, in large stretches of the state, you're far more likely to spot a deer than you are a person of color. But over time, New Hampshire has become less true to the backwoods caricature that Barnicle presented in his columns and more like a multifaceted slice of America that offers at least a little bit of almost everything you'll find elsewhere.

For starters, New Hampshire's political identity has shifted. Between 1948 and 1988, Lyndon Johnson was the one and only Democratic presidential candidate backed by New Hampshire in a general election. The subsequent flip has been dramatic. Starting in 1992, the only time a Republican White House contender beat a Democrat in New Hampshire was in 2000, when George W. Bush eked out a 7,211-vote victory over Al Gore—a narrow triumph that gave the Republican the four electoral votes he needed to make the Florida recount relevant and ultimately win the presidency. And Bush likely would have lost New Hampshire had Green Party candidate Ralph Nader not been on the ballot (Nader won 4 percent of the vote in the state). New Hampshire remains a swing state, but one that has tilted increasingly leftward over the last decade.

Despite this change, "Live Free or Die"—the memorable state motto—still carries real meaning in New Hampshire's collective consciousness. There is a libertarian streak that continues to run deep. Take motorcycle safety. It's not that motorcycle helmets are unheard of in New Hampshire. From November to April, almost all bikers from Londonderry to Laconia wear them. They'd be crazy not to, because in the winter months, helmets keep riders' heads from becoming snow cones. But in warmer weather, motorcycle helmets are roughly as scarce on the highways of the Granite State as New York Yankees T-shirts are in its sports bars. Two other states have no motorcycle helmet laws, even for minors. But I've spent a lot of time in Illinois and Iowa and have noticed that the majority of riders in those Midwestern states don't flaunt the real possibility of their brain matter being sprayed across traffic lanes as a lifestyle statement. In New Hampshire, many people are earnest enough about "Live Free or Die" to behave as if either option were just fine with them.

Even the newcomers tend to take the motto seriously. In the last four decades of the twentieth century, New Hampshire's population growth soared, as residents from more highly taxed nearby states were drawn to its relatively low cost of living compared to southern New England. These were the "selfish" people of Mike Barnicle's telling. Much of this influx came from residents of Massachusetts who settled in New Hampshire population centers just across the border, for example, in Nashua—the second-largest city in the state, behind Manchester. The draw was straightforward: in southern New Hampshire cities like Nashua, you could keep more of your pay-check and still get to Logan Airport in under an hour. And best of all, you'd never be more than a stone's throw away from Dunkin' Donuts.

Dunkin' Donuts is to New Hampshire what Starbucks is to the rest of the country. In Nashua alone, there are no less than four-teen Dunkin' Donuts locations. Fourteen in a city of fewer than 90,000 people! It's impossible to keep an accurate statewide count of branches, as they're continuing to expand so quickly, but the num-ber is well over two hundred. One or two locations probably sprang up since you started reading this book. By contrast, according to the company's online store-locator map, there are only twenty-six Starbucks locations in the state—and most of those arrived recently. New Hampshire is still a place where many people can't bring them-selves to say words like *venti*, *soy*, or *extra foam* with a straight face. To its core, it's a Dunkin' Donuts kind of state: functional and satis-fying enough, without being annoying about it.

When circumstances go awry, Dunkin' Donuts is the one thing that keeps the people of New Hampshire from sinking into apoc-alyptic meltdown. In late October 2011, I was in the state covering that year's presidential campaign when New Hampshire was jolted by a freak autumn snowstorm. This particular nor'easter was nota-ble, even in a state where four or five inches is considered a dusting. "Snowtober," as it became known, dropped about two feet of snow on the southern part of the state, causing even the ever-image-conscious presidential candidates to cancel their events. After the storm had died down, I ventured from the hotel where I was staying to one of the three dozen or so Dunkin' Donuts locations in the greater Manchester area, when I was greeted by a scene that might have doubled as a B story in an episode of *The Walking Dead*. Car after car was pulling into the familiar parking lot, stopping for a few long seconds, and then backing away slowly. It was as if they could scarcely compute what they were seeing: the electricity was out, which meant no Dunkin' Donuts.

I was able to catch a glimpse of one driver's face as the realization of what was happening swept over him. It was like seeing a man who'd just lost his wife, his job, and a kidney, all in the same day. It took him a solid twenty seconds before he found the courage to shift into reverse, amid palpable despair. Where would he go now? What would he do when he got there? How did one even go about the day without being fueled by a medium regular four sugars and a splash of skim milk? This was a bad scene that could become ugly. Thankfully, the power came back on relatively quickly. What did people in New Hampshire do in the meantime without Dunkin' Donuts to fuel them? Mostly, they stayed in their bedrooms. Nine months after Snowtober, Southern New Hampshire Medical Center reported a surge in births.

Although you're never far from one no matter where you are in the state, Dunkin' Donuts storefronts are most common in the four most populated of New Hampshire's ten counties, which carve out the south-central and southeastern portion of the state. Moving up clockwise from the Massachusetts border, they are Hillsborough County (the most populous county, which is flanked by Nashua at 6 o'clock and Manchester at 12 o'clock), Merrimack County to the north (home of New Hampshire's capital city of Concord), Strafford County to the east (whose county seat of Dover is home to the University of New Hampshire [UNH]), and Rockingham County, which is tucked into the far southeastern corner of the state (home of the picturesque, historic seaport of Portsmouth and most of the rocky slice of New Hampshire seacoast). These four counties compose about 74 percent of New Hampshire's population and are where presidential candidates spend the majority of their time, but none of their "cities" feel particularly urban.

Manchester, which sits twenty miles to the north of Nashua along the east bank of the Merrimack River, is home to a little more than 100,000 people. Out-of-towners often characterize it as "blue-collar," but in reality, it's the kind of place where you stand out if your shirt features any collar at all. Gritty. Working class. Tough. All of those words apply. In recent years, however, there has been a proliferation of high-tech companies and other signs of gentrification that include non–Dunkin' Donuts coffee shops with such luxuries as cushioned seating and power outlets, as well as several nice restaurants. The mills that were once the city's lifeblood have since been turned into office space and loft apartments. During primary season every four years, national journalists descend en masse on the Radisson and the nearby Hilton Garden Inn and make use of their expense accounts and Beltway egos, lending further ammunition to the impression that the city remains one in transition. But the fact of the matter is that Manchester, New Hampshire, remains at its core a place where you can easily get into a bar fight if you step on the wrong guy's foot. It's officially nicknamed the "Queen City," but no one calls it that. "Manch-Vegas" is its most popular nickname, but "Manch-ganistan" is its most evocative one.

If the Radisson and Hilton Garden Inn are the unofficial residences of the New Hampshire primary, the New Hampshire Institute of Politics (NHIOP) at St. Anselm College is its workplace. The NHIOP's confines consist of a nondescript auditorium, a TV studio, a few classrooms and offices, and a café stand. Its central role in the presidential campaign is showcased in its hallways and interior walls, which are decked out in a vast collection of photographs from primaries past. Most of the collection captures the typical candidate-of-the-people image that White House contenders in New Hampshire have always sought to project. The black-and-white photo of John F. Kennedy petting a donkey during the 1960 campaign is typical. My favorite piece on display, though, is a vintage poster from the 1968 campaign that features a psychedelic rendering of George Romney's craggy face plastered onto a background that looks more like a notice for a Grateful Dead concert in Haight-Ashbury than it does an ad for the teetotaling Republican governor of Michigan. As the poster demonstrates, even in no-frills New Hampshire a healthy dose of quirkiness has long been a central facet of running for president. Candidates have to find a way to create some flavor of interest, especially if they're as plain vanilla as George Romney or Ohio senator Rob Portman.

If you close your eyes and conjure up the first image that comes to mind after reading the words "US senator," that upper-middle-aged white guy with the nice hair that you're envisioning probably looks a lot like Rob Portman. In the summer of 2014, like a lot of senators do at some point in their careers, Portman was thinking a little bit about running for president. At a time when the nation's first viable female presidential candidate was almost universally regarded as the front-runner to succeed the first black president, the senator from Ohio didn't exactly scream "solution!" to the Republican Party's challenge of expanding upon its old white-guy base in diverse parts of the country. Still, it was clear that the man who had made it onto Mitt Romney's vice-presidential shortlist in 2012 wouldn't be crazy to harbor some national ambitions. His résumé certainly suggested that he could be presidential material. He had won his Senate seat in 2010 by an eighteen-point landslide, beating his Democratic opponent in all but six of Ohio's eighty-eight counties. Well respected by other senators as an amiable colleague, thoughtful on policy, and an effective legislator, in theory, Portman was offering a brand of mainline, center-right Republicanism, likely to be a decent fit for a wide swath of the New Hampshire GOP electorate. Before being elected to the Senate in 2010, Portman was director of the Office of Management and Budget and US trade representative under George W. Bush's administration. And before that, he was Ohio's Second

District congressman for a dozen years. He was smart, well spoken, and handsome in a nonthreatening way. And it didn't hurt that he hailed from one of the country's largest swing states. In sum, he had pretty much all of the ingredients that the recipe book calls for when baking presidential cake.

But Portman was also known for being two things that rarely portend success at the highest level of American politics: he was an exceptionally nice guy, and he was boring. Considering Iowa Republicans' long-established penchant for charismatic hard-right conservatives, if Portman joined the race, New Hampshire would be the place where someone with his bland but competent pedigree would have to stake his ground.

Portman was scheduled to test out what might become his campaign message in New Hampshire with a speech at the NHIOP on August 26, 2014, and I decided to see what he had to offer. I had met him once before, during his 2010 Senate campaign in Ohio, and the strongest impression he left with me at the time was that he was jarringly normal. This was memorable to me because politicians at Portman's level are almost never normal. They may be perfectly agreeable—though many of them aren't—but they almost invariably come across as peculiarly off-putting in a way that can be difficult to pin down. They're just not people you'd want to hang out with in a normal social setting. Like most creatures of Washington, DC, they're usually looking for the next person to talk to at the cocktail party, and there tends to be an ulterior motive behind their every utterance. But Portman, with his honest smile, natural ease, and sincere interest in learning more about the people around him, was different. He embodied the archetype of the affable dad every kid from the suburbs has encountered at one time or another during a visit to a friend's house. This dad always seems to be mowing the lawn or tending the garden, but he's up for shooting some hoops, too. "Hey, buddy," he'd probably say if you stopped by his place unannounced on a Saturday afternoon. "There's some root beer in the fridge, if you're thirsty. I'm gonna run down to the hardware store. Dinner's at 6:30, and guess what? It's taco night! How're your mom and dad doing, by the way?"

The night before Portman's big introduction at the NHIOP, I ran into him at O Steaks and Seafood just down the street from the statehouse in Concord. Portman entered the restaurant exuding that indefinable politician's glow, which should have been a signal for the other diners to at least turn their heads. None did. In fact, no one seemed to know who he was, even though many of them presumably worked in and around politics. I reintroduced myself to Portman. He didn't remember me from four years prior but made no effort to pretend that he did, which was refreshing.

"How many people live in New Hampshire?" he asked after I told him about the book I was working on. His tone was one of genuine curiosity. I told him I thought it was around a million—selling the state short by about 300,000 residents. Portman thought that was "cool"—a place where handshakes in politics were more important than ad buys—much different than how it works in Ohio. Portman took a seat at a separate table and ordered a local IPA. Just one, though.

When I arrived at the NHIOP event the next morning, Portman was already there, chatting with some of the "local business leaders" and New Hampshire politicos who tend to be willing to take time out of their days to come out for events like this even when the primary is still more than seventeen months away. With his salt-and-pepper hair parted neatly, his navy-blue suit and red-striped tie exactly in place, Portman looked like a man who would be cast to play the president of the United States in a 1990s romantic comedy film. It was, however, harder for me to imagine him as the real thing.

In the months before the race actually begins, all aspiring presidential contenders express varying levels of coyness about their possible candidacies. "I'm not making a decision on that yet" and "I'm focused right now on the midterms" are typical responses to The Question. The idea is to make it look like you don't want it too badly, even though everyone knows you do. But when Portman took the stage at the NHIOP on this morning, I could tell right off the bat that his situation was different. His wasn't feigned tentativeness;

it was real apprehension. Portman didn't do any proverbial wink-
ing and nodding at all as he made his way through his dry remarks,
which covered a range of issues, in a voice that barely registered above
a loud whisper. He didn't allude, even in the vaguest of ways, to harboring presidential ambitions of any kind. During the Q-and-A session that followed his unmemorable speech, no one in the audience
even asked him if he was considering it.

I was sure that Portman's aspirations were high and his work
ethic strong, but I doubted that he had the shamelessness or the
single-minded determination required to run for president. The person I saw in front of me was a calm, competent, and capable man who
spoke with some conviction about "the one indispensable economy"
and other such phrases that people who regularly appear on C-Span
use. There was only one part of Portman's profile that I thought
might lift him from the ranks of "just another boring Republican."
The previous year, Portman announced that he had changed his previous opposition to same-sex marriage after his twenty-one-year-old
son came out as gay. In making the switch, Portman had become the
most prominent Republican elected official in the country to support marriage equality. If there was anywhere in the country where a
GOP candidate could run on a pro-gay marriage platform, it was in
largely secular New Hampshire.

Portman, however, didn't bring up the issue at all during his
speech. After he concluded his remarks, he spent a few minutes
signing dozens of decorative wooden eggs—one of those quaint
New Hampshire traditions that every prospective candidate who
speaks at a "Politics and Eggs" event completes. Next, he stood for a
short interview with NH1—a new statewide TV news network that
had not yet launched officially. In the middle of taping the interview,
the cameraman suddenly stopped the young, on-air reporter in mid-
sentence and stepped into his own shot to adjust Portman's tie. "We
can't have wires showing," the cameraman lectured the reporter, as
a man who could become the next president looked on. "That's very
important."

When I finally got the chance to sit down with the would-be candidate for a few minutes, I asked him right away about the gay-marriage issue. "I don't look at it politically," Portman told me. "As you know, I didn't make the decision based on polls or politics. I made the decision on a very personal basis, having never really thought deeply about it, to be frank."

I believed him. Portman said that since he'd made his conversion on the issue public, people had been approaching him at least once a week and "sometimes every day" to extend their gratitude or share their own stories about those in their lives who had struggled with their sexual identities. As he told me all of this, delving more deeply into what happened next after he broke so completely from Republican orthodoxy on the issue, Portman came across as unusually at ease and reflective. For him, indeed, this had nothing to do with politics.

"Yesterday, it is a young man who is very involved in the [Republican] Party, and I don't want to get him in an uncomfortable situation, but this person's view is 'Should I be involved in this party or not?'" Portman recalled, elucidating for me the real-life impact of his public expression of support for gay marriage. "And what he says is that because of me, he's willing to stick it out. Sometimes it's much more personal. It's about the fact that a young man or a young woman now can speak to his or her parents about it in a way they couldn't before because it opened up a dialogue with their family. On the opposite side of the issue, I hear from others who are disappointed, and that's to be expected. It still is an issue where there are big differences within our party."

Here was a thoughtful, nuanced, and intrinsically human reaction to one of the trickiest issues that the Republican Party was grappling with at the time. Portman's words lacked any of the focus-group-tested, sound-bite-ready talking points that I was used to hearing from people who wanted to be president. How it would play out on the presidential stage in the midst of a tough Republican primary campaign was unclear, but I was eager to find out. I never got the chance. About three months later, Portman announced that he would not run for president in 2016, choosing instead to focus on his Senate reelection bid.

As a practical political calculation, Portman's decision proved to be a sound one. Someone of his pedigree and bearing, it turned out, had zero chance of winning the 2016 Republican presidential nomination—not even with a strong showing in New Hampshire. Rob Portman would have had no interest in engaging in the raw demagoguery, embarrassing pandering, and middle-school insult exchanging that would become a fixture of the most viable GOP contenders' daily interactions with one another on the campaign trail. If similarly sober-minded and competent contenders such as John Kasich, Jeb Bush, and Lindsey Graham had internalized what Portman seemed to suspect about what it would take to win in 2016, they, too, might have avoided a lot of unnecessary exasperation leading up to Primary Day and beyond. Then again, if the grown-ups in the room had *all* decided to sit this one out, as Portman did, perhaps the established norms of respectability and decorum would have come crashing down even more spectacularly.

CHAPTER 4

⬛──

THE MOST FORMIDABLE OPPONENT President Richard Nixon
faced in the 1972 Republican primary campaign in New
Hampshire was Paul Newman. One of the film industry's
most bankable stars, Newman was at the time basking in the af-
terglow of *Butch Cassidy and the Sundance Kid* when he decided to
get involved in the race. In doing so, the Hollywood A-lister placed
his bet on a decidedly C-list White House contender. Newman endorsed California congressman Pete McCloskey—a liberal, antiwar
Republican who was running a no-chance primary campaign against
the then popular incumbent president.

Steve Duprey was an eighteen-year-old college freshman who
had been bestowed the important-sounding title of "Carroll County
chairman" for McCloskey's slapdash New Hampshire campaign.
The entirety of Carroll County, which hugs the Maine border just
below New Hampshire's most northerly region, Coos County,
boasted fewer than 20,000 residents at the time. But the position
seemed like a great opportunity for a kid with no experience who

wanted to jump right into politics at the highest level. As it turned out, the gig turned into an even bigger deal than Duprey thought it would be when he was informed that he would be assigned to drive Newman around the state for a three-day post-endorsement sojourn.

How did one prepare to chauffer a movie star around rural New Hampshire? Duprey asked around and discovered that Newman had a particular fondness for St. Pauli Girl beer. On the day of his New Hampshire arrival, the eighteen-year-old Carroll County chairman for Pete McClosky's presidential campaign greeted Paul Newman at the airport with a case of the German pilsner in tow. After exchanging introductions and getting in the car together to head to the first event, Newman got right to the point.

"Got a beer?"

A proud Duprey handed Newman an ice-cold bottle of his favorite brew.

"Got an opener?"

At those three words, the teenager's heart sank.

"No," was all he could muster.

Newman shrugged.

"Don't worry," he said. "I carry one with me."

As they drove around Carroll County together—two real-life outlaws fighting the good fight for a lost cause, one German pilsner at a time—Newman began to take a liking to the kid.

The highlight of the trip came at a one-runway village airport rally in North Conway, where the prominent actor drew a crowd of about 1,000—a previously unheard-of number for a political event in one of the most sparsely populated enclaves of the state where Hollywood and Washington were more or less equally exotic concepts. The problem for McCloskey, however, was that almost all of them were there to see the movie star rather than the congressman. McCloskey never posed even a slight threat to Nixon, who ended up beating him by forty-eight points on Primary Day.

Duprey, however, was one of the few participants to get something of lasting value out of McCloskey's presidential bid. Shortly after their St. Pauli Girl–fueled road trip came to its completion, the actor managed to track down his former road companion's dorm address at the ultra-liberal New College in Sarasota, Florida, and sent him a photograph, signed with the following note: "To Steve Duprey, the best date I ever had."

Duprey, who went on to become a close adviser to John Mc-Cain and a Republican National Committeeman representing New Hampshire, couldn't get the photograph up on his dorm room wall quickly enough. "It was a chick magnet," he recalls.

With no serious threat against him from within the GOP ranks, Nixon set his sights on potential hazards that might emerge from the opposing party in the general election. Maine senator Edmund Muskie had been the Democratic vice-presidential nominee four years earlier and was the clear front-runner to win his party's nomination in 1972. Nixon's famously hard-nosed political team quickly determined that Muskie was the only Democrat with a realistic shot at defeating the president. And so, they sought to take him out.

To help his team of operatives carry out this task in New Hampshire, Nixon had at his disposal a one-of-a-kind miserable prankster who was as unscrupulous in his work as he was effective: William Loeb, the curmudgeonly publisher of the *Union Leader*. Then and now New Hampshire's only statewide daily newspaper, the *Union Leader*'s editorial influence was at the time unrivaled in the state. Since the day he took over the paper's reins in 1946, Loeb had been relentless and unabashed in broadcasting his hard-line right-wing views in front-page editorials that presaged Donald Trump's Twitter missives in their typically cartoonish yet often effective ramblings.

Every four years, conservative Republican White House hopefuls sought the *Union Leader*'s backing, as if it were the golden ticket to the presidency. They did so, even though the paper had endorsed only one winner—Nixon in 1968—of a competitive primary. (Loeb would back his second and last New Hampshire primary victor when he got behind Ronald Reagan's campaign in 1980.) Moderate Republicans and Democrats, meanwhile—two groups that Loeb regarded with roughly equal disdain—did their best to ignore him, as they saw little upside in courting an unreasonable man but saw massive risk in potentially irritating him.

Still, Loeb did not shrink from involving himself in Democratic primaries. In one front-page editorial published before the 1960 contest, he warned New Hampshire Democrats that they would be held responsible for the nation's downfall, in the event that they made the grievous mistake of backing Massachusetts senator John F. Kennedy, whom the proudly opinionated publisher derided as someone who "does not understand the Communist menace."

"If we elect charm in the form of Kennedy to the White House, in the opinion of this newspaper we are just about through as a nation," Loeb wrote in that front-page editorial. In case the severity of his warning had been insufficiently stark, the piece ran under the rather direct headline "You Are Voting for Your Life." Kennedy ended up getting the last word against Loeb that year. In his second-to-last speech of the 1960 general election, the Massachusetts senator stood in front of a massive crowd within shouting distance of the *Union Leader*'s Manchester headquarters. And from there, he let his tormentor have it. "I believe there is probably a more irresponsible newspaper than that one right over there somewhere in the United States, but I've been through forty states and I haven't found it yet," the Democratic presidential nominee said. "I believe there is a publisher who has less regard for the truth than William Loeb, but I can't think of his name."

By late 1971, Muskie had little reason to fear that Loeb would prove more successful at derailing his own campaign than he had Kennedy's. An internal poll that his campaign conducted in September showed Muskie leading his closest Democratic rival, liberal South Dakota senator George McGovern, by a rather comfortable 53 to 6 percent margin in New Hampshire. The accompanying fifty-five-page internal memo that Muskie's campaign aides drafted, however, presaged a troubling sense of overconfidence in the front-runner's ranks. The memo advised that Muskie's popularity in New Hampshire was "strong enough to resist an intense campaign" and suggested that his core strategy be "to refrain from doing anything that might offend anyone." And with that, Muskie had set his own trap for himself.

After having entered the race early, in January 1971, McGovern slowly built up his name recognition, becoming a better candidate each day, as he worked the ground game harder than any of his opponents. This was the first presidential election that took place after the voting age was lowered to eighteen, and as they had for Eugene McCarthy four years earlier, college kids from surrounding states poured into New Hampshire to help organize on behalf of the vocally antiwar McGovern, who had piloted a B-24 Liberator over German-occupied Europe during World War II. Muskie, meanwhile, proved to be unenthusiastic and stiff on the trail, presenting an unflattering contrast to the loose and amiable McGovern. In his book *First in the Nation*, which chronicles the history of the New Hampshire primary through the 1984 election, author Charles Brereton recalls one particular encounter that demonstrated McGovern's charm.

"Hello," the candidate said in greeting a young female voter in Nashua, according to Brereton. "I'm George McGovern. I'm running for president, and I'd like your help."

"I know—I've already met you three times," the woman replied.

Most candidates, at this point, would have apologized for failing to recognize the woman. But McGovern was unfazed. Without missing a beat, he deadpanned, "I know. Eleanor thinks we're having an affair."

As the calendar turned to 1972, Muskie was still well ahead of McGovern in New Hampshire, but he was beginning to lose steam. That's when Nixon's henchmen went in for the kill, via their most powerful New Hampshire ally: William Loeb. The simple goal was to weaken Muskie, the likely Democratic nominee. And for months, the *Union Leader* had already been making clear to its readers where its publisher stood on the senator from Maine, repeatedly referring to him in print as "Moscow Muskie." On February 24, Loeb published what subsequently became known as the "Canuck Letter."

Presented to the public in the state's newspaper of record as a straightforward "letter to the editor," the Canuck Letter was penned, in the *Union Leader*'s telling, by a man named Paul Morrison from Deerfield, Florida. It chronicled an encounter with Muskie and his staff, which Morrison supposedly had witnessed firsthand during a campaign event in the Sunshine State. In the letter, Morrison alleged that someone had asked Muskie how he could possibly sympathize with the problems that African Americans faced, as there were so few black people who resided in his home state of Maine. In response to the question, according to the letter, one of Muskie's aides replied, "No, not blacks, but we have Cannocks [*sic*]." Muskie then laughed at his staffer's supposedly bigoted remark, or so the letter claimed.

The Canuck Letter was riddled with spelling errors—a feeble attempt by a sophisticated political tactician to conjure the patois of an uneducated rube. Further complicating matters, Paul Morrison from Deerfield, Florida, as it turned out, did not exist. But instantaneous fact-checking wasn't easy in 1972, particularly when the publisher was in on the con.

To hammer home his attempt to pin Muskie as an anti-Canadian zealot—for the benefit of New Hampshire's sizable French Canadian population—Loeb printed the bogus letter along with an accompanying front-page editorial written in bold text and headlined "Senator Muskie Insults Franco-Americans." In reality, the term "Cannock" was not generally regarded as much of a slur within New Hampshire's French Canadian community (it was about as marginally offensive as the term "Frenchie" might have been), but Loeb's influence was such that he thought he could easily turn the made-up episode into something worse than it appeared on paper. In his typically aggressive style, he had laid down his marker against the leading Democratic presidential hopeful.

For his part, Muskie tried to ignore the whole episode at first. But when Loeb went on to publish another onslaught against him—this one suggesting that his wife was a drunken, foul-mouthed woman of questionable moral fiber—the normally staid Maine senator decided that he'd had enough. Undeterred by a blinding late-February snowstorm, Muskie stood on the back of a flatbed truck in front of the *Union Leader*'s headquarters. He was just a few hundred yards from where Kennedy had appeared eleven years earlier, addressing the assembled reporters, who were expecting the fireworks to fly. With wet flakes accumulating on his overcoat, Muskie leaned into a microphone and unleashed his rebuke against Loeb. "He has proved himself to be a gutless coward," the leading Democratic presidential candidate said, puffing out his chest as best he could. "It's fortunate for him he's not on the platform beside me."

Muskie's voice was at first inflected with righteous anger, but it soon began to crack with a different kind of emotion—one that was less becoming of the masculine standards of the day. The candidate was, it seemed, on the verge of exploding into tears. Still, most of the initial news reports about Muskie's denouncement of Loeb did not mention anything about crying. And the clip of Muskie's speech that ran on CBS News that night showed an emotional candidate, but one who had stopped short of tears.

It was David Broder's story that ran in the Sunday edition of the *Washington Post* that forever changed how the event was remembered. In it, the famed national political reporter declared that tears had been "streaming down [Muskie's] face." It only later became apparent that Broder had probably mistaken melting snow for tears. The reporter's stature was such in the media world that in short order, editors from the major wire services wanted to know why their reporters had missed the big moment that Broder described, and references to Muskie having cried outside the *Union Leader* headquarters were added to later editions of other publications' stories. This rendition of events was bolstered when a Muskie aide, thinking that it would help to humanize his candidate, "confirmed" to reporters that the candidate had indeed cried just a bit in standing up for his wife against Loeb's bullying.

Until the day he died in 1996, Muskie insisted that he had not shed a single tear that day and that any moisture that happened to have accumulated on his face was, in fact, melting snow. The evidence supporting his case remains substantial. In 1987, Broder wrote a lengthy piece in the *Washington Monthly* that recounted the events of that day. In it, Broder conveyed regret about the manner in which he had described the supposed tears running down Muskie's face and conceded that it was "unclear" whether Muskie had cried.

The extent to which Loeb was in on the fake "Canuck letter" scheme from the beginning remains similarly uncertain. But at the very least, the *Union Leader*'s publisher didn't lift a finger to try to authenticate the letter—the Nixonian origins of which were confirmed in a *Washington Post* story published less than a month before the general election on October 10, 1972. In a front-page article headlined "FBI Finds Nixon Aides Sabotaged Democrats," Carl Bernstein and Bob Woodward reported that the Committee for the Re-election of the President had engaged in "a massive campaign of political spying and sabotage" against all of the major Democratic candidates, including Muskie. The two young reporters, who had been making names for themselves by pursuing the growing story about the break-in at the DNC headquarters inside the Watergate Complex that June, revealed that the New Hampshire incident was a central component of this sabotage campaign. Woodward and Bernstein reported that White House communications aide Ken Clawson had told a *Washington Post* staff writer that he had penned the fake letter himself. Then, when the reporters subsequently interviewed Clawson, the Nixon aide suddenly claimed to have no knowledge of the letter's origins. This denial, it need not be said, wasn't especially persuasive.

Woodward and Bernstein's subsequent reporting in the *Washington Post*, as well as in their iconic book, *All the President's Men*, demonstrated that the Muskie campaign had been under systematic attack from Nixon aides since mid-1971 as part of a concerted effort to undermine the Democratic front-runner, with tactics ranging from theft of sensitive documents to counterfeit campaign literature to additional forged letters.

Muskie went on to defeat McGovern in the March 7 New Hampshire primary by a 46 percent to 37 percent margin. But it was a closer shave for the front-runner than had been predicted, and so McGovern became the latest candidate to "win" New Hampshire by finishing in second place. The momentum he gained after that better-than-expected showing propelled McGovern on an unlikely path to the Democratic nomination.

The impact that Muskie's "crying speech" had on McGovern's ability to close the gap in New Hampshire to the single digits also remains a matter of some dispute. McGovern's team believed that their candidate had already been on an upward trajectory before the events of that day. Not in doubt, however, is that the question of Muskie's "temperament"—largely a result of the manner in which his anti-Loeb speech was covered—went on to dominate the media narrative leading up to New Hampshire Primary Day and beyond. With the simmering Watergate scandal not yet resonating in the public's consciousness, Nixon would beat McGovern in the general election, carrying every state except Massachusetts in one of the biggest landslides in US political history.

CHAPTER 5

T HE PARTY WAS WELL under way inside Fagin's Pub in Berlin, New Hampshire, on an extremity-immobilizing Saturday evening in January 2015. The following morning, I was slated to take part in an eleven-mile winter walk with an eclectic group of activists who were schlepping across the state on foot to promote campaign-finance reform. I still had another thirty miles of icy northbound highway to traverse before getting to my motel in the tiny northern New Hampshire outpost of Errol, but I needed a break, and so I stopped in at Fagin's. As I rubbed my hands together in the entranceway to try to regain some feeling, the record player didn't exactly screech to a halt, but the looks I received from the three local men sitting at the bar were impossible to misconstrue. "Who the hell are you?" they all wanted to know.

The ceiling lights were on full blast, illuminating the place like a supermarket, and it smelled like stale Miller Lite and used hockey equipment. I hovered for a few moments before selecting my seat, a bit concerned about what the consequences might be if I happened to have chosen a regular's favorite stool. But Craig, the affable bartender (who also turned out to be the manager, cook, and unofficial peacekeeper), gave me a friendly nod to let me know that everything was going to be OK. He was taking a steady stream of drink orders from his three costumers, all of whom had come out to watch the New England Patriots take on the Baltimore Ravens in a key playoff game. I'd chosen Fagin's to watch the game over the local Chinese joint—Wang's Garden—and Berlin's other watering hole, Millyard Lounge ("Trust me. You don't want to go in there," I had been told of the latter establishment).

Berlin [pronounced "BER-lin"] is the largest "city" in New Hampshire's Great North Woods, with a population that eighty years ago topped out over 20,000 but has since declined to well under 10,000. The North Country, for short, is the expansive, heavily forested region north of the White Mountains and extending all the way up to the Canadian border. This is not the land of busy ski resorts and picturesque snow-capped peaks that lies just to the south. It is instead mile upon mile of dark, impenetrable woods with a few tiny hamlets sprinkled in. Most of the people who live in the region were born there, and job opportunities generally hover somewhere between scarce and nonexistent. With the paper mill that once served as Berlin's economic backbone now long gone, poverty was rampant and despair palpable in the North Country's hub. At the time when I visited, per capita income in Berlin (approximately $22,000 per year) was only about two-thirds that of the state average (approximately $34,000 per year).

Eager to make an obvious outsider feel more comfortable, Craig poured me a Guinness and told me a bit about the history of the bar. It had been around for about a half century and had once been three stories high during its heyday before a fire had downsized it to one. As Craig told me all of this, I glanced around at the ten empty tables, silent juke box, and handwritten "Wall of Shame" behind the bar, which called out the people by name who had failed to pay their bar tabs.

The place was decked out in the typical New Hampshire sports bar manner, with Boston athletic memorabilia from wall to wall. But there was also a Montreal Canadiens jersey mixed in with the Bruins, Celtics, Red Sox, and Patriots gear. Berlin is roughly halfway between Boston and Montreal, and I was curious about allegiances, so I struck up a conversation with Ted (this is the one and only time in this book that I've taken the liberty to change someone's real name), the man sitting to my right. Ted's complexion was the color of the snow that was piled up along the sides of the road, and his cheeks were candy-apple red. He leaned in close when he spoke, and his breath confirmed that he had already consumed more than a couple of adult beverages by the time I'd arrived. He would enjoy several more before I left.

"It's about half and half," Ted said of Berlin residents' allegiance to the Boston and Montreal hockey teams. Suddenly, his gaze drifted back to the big TV screen behind the bar.

"What the fuck!" Ted shouted, as if his foot had just been run over by a semi-trailer truck. What had actually happened was that the Ravens had picked up a routine first down. "Sorry," he added. Ted was really into the game.

"These fuckin' guys," he continued. "Get the fuck in there, you fucks! He fuckin' kicked him! Sorry."

I was no stranger to sports-bar dwellers who use the word "fuck" about as often as teenagers employ "like," so his language didn't particularly faze me. Nonetheless, Ted apologized after every "fuck" outburst, as if he'd surprised himself by letting another one slip. And still, throughout the night, he continued to throw in a "fuck" or "fuckin'" every five or six words.

In New England sports-fan parlance, *fuck* can mean everything from good, bad, yes, or no—it's all about the context. Usually, though, it meant nothing at all. It's just a filler word to toss in for emphasis, or in place of "um." This was Ted's favorite rendering of the word, that is, "These fuckin' guys, man. These fuckin' guys."

In between fucks, Ted managed to convey that he'd been working for the fire department in Nashua for about a decade. Nashua is not near Berlin. In fact, there is no place in New Hampshire further from Berlin than Nashua—a two-and-a-half hour drive on a good day through the White Mountains and straight down a long stretch of state-owned liquor stores and Dunkin' Donuts branches that span I-93. How was a five-hour commute every workday for ten years tolerable? When I asked him why he didn't just move to the southern part of the state to be closer to his job, Ted answered, "The economy."

He didn't elaborate, other than to say this: "Most of the fuckin' guys I work with at the station fuckin' come up here to hunt and fish and everything. This is my town." Although many of his neighbors had fled, Ted was hanging onto Berlin—at least the *idea* of the place that existed in his mind.

I knew that at this time of night, my dining options anywhere north of here would be nonexistent (it was, after all, nearing 8:00 p.m.), so I decided to make my riskiest move of the evening and try out Fagin's menu. I asked Craig to run through my options. The obvious choice was pizza, which he characterized as "pretty good." But in a moment of blind risk-taking, I decided to go with the chicken fingers. Ted, on the other hand, wasn't about to confuse his system with the intake of solid food. He slammed another beer before providing some more color commentary on how the game was being officiated. "That's fuckin' abuse right there! He fuckin' kneed him! Sorry."

As part of an effort to calm him down a bit, I tried to change the subject to politics. Having lived in New Hampshire his whole life, Ted had seen plenty of candidates come and go over the years. "It's an open presidency, so you'll get fuckin' everybody up here," he said in summing up his assessment of the race. "Which is cool."

The chicken fingers turned out to be pretty good, and so did the conversation. Craig, who was drinking coffee, offered some observations about how candidates benefited or suffered from circumstances and national moods that were well beyond their control. Ted expressed his agreement. Or as he put it, "Fuckin'." Throughout this discussion, I was unable to decipher which political party either man belonged to. New Hampshire is a place where people have lots of opinions about lots of things but take great pride in being removed from typical notions of ideology. "I vote for the *person*, not the party," is something you hear a lot.

As the Patriots began to mount a big second-half comeback, Ted began to make his own transition from "harmless, somewhat brain-dead drunk" to "deeply incoherent, teetering on the edge of a meltdown drunk." And his ability to stay focused on the game waned accordingly. He missed the biggest moment—a Patriots trick play that led to a game-tying touchdown pass—when he was in the bathroom. He wasn't happy about that.

"I was in the fuckin' bathroom," he reminded us, after being told upon his return what he'd just missed. "Fuck!"

Eventually, Ted's sober and acutely embarrassed twenty-year-old son arrived at the bar with the obvious intention of giving his dad a safe ride home. That the son had been in a similar position on previous occasions was clear enough from the way he expertly handled his father's repeated entreaties that he wasn't in need of any assistance. Ted was happy just where he was, sitting there next to me. "He's a fuckin' Patriots fan," he told his son at least five times, gesturing toward me with affection.

After watching the Patriots hang on for a big comeback win, I declined repeated offers of a tequila shot from Ted, double-checked with Ted's son to make sure that he was OK to drive his dad home, and then made my way out—but not before Ted left me with some memorable parting words: "This fuckin' election, man. It's gonna be crazy. You watch. People are mad as fuck." Donald Trump was still five months away from announcing his candidacy, Bernie Sanders more than three months from getting in. At the time, none of the earnest practitioners of journalism were talking about either man as a viable contender. And they weren't talking about how sick of it all people like Ted were, either.

People were mad as fuck.

In geographic terms, the town of Errol is about thirty miles from the Quebec border. In practical terms, it is right in the middle of nowhere. Boasting fewer than three hundred residents, Errol sits at the junction of two roads that wind through the surrounding wilderness like asphalt-covered threads in a giant thorn bush. Errol's remoteness is its draw. Depending on the season, outdoorspeople come from all over the region to snowmobile, fish, hunt, boat, hike, kayak, and try their luck at spotting a moose. That last activity, however, has become increasingly challenging in recent years, as the moose population in northern New England has plummeted.

I arrived at the sensibly named Errol Motel just before 9:00 p.m.—the hour at which I had a few days earlier notified the inn's proprietor he could expect me (there was no online booking). The room he pointed me toward was clean and comfortable, but it was also freezing, because the manager had forgotten to turn on the heat before I arrived. When he called to apologize for the oversight, I told him it wasn't a big deal and that I'd be fine. I donned the long underwear and heavy sweatshirt that I hadn't planned to break out until the next morning, and all was well, as the room heated up slowly. I highly recommend the Errol Motel as a cozy lodging option if you're ever in the area to do some snowshoeing or need to dispose of a corpse. Just remember to bring your own shampoo and soap because the motel doesn't provide it.

By the time the sun came up the next morning, the temperature was on its way up into the double-digits. This development was a distinct blessing, considering that a cold spell the week before had left thermostats in the area bottoming out at −22°F. There hadn't been much precipitation in the days leading up to my visit, but this being January in northern New Hampshire, the motel parking lot was caked in a solid blanket of snow and ice. I made it out by throwing my rental car into drive and then quickly back into reverse. With a four-hour walk ahead of me, I was determined to find some breakfast, hoping that I wouldn't have to hunt for it myself.

I'd been prepared to consider myself lucky if I could get my hands on a pack of Skittles at the gas station. But it turned out that downtown Errol provided everything a traveler could possibly ask for in a place of its size: a general store, a post office, and a couple of restaurants. And, oh yeah, an international airport. Sure, the single-engine planes that skipped across the Canadian border on ten-minute flights probably weren't capable of whisking locals off to weekends in Bermuda, but no one could claim that Errol International Airport wasn't as advertised.

The Northern Exposure Restaurant was the obvious choice over The Hawg Trawf. Northern New Hampshire barbeque is a suspect proposition under even the most ideal circumstances, and at 7:30 a.m., with a long day of walking ahead of me, I figured it'd be akin to committing seppuku without the sword. After downing several cups of coffee and carb-loading on a tall stack of excellent blueberry pancakes, I made my way to the starting point of the walk, which was at Dixville Notch. A "notch" is basically a mountain pass. Dixville Notch—an unincorporated place that usually boasts somewhere in the neighborhood of ten full-time residents—is famous for its role in the New Hampshire primary, not its geological characteristics. Every four years since 1960, the residents of Dixville Notch have gathered shortly before midnight inside the Ballot Room of the Balsams Grand Resort Hotel—one of the North Country's several opulent nineteenth-century hotels—where they cast their ballots at the stroke of midnight. The votes are then tallied in front of the assembled media, and the results are reported on throughout Primary Day, giving Dixville Notch's winner a little attention boost as the voting continues in the rest of the state. The process is then repeated during the general election.

The tradition had lost some steam in recent cycles, as a couple of additional New Hampshire enclaves had gotten in on the act, and the Balsams was currently closed for renovations. But there were plans to reopen the place for the 2016 midnight vote, and the hotel's symbolic significance made it a good launching point for this particular band of long-distance walkers, which called itself the New Hampshire Rebellion.

Formed the previous year by Harvard professor and political activist Lawrence Lessig—who went on to run his own two-month campaign for the Democratic presidential nomination—the New Hampshire Rebellion was designed to draw attention to its pet issue: reducing the influence of money in politics. The group intended to highlight its cause by walking the length of the state at the most inhospitable time of the year. Hence, here I was. In my own experience as a political reporter, it was difficult to escape the conclusion that money was indeed at the root of most of what was wrong with the American political system. As such, I was attracted to the group's high-minded goal and was curious to find out how serious they really were about achieving it, even if it meant spending a few hours lacking the ability to feel my face and toes.

The concept of the multi-day winter walk was inspired by Doris Haddock, who went by the nickname "Granny D." Born in Laconia, New Hampshire, Granny D set off on foot on January 1, 1999, from Pasadena, California, to raise awareness for campaign-finance reform. When she started her walk, Granny D was eighty-eight. By the time she arrived in Washington, DC, fourteen months later, she was ninety. I planned to be the same age, thirty-one, at the end of my walk that I was at the start of it. In fact, I intended to participate only in Day One of what would be a ten-day New Hampshire Rebellion venture to Concord. The eleven-mile southbound hike along Route 26 on this particular day would be one that Granny D probably could have moonwalked in her sleep.

I hitched a ride to the starting point at Dixville Notch with one of the group's participants—a friendly attorney from Massachusetts named Bill, who had gotten involved in the walk after having done some legal work for Lessig's various groups. In chatting with Bill, I acquired my first hint that I had been grossly mistaken in my assumptions about what the participants in the walk would be like. In my mind, I'd been picturing a lot of deodorant-rationing patchouli aficionados, who would be glad to tell you what the *real* crime is, even if you hadn't asked. This perception had been, in part, a reflection of the overall tenor of the flurry of reply-all group e-mails I'd received at a rate of about a half dozen per day in the days preceding the walk. Among the most memorable had been a missive containing the lyrics to a self-penned song (intended to be read, the sender explained, to the tune of "If You're Happy and You Know It, Clap Your Hands"):

If worried 'bout our Congress, take a walk
If money's legal bribery, take a walk
When Congress aids the donors,
And the people are the losers
Our Democracy's in trouble
Take a walk.

After reading that, I was afraid. Once I started the walk, there'd be no way of bailing on these deeply sincere people and their rhythmic clapping and original song lyrics. But I'd already come this far, and Bill was setting my mind at ease.

Bill and I arrived at a parking lot just off the highway where we met the thirty-three other walkers who were taking part in that day's trek back to Errol. Some of them were planning to complete the full ten-day venture to Concord, but others were joining me in taking the more selective approach. When I mentioned to one of the walkers that the sub-zero temperatures of the previous week would have made our impending march a lot more uncomfortable, he told me about the first day of the group's walk from the previous year, which had been marked by the kind of drenching, cold rain that makes a person long for solid precipitation.

Before we took our first step, we first were given a safety talk from a young woman named Xanni, who was a former student of Lessig's at Harvard. Xanni told us that an RV stocked with food and first aid supplies would be following close behind the group at all times. "The signal that you need to get in the car is thumbs down," she added. I wondered about this. Was the walk really going to be so difficult that our ability to say something along the lines of, "I just broke my ankle and need to get in the car, please" would be rendered impossible? Would we all be so out of breath that the use of hand signals would be our only recourse? I didn't ask.

It was at this time that I noticed that many of my fellow participants were carrying homemade signs that said things like "Money Out Of Politics" and "How Are Your Interests Being Represented By Congress?" I wondered how many people were going to see those signs all the way up here. Again, I didn't ask. Several of my fellow walkers were already jogging in place to try to keep warm. One of them, a guy from Concord named Dan, was wearing the kind of sneakers that people typically put on to go for a quick jog on the treadmill, instead of the thick-soled boots I'd assumed would be required for those who wanted to make it out of this with the skin on the bottoms of their feet intact. So Dan won't have toes by the end of the walk, I thought to myself. If anyone else was concerned about the imminent demise of Dan's toes, though, they didn't let on.

After a brief pep talk from Lessig, we took our first steps onto Route 26. Within a minute or so, a man at the front of the pack produced a wooden flute from his satchel and started playing it, Pied Piper–style. It was pretty weird but also surprisingly energizing. I began to set my pace to the pro-campaign-finance reform flautist's rhythm. I was skeptical, however, that I was marching to the tune of impending reform. In spite of the best efforts of people like Granny D, John McCain, and Russ Feingold, American politics had never been more dependent on big money. In the 2012 presidential race, the general election campaigns of Barack Obama and Mitt Romney and their aligned outside groups spent over $1 billion each. There are a lot of problems that result from so much cash infusing our political system. To put it in simple terms, we had become a country where the whims of a malevolent but politically minded billionaire were far more important to electoral outcomes than the votes of a few million people in California or Texas. Since 2010, when the Supreme Court essentially removed the already cracked-opened floodgates of unencumbered political money in its *Citizens United v. FEC* decision, the problem had gotten worse with each subsequent campaign. Smart lawyers and consultants were always figuring out new ways to bring more money into the scam, while enriching themselves in the process and leaving the best interests of run-of-the-mill voters increasingly disposable.

The amount of time that the average candidate had to take out of his or her day to raise ever-increasing amounts of money, rather than thinking about policy, had become a national scandal in and of itself. And when candidates were victorious, they would instantly become beholden to the few groups and individuals who made their wins possible. All of this isn't to say that politicians didn't have good intentions. Many of them did. Just about all of them, though—the ones who get elected, at least—had become increasingly comfortable with working within this toxic system. President Obama, for instance, began his run in national politics as a leading voice in decrying the corrupting influence of big money, but then he went on to raise more of it than any politician in history, mostly through the indirect channels that Citizens United had helped to facilitate. A well-intentioned challenge to this system coming from a flautist and a couple dozen of his buddies on a hike through the New Hampshire wilderness seemed a bit far-fetched to me. Still, I wanted them to prove me wrong. I was eager to hear their plan and to believe that it could work in the same way that I wanted to believe that the Easter Bunny was real when I was a skeptical but optimistic seven-year-old.

And so we walked. It was easygoing at first. The layers I wore kept me warm, my boots proved sturdy, and the flautist stayed in tune. A couple of miles into it, I struck up a conversation with another man named Bill. He was in his sixties and hailed from the nearby town of Columbia, New Hampshire (population 750). This Bill, who wore his beard lumberjack-thick, according to local custom, was soft-spoken and to the point. He told me that he moved his family to the northern New Hampshire hinterlands in 1970, in order to "get out of the rat race." My fellow twenty-first-century urbanites might be surprised to learn that the desire to escape city life for an extreme, rural alternative was a common motivation at a time before mass gentrification. But Bill made this choice for his family when you still had to walk more than five blocks to get a decent locally sourced bean curd roll in downtown Toledo. Back to nature. That was the idea.

I told Bill that I planned to spend much of the next year in New Hampshire. When I had mentioned this intention to people previously, their responses had typically fallen somewhere in the range of "Oh, that's nice" to "Why?" Bill's reaction, though, was markedly different. "You can use my land to camp any time you want," he replied, without a moment's hesitation. My long-term New Hampshire housing prospects were, in fact, unclear, so I hesitated to dismiss the offer out of hand. But as nice as he was, Bill seemed like the kind of guy who might mistake me on a foggy morning for a tasty looking wild turkey and take a shot at me. I was carefully noncommittal but thanked him for his offer.

Eager to change the subject, I asked Bill what had motivated him to join the New Hampshire Rebellion walk. "I think anything you believe in, you have to act on," he said. "I just think you have to put your body on the line. There's not much I can do. I'm not eloquent. But I can walk." Actually, I found this sentiment to be far more eloquent than the typical drivel I was used to hearing from politicians.

During the entirety of the four-hour walk along the side of the only road connecting Dixville Notch and Errol, no more than two-dozen cars passed our group. I counted four of them that honked their horns in what was either a universal signal of solidarity or the New Hampshire way of saying, "Get off the road, so that I don't run your asses over." Just before we reached Errol International Airport, about halfway to our destination, we passed one of the few homes along our route. Suddenly, a middle-aged woman stormed out of her driveway and bolted toward us, as if we were coming to rob the place. "What the hell are you doing?" she shouted. "There's Canadian truckers that come here and don't stop."

There was a long pause until one brave woman stepped forward. "We're fighting to make our government accountable to you, rather than big donors," she said.

The homeowner appeared puzzled about what to make of that comment. But she remained certain about our impending fate. "Someone's gonna get killed," she said. "I guarantee it."

An impending death now promised to us, we continued on our way. Over the course of the next couple of hours, I engaged in some more chitchat and eavesdropped on an extended conversation that three of the walkers were having about cosmology. "I have a friend at MIT, and one of his theories is that the universe actually *is* mathematics," one of the participants said to the other two. OK, these were not a bunch of rubes out for a stroll because they had nothing better to do. But still, the question remained: Why? What were they hoping to achieve in risking their promised demises at the hands of some surly truck driver named Pierre, who had been swilling spiked maple syrup all the way from Quebec City?

One of the participants in the cosmology discussion stood out to me because he was the only person of color participating in the walk. With 96 percent of its residents of the Caucasian persuasion, New Hampshire is the third-whitest state in the country, behind only neighboring Maine and Vermont. New Hampshire's racial homogeny is one of the most persuasive arguments against its special status on the presidential primary calendar, and it's rare to attend a big political event in New Hampshire, either on the Republican or Democratic side, with more than a few black or brown faces in the crowd. But as soon as I began talking to him, it became abundantly clear that Addy Simwerayi's ethnic background was one of the least interesting things about the cherubic-faced twenty-three-year-old.

Addy was born and grew up in the Democratic Republic of the Congo (formerly Zaire), where his father was a political activist whose own pet issue was a topic of more immediate concern than campaign-finance reform. In the Congo at the time, rebel groups had developed a practice by which they would kidnap vulnerable young boys to become their child soldiers and young women to be their slaves. To combat this custom, Addy recalled, his father started a program to educate orphans and widows on preventive measures at a local church. These efforts did not particularly please the leaders of the rebel groups.

It was around 8:00 p.m. on a warm night in the year 2000 when they came for him. Several rebels burst into the house, and Addy, then nine years old, hid under the bed with his mother and six siblings. The home invaders beat Addy's father, hacked at his neck with machetes, and left him for dead. Somehow, Addy's father survived the ordeal and recovered from his gruesome injuries after receiving treatment from his cousin, who was a doctor. Then, as he did every year, Addy's father applied that fall for a US visa lottery and ended up winning the golden ticket out of the Congo for himself and his family. He even happened to have a friend who lived in Hooksett, New Hampshire, who offered to house them all.

The hitch was that Addy's father didn't have enough money to pay the international plane fares for nine people. So he and his wife first came to Hooksett themselves, in order to begin the process of getting situated in the United States, while Addy and his siblings stayed behind under the care of their grandmother and aunt. Things were calm for a while. Addy's aunt made a living for the family buying crops on farms and reselling them in the city for a modest profit. But Addy's aunt also carried the political-activist gene. One day, when she was on her daily bus trip out to a farm, she stood up and began preaching to her fellow passengers about the atrocities that were being committed by the rebel group that had nearly killed her brother. She urged them to fight back. One man on the bus, it turned out, was the wrong person to try to convince, and he had a cell phone on him. A few minutes after Addy's aunt began making her case, a group of rebels erected a crude barricade to block the bus's passage. In events that were later related to Addy, several members of the rebel group then jumped on board. In front of her fellow passengers, one of the assailants took a knife to Addy's aunt's face and cut off her lips. She died three days later.

Addy recalled these traumas to me in the straightforward manner of someone who has told his story many times before. Rhetorical flourishes were not required. With their grandmother the only adult left at home, Addy and his siblings next endured repeated, uninvited visits to their house from unknown men who had heard that their parents were in America and assumed that made the whole family rich. "Where's the money?" Addy recalled one of the men shouting during one particular home invasion. "You have American dollars!" This went on and on—every night carrying the possibility of unspeakable trauma.

Meanwhile, after a brief interlude in Uganda, Addy's parents met a professor at the University of New Hampshire—an advantageous connection that set the gears in motion for the entire family to move to the state. Addy and his siblings touched down in the United States on September 11, 2004. A congressman was there to greet them, and a limousine chauffeured them from the airport. "I'm like, what is this?" Addy recalled. "And we got in there and they had these muffins. I'd never had muffins before, so I puked." He laughed at the memory. "Then they gave me a mint, which I'd never had before, and that just didn't make me feel better."

Addy had his first experience with snow a couple of months later and began to make the kind of life transition that most people can only imagine. The family soon found a permanent home in Manchester, where Addy eventually enrolled in Central High School. He adjusted well, but his youngest brother proved to be less adaptive and was sent back to the Congo to attend boarding school there.

After graduating from high school, Addy completed an internship with the American Friends Service Committee (AFSC)—the Quaker-affiliated social-justice group with which he was employed when I met him on the walk. Addy said that he had first become interested in AFSC because the organization offered free pizza at its meetings every Thursday. But he soon found that he shared his father and his aunt's penchant for advocating for social justice. Addy traveled to Washington with the group to protest the Iraq War and became involved in community-building organizations closer to home. On one of candidate Barack Obama's early visits to New Hampshire in 2007, Addy was among the young people chosen to join the Illinois senator for lunch. He realized even then what a particular privilege it was for someone who was interested in politics and policy to live in the nation's first primary state. "Having that kind of opportunity is something unique to New Hampshire," he said.

After attending Manchester Community College, Addy took on a full-time position with AFSC and became somewhat of a renaissance man of the millennial generation. With an interest in music and entertainment, he had in his spare time begun working as a producer for a teenage hip-hop artist. He also took up script writing during his downtime. Addy planned to return to the Congo one day to start a socially conscious business enterprise, but until it came time to take over the world, more or less, he remained focused on what was going on in New Hampshire.

Addy didn't sound as passionate about campaign finance as some of the more committed members of this particular group. Like me, he was only walking one day. He was more interested in prison reform. But his enthusiasm for "changing the narrative" of the presidential campaign was palpable. He and the other members of his group planned to conduct research on the candidates, ask them questions at their events in the months leading up to Primary Day, and document their responses. In short, Addy wanted to change things. And he didn't know any way to do that, other than by lending his voice—and his feet—to a cause. In the context of the upcoming presidential campaign, this particular liberal-leaning activist had a sensible idea of how to cut through the clutter: by focusing on the more accessible long-shot candidates, rather than the front-runners, who tend to be much less accessible and heavily guarded in their public comments. He figured that it would prove difficult to have a real conversation with Hillary Clinton—widely considered the anointed Democratic nominee-in-waiting—but the Socialist senator from Vermont whom not many people had even heard of at this point? He could work with someone like that.

"We're hoping that someone like Bernie Sanders can rise up and get that voice, and that's going to push [Clinton] to talk about these issues," he told me. It's difficult to overstate how prescient this comment was. Sanders was still more than three months from entering the race. Few people thought he'd actually run, and even fewer believed he had any shot at all at even becoming relevant, if he did. Addy, however, saw things differently.

A few days after the walk, I ran into Addy at a Rand Paul event in Manchester, where he asked the soon-to-be official presidential candidate a question about the militarization of local police forces. The entire exchange with the Kentucky senator took little more than a minute, and none of the reporters who were on hand wrote about it. Nonetheless, I tried to take a step back and think about how unlikely it was that this interaction could even happen at all. There's something wonderful about a process that allows a kid from the Congo to stand face-to-face with a man who might become the next president of the United States and grill him on the topic of his own choosing. Addy embodied what was best about the New Hampshire primary.

We kept walking. At about mile seven or eight of the walk, I spoke for a bit with Lessig, who was near the front of the pack. I found him to be solemn and direct. He didn't have much time for the hints of skepticism that he probably detected in my voice when I asked him how this one group might realistically have an impact on the New Hampshire presidential primary—and by extension—the future of American politics. If the New Hampshire Rebellion could activate 50,000 or so voters who care about campaign-finance reform in this one state, he told me, it would be political malpractice for one of the dozen or so contenders in the field to not to make it a pet issue. There was some logic in that argument, I had to admit. Still, I remained skeptical that the issue would rise to the top of the heap in a political and media environment that much preferred to focus on the things that raise partisan ideologues' collective blood pressure. Campaign-finance reform just didn't fit the bill, or so I thought.

Still, I couldn't stop thinking about Addy. Maybe it was possible that determined individuals like him really could help to cut through the clutter and take the conversation directly to the candidates. Lessig was sure that they could. For the next few months, he told me, the New Hampshire Rebellion would train more people like Addy to ask pointed questions of presidential candidates at town hall meetings around the state. The one that they wanted to hammer home repeatedly was this: "What are you going to do to fix the system of corruption in American politics?" They would also ask other questions that the media were mostly ignoring, and they would repeat them until New Hampshire voters—and then the campaigns themselves—*had* to start paying more attention. It was a movement to show whether ideas, not money, still won presidential primaries—democratic activism in its most basic form. You didn't need a cable news show, or even a microphone, to engage in it. You just had to have the courage of your convictions. And you also had to be in New Hampshire, where the tone would be set for the rest of the country.

CHAPTER 6

A MONTH AND A HALF before I visited Bill Shaheen's law office in the seacoast town of Dover, his wife, Jeanne, had been elected to a second term in the US Senate. As a Democratic incumbent, she had managed to win in what was otherwise an excruciating year for members of her party. Shaheen was impressive in beating back a hard-fought campaign by her Republican challenger, former Massachusetts senator Scott Brown, whose charm and political dexterity had nearly been enough to overcome perceptions that he had—prepare to clutch your pearls—harbored politically opportunistic motives in relocating to New Hampshire to run for her seat. But Shaheen had too much clout, and her ties to the state ran too deep. The first female senator in New Hampshire's history, she had served three two-year terms as governor prior to ascending to the Senate. She was the only woman in the history of this country who has been called both "Governor" and "Senator"— a singular feat befitting her unrivaled status as the gatekeeper to

Democratic political life in New Hampshire, both as an officeholder and influencer. In short, Jeanne Shaheen was a one-woman Granite State institution.

And so, I expected a certain level of stateliness when I walked into the corner office that was occupied by the other half of New Hampshire's most prominent political couple on that wintry morning. I'd never met Bill Shaheen before, but I knew that he had been almost as much of a power player in New Hampshire politics over the previous four decades—albeit mostly behind the scenes—as his wife was. He'd recently been elected as the DNC committeeman for New Hampshire and remained one of the most sought-after political operatives in the state for any Democratic candidate running at any level. So I was a little surprised when I entered Bill Shaheen's office and saw that the person sitting behind his desk was dressed more like a hardware store clerk than a custodian of New Hampshire's Democratic establishment. Shaheen wore a flannel shirt with a brown woven belt, which held up a pair of stonewashed jeans that I surmised had been purchased sometime before the fall of the Berlin Wall. He had a thick, northern New England accent and facial features that were as craggy as the nearby mountains. After I offered a brief introduction and sat down in the chair in front of him, he kicked up onto his desk his Nike low-tops, which were lined with white tube socks. His personality was as no-frills as his clothing—nothing like the silky smooth, expensively suited hucksters who tend to pull the levers of politics in Washington. Bill Shaheen was New Hampshire through and through. I liked him right away.

In spite of his dressed-down appearance, Shaheen did allow himself the indulgence of decorating his office with photos of himself and his wife posing with various Democratic presidential candidates over the decades. "Bill, thank you for ALL your help! You're the best. Hillary," read the inscription from the former secretary of state, whose 2008 New Hampshire presidential campaign Shaheen had co-chaired until he stepped down upon receiving blowback for raising Barack Obama's adolescent drug use as a campaign issue. But from the beginning of our conversation, Shaheen was intent on hammering home the idea that he wasn't a pretentious guy, as if his wardrobe choices hadn't already made that abundantly apparent. "I come from shoe shop people," he told me with pride, noting that neither of his parents had completed high school.

Shaheen's first taste of presidential politics was imbued with the flavor of glue (he licked stamps for JFK while he was a student at Dover High School in 1960). After a stint in the army, he graduated second in his class from Ole Miss Law School in 1973 and then returned home to New Hampshire, where he became the city attorney in Somersworth and had his first child with Jeanne. Then one winter night in early 1975, he attended a political event at the Ramada Inn in Dover with about two dozen other people. The highlight was Jimmy Carter, a soft-spoken and little-known former governor of Georgia. Just about everyone else in attendance that night had been only mildly curious to hear what Carter had to say. Shaheen was more than curious. As one of the few people in the room who had some personal experience living in the Deep South (Jeanne had taught at the first integrated high school in Mississippi), he liked what he saw in Carter, who had famously vowed that segregation in Georgia was over forever. Standing before him was a good, honest man—not to mention a skillful politician and a centrist who could win in parts of the country that had become increasingly challenging for Democrats. And more important, Shaheen told me, sneakers still propped up on his desk, he could see that "Carter's heart was in the right place."

As Carter lingered for a while after the event, Shaheen approached him and said five words to the long-shot presidential candidate that would change both of their lives: "I want to help you." Shaheen may have been brand new to presidential politics, but so was Carter. And lacking other good options in New Hampshire, the Georgian took him up on the offer. Soon after that meeting, Chris Brown—a young man who had coordinated Carter's earliest Granite State efforts even before Shaheen got on board—called a statewide campaign meeting to elect a New Hampshire chairman. About three hundred people expressed some interest in attending.

Eight of them actually showed up. As Shaheen recalls, all eight offered reasons they couldn't take on what would be a demanding job—even for a candidate like Carter, who had very little chance. Shaheen, meanwhile, was the only one in the room who couldn't come up with a good excuse on the spot. "I looked around the room and said, 'Oh, fuck, what are we going to do now?'"

Shaheen agreed to the job before he notified his boss, who was a retired judge. "Listen, Judge," Shaheen recalls telling him. "I'm going to help this guy Jimmy Cah-tah become president."

"Jimmy who?" his boss replied.

"Jimmy Cah-tah."

"Is he the guy who rides the white horse and sings songs?"

"That's Jimmy Walk-ah," Shaheen said. "This is Jimmy Cah-tah. He's a peanut fah-mah."

Shaheen told his boss that if he wasn't going to be fired, he intended to take two and a half days per week to devote to the judge. Shaheen would work for Carter the other four and a half days a week (he intended to work through every weekend). His boss agreed to keep Shaheen on but under the condition that his pay be cut in half. That sounded fine to Shaheen, who then explained the situation to Carter. The candidate offered to make up the difference in his salary, but Shaheen declined. "I'm not doing this for you," he recalls telling the Georgia Democrat. "I'm doing this for my country. You can't pay me. I'm not taking your money. And if you were going to pay me for the hours I'm about to work, you couldn't afford it." That kind of financial sacrifice is rare in the modern, highly lucrative world of political consulting. But it is not unheard of among the small group that composes New Hampshire's most sought-after senior campaign chairmen and women—people like Bill Shaheen, who continue to offer part-time services to candidates for free.

In this particular era, long before micro-targeting took hold, one of the Carter team's vote-getting techniques in the early days of the campaign was to approach people at random on the streets of New Hampshire and offer them little bags of peanuts. Eventually, they had to stop because opponents suggested that the former peanut farmer's campaign was illegally giving away something of value, in order to win votes. In New York, people who want to influence elections are disgraced for dispensing no-show patronage jobs and six-figure bribes. In New Hampshire, they're shamed for offering peanuts.

After the peanut setback, Shaheen and the rest of his newbie New Hampshire crew continued to grind it out. "We worked all the time," is the way Shaheen remembers the next year of his life heading into the February 1976 primary. "We worked so hard that we burned a couple kids out." They were innovative as well as dogged. At a time when New Hampshire voters still selected delegates to the national party convention directly, Shaheen's mother—an eighth-grade-educated ward clerk—warned her son that Carter's voters were going to be confused about which prospective delegates they should pick. As a solution, she suggested that the campaign distribute to supporters sample ballots that highlighted the delegates they'd identified as Carter supporters. Shaheen crunched some numbers and determined that he needed $15,000 to complete the task. But when he asked the national campaign for the cash, his request was denied. Fortunately for him, and for the future president, a Carter campaign official from well-funded New York—who had identified the importance of New Hampshire to Carter's hopes of winning the nomination—came through with the funds.

Carter's original strategy had called for replicating the relatively laid-back style of campaigning that presidential candidates had typically employed in New Hampshire up to that point, limiting interviews and appearances in private and public venues. But to the frenetic and personable candidate, that strategy made no sense. From his first appearance in the state, Carter worked as hard as his young staffers did. In fact, he worked harder than any candidate who had ever run for president in New Hampshire, packing his schedule with as many small events and local interviews as he could fit in from dawn to dusk.

New Hampshire voters were impressed, and so were Carter's opponents. As a staffer working for Arizona congressman Mo Udall—widely considered the leading "liberal alternative" to Carter—put it, the former Georgia governor worked "for a year as though it were the last six weeks of the campaign. That saturation campaigning made him impossible to beat."

On the heels of a big January victory in Iowa, Carter proved that a Georgian who sounded the part could win way up north in New Hampshire, as he ended up with 28 percent of the vote in the February 24 primary—good enough for a six-point victory over Udall in a deeply splintered field. With his New Hampshire victory, Carter was on his way to the Democratic nomination and the presidency.

With his hands folded behind his head and his low-tops still resting atop his desk, Shaheen summed up the approach he had used when running a campaign in New Hampshire four decades earlier, a principle that remained unchanged into the second decade of the twenty-first century. "When you're doing this for nothing, you can't fake it," he said. "The amount of time you put in, you can't equate it with money. It's *all* the time. I think about it, I dream about it. If I don't believe in it, I'm not doing it."

CHAPTER 7

I T'S HARD TO REMEMBER in retrospect, but at the outset of the
2016 presidential campaign, the most fascinating Republican
contender was widely considered to be none other than Rand
Paul. Labeled "the most interesting man in politics" on the cover
of *Time* magazine, Rand was thought to be a serious threat to win
the GOP nomination that his father, Ron, had sought twice before.
Rand, it was commonly accepted, was a much better politician than
his father ever was. Why? Because the son had no problem with
being opportunistic and modulating some of his views at just the
right time, whereas the father would never dream of compromising
his principles. Rand was running for president to win; Ron had run
to make a point. Little did we know at the time that running to
make a point in 2016 would turn out to be just the right blueprint for
electoral success in New Hampshire, whereas playing the game the
way everyone expected it to be played meant certain doom.

In spite of his political dexterity, Rand Paul didn't merely harbor libertarian views. His every observation about life often seemed

filtered through the eternal battle he saw being waged between "individual liberty and government overreach"—a perspective that his father had imbued in him since his first bedside reading of Ayn Rand. Like his dad, it seemed to me, Rand was the rare top-tier presidential contender who got into politics more to implement his worldview than to achieve power for its own sake. That didn't mean that his estimation of his own greatness wasn't ironclad. It was. The wrinkle was that in his heart of hearts, Rand Paul was an honest-to-God ideologue whose ambition to become president of the United States was merely an offshoot of that self-certainty.

But what Rand Paul had in conviction, he lacked in conviviality. One afternoon, when he was stumping in New Hampshire before the 2014 midterms on behalf of Republican congressional candidates in the state, I had been chatting with a couple of his staff members in a Manchester hotel lobby when the soon-to-be presidential candidate sauntered over to pass a few spare minutes with us. I had already interviewed Paul earlier in the day and had a beer in front of me, rather than a tape recorder, so it was clear that this would be an informal chat. I asked him about his recent charity trip to Guatemala, in which he had exchanged his politician's suit for his ophthalmologist's lab coat, in order to perform life-changing cataract surgery on dozens of patients. It had been the latest iteration of the annual medical charity trips that Paul took to the developing world—an excursion that was wholly commendable and offered an opportunity to see who Paul really was as a person. For most people, my question would have provided a chance to reflect on what it was like to give a person the gift of sight after years—and even decades—of blindness. What a powerful thing! Instead, he launched into a riff about an inexpensive piece of medical equipment that had been banned by the US government but had allowed him to perform the surgeries more economically in Central America. Somehow, Paul had taken my casual inquiry about his international charity work and immediately turned it into a diatribe against overregulation.

Fundamentally, Paul was an introvert who would rather be doing anything but talking to voters and reporters, if it weren't for the inconvenient problem of believing so strongly in his ideology. Sure, he might show up at the Kentucky Derby to knock back a bourbon for the cameras, but anyone who spent even a little bit of time with him had to become aware that he regarded humanity with a professorial distance that made Barack Obama's cerebral and sometimes aloof bearing seem downright gregarious in comparison. The distinct impression that I felt every time I interviewed Rand Paul was that my questions were boring him. And when he mixed with crowds on the trail, his eyes typically appeared to glaze over, while he kept his hands planted deep in his pants pockets—the picture of barely contained misanthropy. Pushed by his aides to do so, he would make an effort to shake every hand in the room, but he did it with the enthusiasm of a newly arrived prisoner greeting his cellmates.

Paul also had an unfortunate tendency to speak before he'd thought his comments through. I had witnessed this habit during one of his early New Hampshire visits, when he told a well-lubricated nighttime crowd outside the minor league baseball stadium in Manchester, "I think the first executive order that I would issue would be to repeal all previous executive orders."

The next morning, Paul's top political aide, Doug Stafford, took the prudent step of walking back the comment, telling a reporter that the senator's remark "was not made to be taken literally." OK, fine. A politician said something off-the-cuff that he didn't really mean—it happens from time to time. The problem with Stafford's statement? Paul hadn't gotten the message. In an interview I conducted with him later that morning, Paul reiterated his belief that repealing every previous executive order was "a nice idea" and that "you could sunset them all and really repeal them all, and then you could start over." All of them? Even the Emancipation Proclamation? What about President Truman's executive order that desegregated the military? I noticed that Paul's eyes widened a bit as he perked up for the first time since we'd begun our conversation. "Well, I mean, I think those are good points, and it was an offhand comment," he said. "So, obviously, I don't want to repeal the Emancipation Proclamation and things like that." Right, it's nice to have things like that.

Despite his shortcomings as a candidate, I have to admit that at the outset of the race, it seemed to me that Paul would be well-positioned in New Hampshire—the early voting state whose libertarian streak is codified in its motto. For all of his faults, Paul exuded the "live free or die" ethos. He and his political team knew that in order to have a shot, New Hampshire was something close to a must-win. They also knew that their best chance of winning there was to string together an oddball coalition of college stoners, dangerous-looking men with "Private Property" signs posted at the end of their long gravel driveways, and some run-of-the-mill conservatives who'd grown tired of the typical Chamber of Commerce–friendly Republican nominees of years past. The formula made sense, in theory. But a few days after my winter walk in Errol with the New Hampshire Rebellion, I happened to be the lone journalist to bear witness to a moment that, for me, summed up in one neat little ball the reason this particular Republican rebel's candidacy probably was doomed from the get-go.

It all started with a chipped tooth. During my sophomore year of high school, my face had an unfortunate collision with the frame of a tennis racquet—an encounter that left me looking a bit like one of the mountain men from *Deliverance*. I had a veneer put on to cover the chip, but the problem with veneers is that they tend to break every few years when a chicken wing or a crouton connects with them at just the wrong angle. The night before Rand Paul came to New Hampshire for his latest trip there, I was at Mint Bistro—my favorite restaurant in downtown Manchester—and I'd just bitten into an Asian short-rib nacho when I heard the familiar crunching noise, which signaled that I had a couple of trips to the dentist's office and a bill totaling several hundred dollars to look forward to later in the week. In the meantime, I would have to spend the following day reporting on a presidential candidate with a jagged hole where my left front tooth used to be.

Although he had not yet declared his candidacy officially, Paul had scheduled a full day of retail-style stops around southern New Hampshire with nary a wink and a nod about his 2016 intentions.

The guy was running, and he didn't make any effort to play it coy on this particular day. He spoke—mostly with his hands tucked into his pockets, and always in a monotone, bored-teenager murmur—about old Republican ideas such as eliminating the Department of Education and newer ones such as preventing the government from spying on citizens' cell phones. The latter proposal was a particular hit during his visit to the Londonderry Fish and Game Club, for what was billed on as a "Second Amendment Supporter Event." The gathering was labeled on Paul's schedule as being "open press," but club president Rick Olson had other ideas. I was a late arrival, and the crowd inside the aluminum structure that served as the group's headquarters was pretty substantial. As such, I had to rely on my years of training as a campaign journalist to bend and contort my body in the manner required to board a rush-hour train in midtown Manhattan, in order to get inside.

When it came time to begin the proceedings, Olson announced that he and his fellow club members first had to take care of "some executive club business" and thus would kindly have to ask the members of the media on hand to leave the premises temporarily. After a few moments of inaction leading into some meek sighs of protest from my fellow members of the fourth estate, the several dozen journalists who had assembled near the stage began filing out of the aluminum structure. On a whim, I decided not to join them in exiting. This wasn't a particularly brave or noble act on my part—it was just that I was already standing toward the back, and I was pretty sure that if I could keep my audio recorder partially concealed, everyone would assume that I was a card-carrying member of the gun club. I'm not saying that my missing front tooth helped to sell the idea that I was just another pistol-packing, "don't-tread-on-me" club member, but it certainly didn't hurt.

Once all of the other journalists had finished filing out of the room, Olson quickly dispensed with any pretense that the line about "club business" was sincere and handed the microphone over to Paul, who no doubt took the stage harboring the reasonable assumption that no one from the outside world was listening. In his remarks,

Paul wowed the crowd by telling them the story about how he had launched his 2010 Senate campaign at a "machine-gun festival." Apparently, there were no surface-to-air missile festivals in town that weekend. He talked about his support for demilitarizing local police forces and arming commercial pilots ("a no-brainer") and his opposition to no-knock warrants and limiting magazines. "From a practical point of view, I'm not that great a shot, so I need a few more chances," Paul joked.

His rhetoric was jarring, though not especially surprising, considering the speaker and his venue. It wasn't until the Q-and-A session that followed his speech that Paul really let his guard down and went full-on true-believer to an extent that I considered to be beyond the pale for someone who deigned to harbor realistic hopes of becoming president. The question that Paul received was about the United Nations, and he took it as an opportunity to tee off on some of the "highly objectionable" UN treaties that he said threatened to encroach on American sovereignty. That part of his answer was all well and good and in keeping with statements that he had made previously. But when someone in the crowd followed up with a suggestion to "get the UN out of the US," Paul responded with a buoyant "Hear, hear" and proceeded to escalate his rhetoric into the domain of isolationist radicalism.

"The concept of having a body where we discuss diplomacy and discuss things isn't a bad one necessarily," he began. At that point, I sensed that a big, bright-red "However" was on the way, and Paul didn't disappoint. "There's a lot of reasons why I don't like the UN," he continued. "And I think I'd be happy to dissolve it."

Rand Paul would be "happy" to dissolve the United Nations? There, in an instant, the vocal critic of the UN had gone on the record as a proponent of discontinuing the international body entirely, like it was an out-of-date toaster. This was John Birch Society stuff. And even worse, when the words came out of Paul's mouth, it sounded as if he was coming up with the idea on the fly. "I *think* I'd be happy to dissolve it." Sure, that sounds cool. Why not? It was a line that Paul—-who had long been taking pains to say that he was merely a "noninterventionist" and not an isolationist—would never have conceived of uttering in a foreign policy speech at the Council on Foreign Relations or during an appearance on *Meet the Press*. But here in small-town New Hampshire, during what he believed to be a closed-door gathering of like-minded souls, it was a surefire applause line, and he couldn't resist indulging just this one time. And that, ultimately, was the problem: that it was just one time. This was not a year when the Republican rank and file wanted its candidates to wink knowingly every now and then in private settings. No, they wanted their zealotry wide out in the open where everyone could see it. With Donald Trump's anti-NATO screeds still far off on the horizon, Paul was trying to play the cute political game within the established norms. It was the way the nomination had always been won before—the way his dad could never bring himself to engage, as he built his own formidable movement within the party. As it turned out, Rand Paul proved to be neither the most interesting man in politics nor the most interesting man in his own family.

At the time, however, I merely assumed that by saying aloud what he actually thought, Paul had really screwed up. Surely the mainline conservative Republicans and moderate independent voters who had long composed the majority of the New Hampshire GOP primary electorate would never stand for this kind of extreme rhetoric. You couldn't just come up to New Hampshire and say whatever you wanted, even in private, just because it stoked the basest impulses in the most hard-line voters, right? As it turned out, you could indeed do just that—and a whole lot more—but only if you were a candidate who possessed two traits that Paul lacked: sparkling charisma and utter shamelessness. As future events would demonstrate, it wasn't Rand Paul's occasionally extreme rhetoric that prevented his campaign from getting off the ground. It was rather his inability to match his jarring words with the kind of self-aggrandizing populism that only a certain billionaire with an unhealthy TV ratings obsession could provide.

CHAPTER 8

W HEN HE RAN FOR president a second time in 1976, Ronald Reagan made New Hampshire a strategic focus from the get-go. With popular former governor Hugh Gregg running his campaign in the state, the conservative challenger to incumbent President Gerald Ford held what were dubbed "citizens' press conferences" around the state, in which Reagan would first read from a prepared script and then take questions from the crowd, early precursors to the town hall meetings that John McCain would make famous in the 2000 campaign. New Hampshire Republicans were largely impressed with the two-term former California governor, whose sunny demeanor and hard-line principles made for a potent combination on the stump. But what may have cost Reagan victory in New Hampshire that year—and, ultimately, the GOP nomination—was a January speech he delivered in Chicago, in which he appeared to come out in favor of cuts to federal spending that would increase tax burdens on the states. The Ford campaign pounced, contending that Reagan wanted New Hampshire to impose a general sales and income tax on its residents for the first time—a charge that was roughly akin to a presidential candidate in Wisconsin being accused of wanting to ration beer and cheese. Gregg and the rest of Reagan's New Hampshire team tried to keep expectations low, but when Ford ended up eking out a win on Primary Day by less than 2,000 votes, the president's narrow victory was all he needed to claim the momentum.

Four years later, Reagan, by then the front-runner for the Republican nomination, didn't work New Hampshire on the ground as extensively as he had in 1976. The initial 1980 blueprint for his campaign was in keeping with Reagan's overall efforts to remain "above the fray"—a strategy that has worked about as well over the years in New Hampshire as the "prevent defense" has in the NFL.

The reality check came on January 21, 1980, with Reagan's unexpected defeat in Iowa at the hands of George H. W. Bush. Reagan's campaign team had for the most part kept the candidate far away from Iowa. He had even spent the night of the caucuses at his home in Los Angeles, rather than demonstrating any urgency to win what he derided (accurately) as a "straw vote." That tactic proved to be a massive mistake. Reagan's defeat in Iowa was a stunning upset and a major setback for his chances. Working in his favor was the unusually long thirty-five-day period that year between the Iowa and New Hampshire votes, during which he could try to save his candidacy. Still, the task before Reagan was an especially daunting one, as his own New Hampshire internal polling showed him losing to Bush by twenty-one points. It was time to get into the thick of the fray.

The most famous moment of Reagan's 1980 primary campaign transpired inside the Nashua High School gymnasium three days before the February 26 primary. What went down there amounted to one of the all-time great political setups. The *Nashua Telegraph* had agreed to sponsor a one-on-one debate between Reagan and Bush, which would have excluded four of the other major Republican candidates in the race, who were in the state at the time: Illinois congressman John Anderson, Illinois senator Howard Baker, Kansas senator Bob Dole, and Illinois congressman Phil Crane. But when the Federal Election Commission ruled that the newspaper's sponsorship of such an event would have amounted to an illegal campaign contribution to Reagan and Bush, the Reagan campaign agreed to settle the matter by paying for the forum itself. At the last minute, Reagan decided to invite the four other GOP contenders to the debate—clearly, in retrospect, an attempt to goad Bush. It worked. Bush, quite understandably, was livid. These weren't the rules to which he had agreed.

Just before the debate started, with Bush already on stage, a confident Reagan entered the gym with the four newly invited candidates in tow. Bush was visibly irritated, and so was the forum's moderator, *Nashua Telegraph* editor Jon Breen, who also wanted to host the one-on-one debate to which the Reagan and Bush camps had agreed. When it was announced that the other four candidates would not be allowed to participate, an irate Reagan began to protest in front of the already riled-up 2,000 or so spectators in attendance. Then, in a last-ditch effort to reestablish his authority, Breen ordered the sound technician to turn off Reagan's microphone after the candidate asked to address the crowd.

"I am paying for this microphone, Mr. Green [*sic*]!" Reagan shot back.

Breen was not persuaded. Eventually, the four other candidates agreed to leave the stage, and the one-on-one debate that Bush called for went forward. As far as the impact of the moment, that Bush ultimately got his way mattered about as much as it did that Reagan got Breen's name wrong. What actually counted was that Reagan had shown himself to be a man who took charge and got what he wanted—not anything like the pedantic and publicly apprehensive Bush, who couldn't even summon the courage to look his opponent in the eye, as he whined about the rules. For the next three days, the "paying for this microphone" clip ran on local and national news shows over and over, helping to cement Reagan's tough-guy image and the perception that Bush probably would have been more comfortable on the croquet court than he would staring down the Soviets. Reagan ended up winning the state by a previously inconceivable twenty-seven-point margin. It wasn't just an iconic sound bite from the 1980 campaign—it was the moment that turned around Reagan's political career and launched him to the presidency. That, at least, has long been the popular interpretation.

Here's what actually happened. Reagan had already begun gaining ground in New Hampshire *weeks* before what became known as the "Saturday Night Massacre" in Nashua. As it did in 1976, the *Union Leader* endorsed the former California governor. Loeb provided editorial cover in his typical manner. The cantankerous publisher denigrated Bush simultaneously as both "an oil man from Texas" and a pawn of the "entire Eastern establishment." (Reagan would end up beating Bush in Manchester itself by a margin of 74.8 percent to 9.4 percent.)

Loeb's backing helped, but Reagan also lifted himself. Most notably, he learned from the mistake he'd made in Iowa when he acted as if stumping vigorously was somehow beneath him. From the moment the campaign moved to New Hampshire, Reagan determined that he would go all out and make himself available in face-to-face interactions with as many voters as possible—as he'd done four years earlier—even if it was his birthday.

Fewer than three weeks removed from his crushing Iowa defeat and more than two weeks before the "Saturday Night Massacre" had all but sealed his New Hampshire victory, the Gipper wasn't in a mood to spend much time celebrating sixty-nine candles on February 6, 1980. He had a packed schedule of retail events around New Hampshire on a seasonably cold day, and he wanted to get closer to real people than was generally possible. A major nuisance for Reagan at that time was his Secret Service detail, which frequently kept him at much more than arm's length from New Hampshire voters—a maddening physical obstacle for the gregarious candidate. But with the slaying of Bobby Kennedy in 1968 and the attempted assassination of George Wallace in 1972 still fresh memories, early and stringent Secret Service protection for serious presidential candidates had become de rigueur. Reagan had been assigned a detail even before he announced his candidacy in November of the previous year. On the final stop of his birthday swing through New Hampshire, however, he was determined not to let the Secret Service get in the way of making some personal connections.

It was well after dark by the time the candidate and his substantial Secret Service and staff entourage arrived at the University of New Hampshire's campus in Durham and made for the Tau Kappa Epsilon (TKE) fraternity house. Reagan had become a TKE member himself while attending Eureka College all the way back in 1929, and he was warmly greeted by the newest generation of brothers at UNH. After he made some informal remarks about what the fraternity had meant to him, it wasn't long before someone offered Reagan a beer, the purpose of which—it was explained flatly—was to wash down his slice of birthday cake. Then, as now, there were few more enticing social achievements for a college kid than getting a famous person to drink their terrible beer.

Ever the polished performer, Reagan knew when it was time to call it a night. After about ten minutes of handshakes and photo-ops, the candidate and most of his support staff bid the fraternity brothers a fond farewell and headed for the airport. But for a group of campaign advance men and Secret Service agents who were now off the clock, the party was just getting started. Paul Young, who was president of the UNH chapter of TKE at the time, still remembers what transpired.

"The Secret Service agents are showing us their guns, they're getting hammered. They're smoking dope with the advance people. They get them hammered. At the time, we had fire extinguishers hanging on the wall. They took them and sprayed down the girls who were there with water."

After a few more hours of collegiate revelry, Reagan's advance men decided they'd best head out. Things turned particularly hairy at this point, when a carful of boozed-up Reagan advance staffers drove directly into a stone retaining wall. Unable to restart the engine and out of clear options for how to rectify their predicament in the pre–cell phone era, they took off on foot. The next morning, as Young recalls, the cops made a cursory call to the fraternity to try to get an idea of what had happened, but nothing ever came of it. "That was campaigning in the old days," Young said.

Knowing what we do now about the extracurricular activities of some Secret Service agents in recent years, it might not seem particularly astonishing that a few of the men who were tasked with guarding the life of a future president once used their downtime between shifts to put on an impromptu wet T-shirt contest on a college campus before engaging in some—at best—questionably sober driving. But when you stop to consider that Reagan was a man who, a little more than a year beyond the event in question, would barely survive an assassination attempt, it is quite a bit more jarring.

CHAPTER 9

IN MARCH 2015, I took my first reporting trip to New Hampshire as a newly minted employee of the "Huffington Puffington Post," as Rush Limbaugh referred to it. I took the train from New York City to Boston, where I planned to rent a car and drive up to see Texas senator Ted Cruz, who was on his inaugural New Hampshire swing as an official presidential candidate. The previous week, Cruz had become the first major GOP contender to announce his candidacy—a smart move to generate some early publicity for a candidate who at the time was widely considered a heavy underdog and had fewer friends in Washington than Kim Jong Un. Somewhere in Connecticut, I got up from my seat to hit the café car and ran into a Republican political operative I'd known for a long time who was also heading to New Hampshire and wasn't particularly sympathetic to the junior senator from Texas. I mentioned that I was on my way up to cover the Cruz festivities. "Oh yeah?" he replied. "I've got something for you."

The man who was hosting Cruz at his very first event as a 2016 contender, as it turned out, was none other than Jack Kimball—a

former New Hampshire Republican Party chairman who had resigned from that position in 2011 just before the party's executive
committee was poised to force him out after a brief six-month tenure. Kimball had always been an outcast in state GOP politics, but
he had more or less been tolerated as an absurd curiosity. Still, main-
stream New Hampshire Republicans were embarrassed that they'd
once elected someone to lead them who frequently called for President Obama's arrest and espoused similarly extreme views every
time he stepped in front of a microphone. But my tipster let me in
on an additional item of note: that Kimball was an avid social-media
user who had taken a particularly active interest in spreading conspiracy theories on his publicly accessible Facebook page. I took a
look right away and found that his were the types of missives that
give people who wear tinfoil hats a bad name. They included a post
on the previous day in which Kimball linked to a YouTube video
titled, "Military Takeover Plan Revealed: Is Your State Next?" A
week and a half earlier, he had warned his friends in a post he'd
written: "Urgent Urgent Urgent The US has gone to defcon 3 (yellow) and there has apparently been some air battles between our Air
Force and Russia off the coast of Alaska. Just happened a short time
ago. Check out this video then go to the defcon message board for
further information (google it). Spread the word."

Kimball's paranoid views had become a matter of local public record when NHJournal.com—a news site operated by state Republican operatives—obtained an e-mail in which he had warned
friends and family to "be alert" because, he said, his daughter and
son-in-law had recently witnessed dozens of white military vehicles
in Maine heading south toward New Hampshire. "Don't know what
they were doing or where they were going but the white vehicles
sound more like UN trucks," he wrote. Another local website, the
Portsmouth Patch, then reported that one of Kimball's friends subsequently replied to let him know that the trucks had belonged to a
convoy of National Guard medical units returning from a training
exercise and did not, in fact, constitute the early movements of a UN
attack on the homeland.

A somewhat chastened Kimball then explained that his initial "be alert" e-mail had merely been in keeping with the extent of the dangers out there. "We're all concerned about what's going on with Obama," he told the *Portsmouth Patch*. "We've all been talking about what's happening. We've got Chinese troops arriving in Hawaii . . . and Kansas. There's a lot of things going on that are very suspicious. There are a lot of people that are very vigilant."

I checked with a few New Hampshire Republicans of sound mind to make sure it was really possible that Ted Cruz's first introducer as a presidential candidate had said so many things publicly that were so batshit crazy. It was all true, I was assured by multiple sources, and so I banged out a story before joining up with Cruz later in the day, giving it the headline: "Ted Cruz's First Campaign Stop Hosted by Conspiracy Buff Who Wants Obama Arrested." It was the sort of thing that I knew would get clicks, but it was also legitimately newsworthy because it revealed the kind of people with whom a would-be president was comfortable associating on the campaign trail. At best, it was a sign of incompetence by Cruz's not-yet-ready-for-primetime staff. At worst, it suggested that the Ivy League–educated Cruz was more than willing to ride shotgun on the Crazy Train if it helped lead him on a path to the White House.

I also knew that in writing my article, I had brought negative attention to a man who was—shall we say—unpredictable in how he might react to criticism. So it was with more than a little trepidation that I entered VFW Post 8641 in Merrimack, an upper-middle-class town of 25,000 people tucked between Nashua and Manchester whose biggest draw is its one-hundred-store outlet mall. Cruz's first New Hampshire event as a presidential candidate was being sponsored by something called the "Conservative Business League of New Hampshire." This was a newly formed group that would serve as Kimball's attempt to put a sensible-sounding name to his specious views.

The place was packed when I got there just before the 3:00 p.m. start time, and camouflage was by far the most popular color in the crowd. In New Hampshire, at small events for candidates who don't have Secret Service protection, it's typically possible to enter the venue as a member of the media without displaying any accreditation. In fact, I didn't even own a media credential throughout the vast majority of the 2016 campaign. So in entering the Cruz event, I attempted to perform my usual move of sliding past the press check-in desk without talking to anyone. It didn't work this time, as a burly, mustachioed man sitting on the other side of the table stopped me in my tracks. His bearing was that of the kind of guy who worked at the DMV and took great pleasure in failing people on their driving tests after parallel parking half an inch too far from the curb.

"Hold up," he shouted, even though I was standing two feet away from him. "Are you media?"

"How could you tell?" I replied, unable to disguise my irritation. I put my laptop bag down on the table, wondering whether I should just identify myself as a card-carrying member of the "Huffington Puffington Post" and get it over with.

"You have the look about you," the walrus-like enforcer shot back.

As I signed myself in, I decided to continue to engage him. "What look?" I asked.

He didn't answer right away. Instead, he let me finish writing down my contact information. Then he paused for another few seconds. If he had been carrying a cigar, I was sure he would have lit it right at that moment.

"Oh," he said finally. "I keep that to myself."

As I backed away from the table, the man at the desk added one more thing: "It's because you look lost." And then he finally smiled. It wasn't the creepy, knowing smile of a dangerous and paranoid vigilante. It was just the smile of a friendly campaign volunteer who was screwing with me a little bit—the smile of a regular New Hampshire guy, who happened to like Ted Cruz.

I made my way into the middle of the crowd of a couple of hundred people and waited for the event to begin. Before too long, a familiar tune began to reverberate from the PA system: "Where the Stars and Stripes and the Eagle Fly." For the uninitiated, the catchy, aggressively patriotic song was recorded and released by country singer Aaron Tippin shortly after 9/11. As such, it was the perfect fit for Ted Cruz's campaign kickoff. Cruz had recently said in an interview with *CBS This Morning* that he had lost his previous taste for rock and roll in the wake of that sunny Tuesday morning and had simultaneously acquired a new appreciation for country music. Kind of weird, right? Why did that happen? Because the response of the country music community to 9/11 resonated with him, you see, and so he adjusted accordingly. "My music taste changed on 9/11," Cruz said in the interview. (Really, he said that.) "I actually intellectually find this very curious, but on 9/11, I didn't like how rock music responded," he added. "And country music, collectively, the way they responded, it resonated with me."

Set aside, if you will, the historical reality that many of the most prominent classic rock artists at the time—including Paul Mc-Cartney, The Who, David Bowie, Elton John, Eric Clapton, John Mellencamp, Mick Jagger, and Keith Richards—had headlined the big benefit concert for New York City's first responders the month after 9/11 at Madison Square Garden. And never mind that Bruce Springsteen and Neil Young actually *wrote songs* in the aftermath of the attacks that were directly inspired by the events of that terrible day. Even if the rock musicians that Cruz professed to having been a fan of previously hadn't responded in such a way, the very idea that his musical tastes would be forever changed by the nation's worst terrorist attack provided a fascinating glimpse into this particular politician's thought process—a "very curious" glimpse, to put it in his words.

In any case, "Where the Stars and Stripes and the Eagle Fly" was the most obvious, focus-group-tested song choice for Cruz to play at his campaign kickoff, and that's why he picked it. Over my years covering Republican presidential candidates, I'd heard the thing played hundreds of times. The lyrics had already been ingrained in my head from campaigns past. But by the time the chorus rolled around this time—"There's a lady that stands in a harbor for what we belieeeeeve"—it became clear that something was off. This was usually the big moment when the candidate revealed himself to the cheering crowd, but Cruz was nowhere to be seen.

People continued to clap confusedly a couple of minutes later when the song came to its end. Then, near silence. As rally-goers exchanged perplexed glances, Jack Kimball took it upon himself to save the day. The man who spent much of his time online trying to convince others not to trust anyone asked everyone on hand to trust him. "Honest to God, folks," Kimball said. "I'm not lying. He's here."

Over on the other side of the room, the house DJ took it from the top. It was time to reprise "Where the Stars and Stripes and the Eagle Fly."

I was born by God's dear grace
In an extraordinary place
Where the stars and stripes and the eagle fly.

Just as it was starting to appear like another false alarm, Cruz at long last entered the room. The sharp-chinned candidate made his way through the crowd of supporters in routine fashion, shaking hands and taking photos. Nothing seemed out of the ordinary. But then, as he got a bit closer, I noticed what at first appeared to be a halo around his head. Upon further inspection, I could see that it was a pale headset microphone—the kind worn by telemarketers, televangelists, and Britney Spears. Cruz had worn the same device during his official campaign announcement the previous week at Liberty University, but that was during a speech to 10,000 people! This was a small crowd in New Hampshire. Voters here—as everyone knew—wanted to look their candidates in the eye, have a real conversation, and get to know them. This was the state where natural conversation was supposed to come at a premium. It was not a place for headset microphones—at least it never had been. But Cruz, it was clear, would be running his campaign a bit differently.

As I stood behind the full bar that the VFW hall had on offer, I scribbled some of these less than prophetic thoughts into my reporter's notebook as Cruz was ascending the makeshift stage. Just at that moment, a Cruz supporter who subsequently mistook me for a bartender turned to me and asked, "You got any hard stuff back there?" In retrospect, I probably should have just poured a couple of tequila shots for both of us.

On stage, Kimball was in the process of delivering his introductory remarks, with Cruz standing by his side. I avoided looking Kimball in the eye, concerned that he might point me out in the crowd and accuse me of being something horrible, like an anti-American traitor, a pro-government spy, or a reporter. Kimball was ranting and raving, as was his custom, but it was hard for me to make out what exactly he was saying. And I wasn't the only one. "You've got a microphone, Jack," someone in the crowd said back at him, but not loudly enough for him to hear. "You don't have to yell."

After Kimball had finished, Cruz delivered what became his standard, red-meat-laden stump speech, replete with its calls to "abolish the IRS," "repeal every word" of Obamacare, and "reignite the power of America." The crowd loved all of it, especially when the Canadian-born candidate practically vomited with disdain in decrying "all these illegals" who are "taking our food stamps and our homes." His hair slicked back with extra-shiny gel and his microphone headset amplifying his voice, Cruz cut the figure of a disagreeable preacher trying to warn the faithful about how bad Hell really was, or perhaps an unscrupulous college basketball coach delivering a recruiting pitch to an elite high school sophomore. He also offered plenty of the pregnant pauses that would become his rhetorical calling card—the kinds of carefully crafted moments of melodrama that often made you wonder in later debates whether this was a B-list actor, merely playing the role of a firebrand presidential candidate.

Eventually, the DJ hit play on "Where the Stars and Stripes and the Eagle Fly," and it was off to the next one. That night, I headed to the Radisson in Nashua—a mid-level hotel that, for some reason, had the architectural features of a medieval castle. Yes, turrets and all. Cruz was slated to speak at an event there that was being put on by the Young America's Foundation—a group of college-aged conservatives who were in town for a weekend conference (think a bunch of Alex P. Keaton clones but with LinkedIn accounts). I arrived early and started working on the story I'd file later that weekend, as the group's young participants mingled in one of the hotel's conference rooms. Gatherings of young conservatives tend to have all of the atmosphere and unendurably awkward sexual tension of the first hour of a high school dance, complete with the bar stocked with coke, ginger ale, and cranberry juice. And this one fit the bill perfectly. In small packs, dangerously awkward young men in suits that were two sizes too big for them held court on cool, millennial-oriented topics, for instance, Austrian economics and summer internship opportunities at the Heritage Foundation. On the other side of the room, young women in business skirts that their mothers probably would have deemed too short stared at their phones.

This, it was safe to say, was a far different crowd than the heavily camouflaged, "they're coming for us!" concealed-carry set that Cruz had spoken to earlier in the day. When Cruz took the stage to address this particular group, it was clear instantaneously that the Princeton- and Harvard Law–educated candidate was well aware that he was going to have to change up his act. As he did earlier in the day, Cruz spoke fluidly and clearly without notes (the former national champion college debater was not going to get out-talked by anyone in this campaign). But his talking points were entirely different than they had been earlier in the day. With his microphone now clipped to his suit lapel instead of attached to his head, Cruz tried to play an unconvincing version of the Cool Dad that Rob Portman didn't have to pretend to be. He made a reference to the already concluded HBO vampire series *True Blood*, boasted about how he had coopted Barack Obama's grassroots-driven 2008 campaign strategy in his own Senate bid, and did a couple of goofy impressions of Ronald Reagan and Jay Leno. None of these references were contemporary, exactly, but they were closer to modern times than the Revolutionary-era motifs that he had emphasized that afternoon. "I think every young person, after you go in to vote, oughta walk out and punch your parents in the nose," Cruz said in what was his most memorable canned line of the evening. "I mean, it is as if your parents went out and took a credit card in your name [and] said, 'Savannah, we're going to Vegas. We're going to party it up, we're having a great time, and guess what? You get to pay the bill!'"

Savannah liked that one. She and her fiscally responsible, socially tolerant friends even looked up from their phones to laugh. And this was Cruz's super power as a candidate: a rare ability to tailor his message in both substance and style to whichever group he happened to be addressing at the time, done without losing his credibility as an across-the-board arch-conservative. It was impressive. But it wasn't "authentic" in any kind of reading of the word. Wouldn't the legendarily savvy voters of New Hampshire dock Cruz some points for modifying his tenor to accommodate each specific audience? The candidate didn't appear to be concerned, as he would soon demonstrate in a third setting on his inaugural trip to the state.

The next morning, Cruz completed the final leg of his New Hampshire campaign kickoff at the Portsmouth Country Club—a subdued but elegant facility that boasted putting greens and fairways as pristine as the silverware and white tablecloths in the ballroom. At the civilized brunching hour of 11:00 a.m., Cruz delivered a restrained, statesmanlike speech in front of the kinds of navy-blue-sport-coat-and-khaki-pants-wearing Republicans for whom participation in a "tea party" typically involved finger sandwiches and fine china, rather than tricorn hats. Once again, he'd read his crowd perfectly. This guy was good, I realized. It would be a mistake for any of his opponents to dismiss him as a fringe player in this campaign. He could go far—even in New Hampshire, which figured to be the fiery Texan's least hospitable early voting state.

I was mulling over all of this as I walked out of the Portsmouth event toward my rental car, when in the middle of the parking lot, a male voice shouted unmistakably in my direction.

"Hey! Are you a reporter?"

The familiar question made me cringe instantaneously. I swiveled around and saw that the voice had come from a man who was decked out in standard country-club garb with khakis, boat shoes, and all. Standing next to him, however, was his friend, who was dressed a bit differently. This gentleman was decked out in white breeches, the gold-buttoned coat of a Revolutionary War–era patriot, and, yes, a tricorn hat. It wasn't all that rare to see grown men playing dress-up at Republican political events in 2015, but as I mentioned earlier, I didn't expect to encounter this sort of thing at a venue where greens fees were $85 per round for nonmembers.

"Yeah," I shouted back.

"What paper do you work for?"

"The *Huffington Post*."

The sheer delight that illuminated the guy's expression was instantaneous.

"Oh, boy," he said, with the kind of disdain that might have been warranted had I told him that I worked for the *White Power Gazette*. "You know, Rush calls it the—"

"Huffington Puffington Post?" I ventured.

Indeed. The man folded over into a belly laugh, as did his dress-up playing companion, who took his turn next.

"Don't mind him," the reincarnated Paul Revere said. "He just doesn't like people who work for *Communist* news organizations!"

The ensuing laughter at his own joke from the man in tights was animated and prolonged. It offered me plenty of time to come up with a comeback. As I reached for my car keys, I thought briefly about shouting something back about how I admired his pantaloons. But New Hampshire is a small state, and Primary Day was still more than ten months away.

CHAPTER 10

T HE PERSON WHO KNOWS more about the New Hampshire primary and its history than anyone who has walked the earth has a name: Bill Gardner. For more than four decades, Gardner has kept his state at the top of the national political conversation—a singular achievement that has no counterpart in Iowa or anywhere else. Gardner was first elected in an upset victory as New Hampshire's secretary of state in 1976 at the age of twenty-eight. His comprehensive knowledge goes back to the events leading up to 1920, which he's glad to share, in the most minute detail, with just about anyone who enters his modest second-floor office inside the statehouse in Concord. The man isn't just an amateur historian. He's a walking, talking encyclopedia of New Hampshire politics.

Before ascending to the job, Gardner was a Democratic state representative, but the equal regard with which New Hampshire politicos from both parties hold him reveals how vital he is to the state. To put it simply, everyone in New Hampshire likes Bill Gardner. A gentle soul with the low-key demeanor of a librarian, he has the

attention for detail of an accountant and the single-minded determination of the eponymous character from the movie *Rudy*. Gardner's personal bible is the New Hampshire Manual for the General
Court—a guidebook on state law—where his own version of the
Ten Commandments is summarized in RSA Section 653:9, which
mandates that New Hampshire's presidential primary election "shall
be held on the second Tuesday in March or on a date selected by
the secretary of state which is 7 days or more immediately preceding the date on which any other state shall hold a similar election."
Under Gardner's interpretation, a "similar election" has meant another state's *primary*—an understanding of the statute that has allowed Iowa to hold its caucuses first without complaint from New
Hampshire.

As codified by those words, Gardner's chief responsibility has
been to set the date of the primary every four years and do absolutely
anything it takes to make sure that New Hampshire goes before any
"similar election." It hasn't been easy. During every presidential election cycle since he has been in office, one or more states—often with
the overt backing of the RNC or the DNC, or both—has tried to
usurp the established process and find a way to knock New Hampshire out of its prime position. These efforts have been conducted
with varying degrees of seriousness. Whether in 1969 (seven years
before Gardner had assumed office), when a young Nevada assem-
blyman named Harry Reid tried to put a bill through that state's
legislature to leapfrog New Hampshire, or in 2014, when the Utah
statehouse briefly tried to schedule its 2016 presidential primary a
week before New Hampshire's, the challengers to New Hampshire's
throne have failed every time.

"You can plant saplings on the main street of a city, but they
never grow right because they're artificial," Gardner summed up his
case against allowing new states to take over New Hampshire's traditional role. "In the woods, they grow right because they begin with
a seed that germinates, and they grow stronger over time, and they
become a tree. But they don't become that tree when they're planted
artificially."

Gardner oversees a primary election process that still uses paper ballots, so it is perhaps not entirely shocking that he doesn't even have a computer in his personal office. It is there in the statehouse that the candidates themselves typically show up to pay the $1,000 fee and sign the paperwork that allows their names to be placed on the primary ballot. After they complete that administrative paperwork, they can typically look forward to an earnest conversation with the secretary of state about the importance of New Hampshire, why New Hampshire has earned its role in the process, and whatever New Hampshire–related anecdotes happen to be on his mind that day. For Gardner, face-to-face interaction has always been the coin of the realm. Once he gets going on a story, it's nearly impossible to interrupt him, and it's best not to try.

Gardner is keenly attuned to New Hampshire's reputation for clinging to an undeserved sense of entitlement. He's well aware of the charges of arrogance and undemocratic privilege masquerading as quaint tradition. But rather than seeking some kind of compromise, he'll argue the merits of the state's special status to the death: how New Hampshire has *earned* its spot at the head of the table through a century of experience; how the state is the last bastion of hope for the presidential underdog, particularly in the post–Citizens United era, when the candidate with the most money would otherwise triumph every time. "It gives the little guy a chance," he told me in summing up the case. "You don't have to have the most money or the most fame to have a chance here."

More than any other line of attack, Gardner has fretted in recent years over the accusation that New Hampshire's pale-white electorate, which doesn't look anything like an increasingly diverse America, makes it particularly unsuitable to be leadoff batter in the game of picking presidents in the twenty-first century. In responding to that particular criticism, Gardner will often concede the point that his state is not a hotbed for diversity, before he points to the past to call into question the extent to which that matters. John Hale, the nineteenth-century senator who took an early stand against slavery, was a New Hampshire guy, Gardner will point out, as was civil rights leader Jonathan Daniels, who was murdered in Alabama in 1965 while saving the life of a seventeen-year-old African American activist. But in spite of these interesting historical notes, it is readily apparent that this particular case against New Hampshire is the one that nags at him the most.

During his lengthy tenure, Gardner has clashed with national figures from both parties. Most recently, RNC chairman Reince Priebus in 2015 said ominously that Iowa and New Hampshire shouldn't "get too comfortable." But over the decades, more often than not, it has been prominent Democrats—including Harry Reid, Barney Frank, Howard Dean, and others—who have been most vocal and persistent in challenging New Hampshire's status.

In October 1983, Nancy Pelosi—who was then the chair of the compliance and review committee for the DNC—led a delegation to New Hampshire to express national Democrats' concerns that the early primary date that Gardner had set for the 1984 primary was in violation of Democratic Party rules. Actually, she wasn't so much "expressing concerns" as she was demanding that Gardner—and by extension, New Hampshire—back down and hold its primary on the same day that neighboring Vermont (of all places!) held its contest. Gardner took the meeting with Pelosi and explained politely to her that he was obligated by state law to schedule New Hampshire's primary *before* Vermont had its own contest.

"You just can't do this," Gardner recalls Pelosi telling him.

"Well," he replied in his matter-of-fact way. "I *have* to do this."

Although New Hampshire's first-in-the-nation status had been in effect for more than six decades at that point, Gardner's defiance was not what Pelosi had expected when she flew across the country to confront a mere state-level official, whom she'd been told was a fellow Democrat and would bend to her will. When she was leaving his office, as Gardner remembers it, she turned back to him to offer some memorable parting words.

"You know, you probably think you have a political future ahead of you," she told Gardner. "If you do this, you will not be elected again because the people of your state will know that it was because of you that they were not able to be a part of the Democratic National Convention."

On the off chance that threat not to seat New Hampshire's delegates at the DNC proved not to have its intended effect, Pelosi next sat down with the state's newly elected Republican governor, John H. Sununu, who would go on to become President George H. W. Bush's chief of staff later in the decade. Pelosi told Sununu that he was going to have to straighten out this Gardner guy. Sununu's response: he couldn't do it. The authority didn't rest with him. Pelosi left in a huff.

Gardner, meanwhile, firmed up the date for the 1984 New Hampshire primary: February 28, exactly one week before Vermont's primary. Pelosi and her fellow national Democrats, however, weren't prepared to give up just yet. The day before Granite State voters went to the polls, the DNC put out a press release that characterized that year's New Hampshire primary as an illegitimate event, even though the candidates themselves had campaigned there and the media continued to ascribe tremendous importance to it.

This last desperate gambit on Pelosi's part had no effect, either. On the morning of the primary, the *New York Times* reported, "Walter F. Mondale now holds the most commanding lead ever recorded this early in a presidential nomination campaign by a non-incumbent, according to the latest New York Times/CBS News poll." That survey had former Vice President Mondale at 57 percent, civil rights activist Jesse Jackson at 8 percent, astronaut-turned-Ohio-senator John Glenn at 7 percent, and little-known Colorado senator Gary Hart at 7 percent. If it had the opportunity to do it over again, the *New York Times* might have characterized the race a bit differently. As a driving snowstorm blanketed New Hampshire, Hart pulled off what remains among the most shocking upsets in the history of the primary. And he did it rather easily, defeating second-place Mondale by 9 points. Hart's unexpected New Hampshire triumph turned the Democratic race upside down, but the former vice president was able to hold off the insurgent to secure the nomination in the end.

A couple of weeks before the DNC gathered that July in Pelosi's hometown of San Francisco to nominate Mondale and New York congresswoman Geraldine Ferraro to the Democratic presidential ticket, the delegation from New Hampshire received a message from party officials: we didn't really mean it. The New Hampshire delegates were all seated at the convention, and Bill Gardner had won again. In every presidential election cycle since, one or more states have explored the possibility of trying to roll Bill Gardner—stubbornly quixotic efforts that, in the aggregate, amount to something close to the definition of political insanity.

CHAPTER 11

I T WASN'T UNTIL APRIL 2015 that the 2016 presidential campaign
was fully under way. Rand Paul came in on the heels of Ted
Cruz to become the second major Republican to get into the
race officially. Then Marco Rubio, Carly Fiorina, Ben Carson and
Mike Huckabee all followed within a month. In terms of impact,
however, all of those GOP presidential announcements combined
were dwarfed by Hillary Clinton's campaign launch. In an effort
to avoid the overarching mistake of her 2008 bid, in which Clinton
largely embraced her image as the "inevitable" Democratic nominee,
this time around she may have been the first candidate in modern
history who sought to begin a presidential run with as little fanfare
as possible, calculating that her stature alone would be more than
enough to push out any significant competition.

On a sparkling spring afternoon, Clinton announced she was
running in a web video and then hit the road from her home in
Chappaqua, New York, with a slate of low-key events in Iowa that
were designed as a woman-of-the-people-style road trip. This was

not the high-flying former first lady, US senator, and secretary of state—the most extensively credentialed nonincumbent White House hopeful in the nation's history. It was just Grandma Hilly, gassing up the ol' "Scooby Van" for a road trip out in the country to meet some nice gals and fellers—or as her campaign called them (presumably after extensive focus-group testing): "ordinary Americans." It was the candidate herself who decided to name her Secret Service agent–occupied SUV after the colorful vehicle featured in the 1960s animated cartoon franchise. This was Clinton's attempt to convey a downhome aesthetic and sense of whimsy—at odds with the usual surroundings of a woman who had been riding almost exclusively in limousines and private planes for a quarter century. But Clinton's "Scooby Van" had none of the flower power adornments that characterized the original "mystery machine." Her ride was actually just a plain ol' black Chevy Express Explorer. You know, a van.

This was a candidate who, for a little while, had free rein to set her own narrative. And she did so as she refused to answer a single question from the media during her *first couple of months* on the trail. The implicit message was this: the Clinton campaign didn't need the media. The media needed her. The theory made sense, as long as she was the most intriguing candidate in the race.

When Clinton made her first New Hampshire trip as a 2016 presidential candidate, I didn't have to think too hard before deciding to skip the spectacle. Clinton's first New Hampshire foray of the cycle was orchestrated by her handlers, as if she were a rare and precious falcon being put on display before a clumsy group of amateur bird-watchers. "You may admire the specimen from afar, but if you should dare move within arm's reach, you'll be asked to leave."

Before I ducked out of the state to avoid the New Hampshire grand opening of the Hillary Exhibition, I committed the grave mistake of attending the state Republican Party's "#FITN Republican Leadership Summit" at the Crowne Plaza Hotel in Nashua, right down the street from the Radisson Castle. The summit drew no less than nineteen declared or prospective Republican presidential contenders and was the first major New Hampshire cattle call of the 2016 campaign. After giving up a perfectly good Saturday afternoon to attend, I watched as GOP White House hopefuls took turns making speeches inside a stale and musty hotel conference room to local officials, activists, and a few crazy people who probably weren't even registered to vote but greatly enjoyed yelling things when there were cameras around. It was almost impossible to learn anything about the candidates, since they didn't interact with one another the way they did in debate settings, and questions from the audience were few and far between. Cattle calls were some of the more indefensible aspects of the early primary state ritual, as their main purpose was to serve as easy moneymakers for the state parties and conservative interest groups that hosted them. They offered no inherent value to anyone else. Still, the candidates, by and large, felt compelled to attend ("Well, if *he's* going, I guess I'd be crazy not to go, too!").

The closest thing to breaking up the monotonous string of well-worn stump speeches from the potential and already declared candidates came when a woman in the audience asked John Bolton—the former US ambassador to the United Nations and transcendentally mustachioed Iraq War apologist—what he planned to do about President Obama's recent activities. These activities, she said, included "smuggling the Muslim Brotherhood into the White House" and "amassing his own tanks and assault weapons" in preparation for a coup against other elements of the federal government. When the Yale-educated Bolton's response was not to dress down the woman for spewing such nonsense, but instead to pivot immediately to the "radical ideology" that he said Obama had acquired at Harvard Law School, I decided I'd had enough.

In search of some sanity as the calendar turned to May, I took it upon myself to attend an event that a year earlier would have generated all kinds of fanfare but was now largely being ignored by the media: a visit by New Jersey governor Chris Christie to New Hampshire. In October 2011, I'd been at Dartmouth College in Hanover, where the charmingly overbearing New Jerseyan had come to town on an idyllic autumn day in order to lend his official endorsement to

Mitt Romney. It was Romney's first attention-grabbing endorsement of the race. Christie was hands down the most dynamic Republican politician in the country at the time. Amid the crush of dozens of cameras and a hundred or so reporters who were on hand for the event, I recall marveling at how effortless and convincing the New Jersey governor appeared as he lent his support to Romney. It was like watching the coolest, most confident kid in the class stand up for a socially awkward nerd, who'd just been stashed in the dumpster by some bullies.

By 2015, that luster had vanished as quickly as the one hundred pounds or so that Christie had lost in the interim. The Bridgegate scandal, which had broken wide open in January 2014, was the most direct cause of his fall from grace. Just three months after being re-elected in deep-blue New Jersey in the kind of landslide that should have padded an already robust presidential résumé, it was revealed that some of Christie's closest confidants had ordered the closing of traffic lanes heading to the George Washington Bridge, which connects New Jersey to Manhattan. It was all part of a half-baked plot to "punish" a small-town Democratic mayor who had declined to endorse Christie during the campaign. As ludicrously ill-conceived as the scheme was, and though investigators found no evidence that Christie had any knowledge of it before it became public, the episode confirmed the perception of the New Jersey governor as a score-settling bully who ruled by intimidation. It didn't help matters for Christie that New Jersey's fiscal house was about as tidy as a crack den, not to mention that he had alienated a lot of Republicans with his enthusiastic embrace of President Obama during his visit to the Superstorm Sandy–ravaged state just days before the 2012 election.

In his self-assured way, Christie continued to act in public as if nothing were amiss, and he was a frequent and conspicuous visitor to New Hampshire during the 2014 midterms in his role as the Republican Governors Association chairman. As Christie's poll numbers both in New Jersey and nationally continued to nosedive, the scope of his 2016 bid was narrowing significantly from the original idea of running a well-funded national campaign from the get-go. By

January 2016, it was clear that his dwindling hopes of making a serious White House run rested entirely on winning (or coming damn close) in New Hampshire. And so New Hampshire was where he would make his stand.

It was a long shot, yet it seemed conceivable to me. Sure, Christie had a bridge-load of problems. But he was also a magnetic Republican with almost universal name recognition and enough remaining credibility to pick up the pieces in the event that some other favorite such as Jeb Bush stumbled and left him an opening. Most important, there was no better communicator in the race. Over the previous few years, I'd seen Christie wow crowds at town hall meetings in and outside of New Jersey with the rhetorical prowess of a once-in-a-generation politician. In an era when authenticity had become perhaps the most coveted and elusive characteristic for presidential candidates, Christie oozed it. Plus, New Hampshire voters by and large had a particular soft spot for comeback stories.

I felt pretty strongly that writing off Christie's chances would be a mistake. So I was surprised when I arrived at the VFW Hall in Hudson to find that there were only a few non–New Jersey reporters on hand to cover the event and just one from a national outlet. But that's the nature of presidential political coverage. It tends to be like a youth soccer game, in which the ball is the leading candidate of the moment and the players are journalists drawn to it like a magnet, while the wider field is mostly ignored.

Christie's talented advance team had organized the event like a wrestling ring, with Christie in the middle, and concentric circles of chairs surrounding him. And he came ready to perform. When the candidate opened the floor to questions, a man wearing a US Navy hat rose from his front-row seat and asked him how he would handle the threat from ISIS (or ISIL, the Islamic State). It's often said that in the end, voters don't make their decisions based on foreign policy, but it was already clear that the generalization didn't apply to this election at all. Poll after poll showed that international affairs were a top concern for Republican voters, especially in New

Hampshire, perhaps driven by the images of gruesome beheadings at the hands of ISIS that had become regular fixtures on TV news. After asking Christie how he would address ISIS, this particular retired navy man added the observation that if he had been commander in chief when the terrorist group began executing American captives, he would have "darkened the sun" with American bombers to fight back against the "psychotic" men who carried out the crime.

Most candidates in this situation would simply have nodded in agreement. Not Christie. He liked to fight, even when it was about ISIS. "I don't think they're all psychotic," he shot back. "I think they know exactly what they're doing." It was a line that would oddly presage perhaps the most pivotal moment of the New Hampshire Republican primary campaign several months later. But at the time, it simply left me impressed. To me, Christie's tactic of arguing even when he was agreeing came across as so much more effective than if he had merely offered boilerplate affirmation. New Hampshire voters don't mind a candidate who sees things a little differently than they do. Authenticity and passion matter so much more, and Christie had both in spades.

Christie was similarly assertive—if far more controversial— when he was asked about how he planned to take a harder line against Iran. September 11, Christie said, served to reinforce the principle that security took precedence over privacy rights—or as he put it, "You can't enjoy your civil liberties if you're in a coffin." Well, that was a doozy. Way over the top, you might say, and quite a bold statement of principle to make in a state where "Live Free or Die" is taken seriously. But Christie's histrionic image was clearly aimed at trying to win back GOP voters who were veering into Rand Paul's noninterventionist camp.

In the entirety of Christie's long Q-and-A session, campaign finance didn't come up once. In fact, it had dropped off of the campaign radar generally. I wanted to believe that the people I'd spent the day with in northern New Hampshire really were going to have an impact on the primary—even a small one—but I wasn't seeing it, not at this particular town hall, nor at any of the other campaign events I'd attended thus far.

The next day, I stopped by the New Hampshire Rebellion's modest basement headquarters in Manchester and found that the group was very much still around, though their ranks weren't exactly bursting at the seams. With its college dorm room wall décor and sparsely furnished confines, no one was going to mistake the place for the kind of well-heeled super PAC whose monumental influence the group was seeking to diminish. On this particular Wednesday afternoon, four of the organization's five full-time employees were on the clock. Jeff McLean—the Rebellion's thirty-something director—walked me through what they'd been up to since that frosty January day when I'd joined them in Dixville Notch. It pretty much boiled down to this: more walking around New Hampshire. The group was planning a six-mile Memorial Day weekend walk traversing the Upper Connecticut River Valley towns of Lebanon and Hanover and then a couple of longer seacoast walks planned for the Fourth of July weekend.

It is nice to go on a good, long walk, I conceded. It's good exercise, a solid opportunity to meet like-minded people and march to the flautist's tune. And I was sure that the walks were raising some awareness. But was more walking really the answer to such a big problem? McClean argued that as small-ball as they might seem, these events were vital to the New Hampshire Rebellion's mission, in that they allowed supporters of campaign-finance reform to realize that they weren't alone and it gave them an extended opportunity to talk about how better to solve the problem.

Yeah, I was still skeptical.

McClean also showed me a website the group had recently launched called Questionr.us. It was equipped with a convenient tool that allowed users to search for a presidential candidate's public events by city, state, and zip code, and it laid out the New Hampshire Rebellion's mission of asking each candidate the same question: "What specific reforms will you advance to end the corrupting influence of money in politics?" It also allowed users to upload and share video or audio of candidates whom they'd queried. They'd already posted answers from seven declared and soon-to-be-declared candidates.

But when I asked him whether he'd seen any real progress, McClean didn't try to sugarcoat the reality. He acknowledged that it was going to be a tough haul to reach their goal of convincing about 50,000 primary voters to care about their issue and then—if everything went exactly right—turn support for campaign-finance reform into a decisive factor in the 2016 New Hampshire primary. "It's the root issue—it connects every other issue that people care about," he said. "Money's a good thing, but as soon as you put it into the political system, it breaks everything." He didn't have to convince me. But in order to see any progress at all, the cause would need a candidate or two to champion it. And no, Lawrence Lessig wasn't going to cut it.

CHAPTER 12

T HE TONE FOR THE volatile 1988 campaign in New Hampshire was set when an unassuming, self-effacing kid from Queens who had pulled himself up by the bootstraps and made it in the world of real estate decided to give politics a whirl. His name was Donald J. Trump, and in the fall of 1987, he was flirting with a run for president of the United States.

That year, believe it or not, Trump was actually playing hard to get. A group of New Hampshire supporters set up a committee to draft him into the race, begging the forty-one-year-old tycoon to make America great again decades before he came up with the slogan. Trump arrived in the state in typical style at the Hampton helicopter pad in October 1987. He was then chauffeured to the Portsmouth Rotary Club, where he keynoted an event that was hosted by the draft committee. Around five hundred people packed the place that night to catch a glimpse at the celebrity not-yet-candidate, who spoke in hyperbolic terms about how the Japanese were "just killing" the United States on trade deals. In the end, Trump passed on entering the race and barely qualified as a footnote in the historical sweep of the 1988 campaign. Looking back on it now, however, it's difficult to shake the belief that he might very well have defied all of the pundits then, too, had he decided to give it a whirl.

Trump certainly would have had no shortage of capable state-level operatives at his disposal, many of whom would have jumped at the opportunity to lend their services to a political neophyte with plenty of his own cash to back up his grassroots appeal. To be an established New Hampshire political operative has long been one of the greatest gigs in America. The club is a small one, and the bar to entry relies almost entirely on two straightforward factors: personal connections and your ability to convince prospective world leaders that you can help get them elected. If you're good, every four years (eight at the most) the most viable presidential candidates will claw each other's eyes out for the right to pay you a hefty sum to advise them on how they might secure a few thousand additional votes. And if you're not good—let's say, for instance, that you've never come close to being on the winning side of a New Hampshire primary before—there is still going to be work for you. The mid- to lower-tier candidates will line up in the barren lobby of your Concord law firm or Manchester PR practice just for the opportunity to throw wads of cash at you, in exchange for your database of personal cell phone numbers for town councillors in Bedford and intricate knowledge of which diners in Keene draw the biggest Tuesday lunchtime crowds. You've truly made it once you're granted the universally acknowledged, if somewhat ill-defined title of "consultant." It's a designation that is official once it appears after your quotation in the *New York Times* or engraved on a CNN chyron, and it's a reward that usually comes with a lucrative lifetime tenure.

Unquestionably, these mostly white, mostly male facilitators who have earned the designation of "New Hampshire political consultant" do provide valuable services to the candidates, who are mostly clueless about the ways of the state when they arrive for their first Politics and Eggs event. Even the most aggressive, sleep-shunning White House hopeful can only shake so many thousands of hands in a state that contains 1.3 million living souls. So the central job of the New Hampshire political consultant (and, to a lesser extent, the lower-level aides and volunteers who work on the campaign team) has always been to act as the center point in a series of concentric circles of outreach. Think of the job as a one-person social media app. A New Hampshire political consultant, for instance, might call a dozen of the most plugged-in activists and local officials to highlight a candidate's upcoming appearance in the state or a new policy rollout. Those contacts, in turn, would then call a dozen of *their* associates in the next circle outward, and so on.

Although there have been notable exceptions over the years—and a few feuds have run into the decades—political consultants in New Hampshire generally tend to get along with each other. The tight-knit industry is kind of like a Yankee version of the southern good ol' boys club. In general, New Hampshire political consultants are likely to be far more forthright with reporters and more agreeable human beings than are many of their counterparts in Washington. New Hampshire political consultants also like to have fun, especially even when they're practicing the dark arts. Every presidential campaign cycle in New Hampshire sees its share of staffer-driven chicanery—some more so than others. The 1988 Republican primary was notable in that it featured some truly top-notch shenanigans.

That year, Vice President George H. W. Bush was the clear front-runner for the Republican nomination and appeared poised to atone for the drubbing he had received in the state eight years earlier. But just like Ronald Reagan in 1980, Bush came limping into New Hampshire in 1988 after suffering an embarrassing third-place finish in the Iowa caucuses behind Kansas senator Bob Dole and televangelist Pat Robertson (a particularly surprising result, considering that Bush had defeated Reagan in Iowa in 1980). Bush's strongest asset in New Hampshire was the support he had from Republican governor John Sununu. An MIT-trained engineer and a bit of a cantankerous genius, Sununu was able to complete complex mathematical problems in his head, and he knew his state as well as he did equations. Sununu was well aware that in order to mount his comeback, Bush

first had to start looking like a winner again, and in order to do
that, he had to attract more prominent endorsements than Dole did.
Sununu could try to cajole and persuade—but that would only get
him so far, so he turned to an innovative trick he had up his sleeve:
license plates.

By design, there isn't a lot of political patronage in New Hampshire politics. Unlike in other states, there is no endemic history of
sleazy state legislators trying to bolster their $100-per-year salaries
through backroom deals. It's not a part of the culture, and there is
little opportunity for unscrupulous officials to enrich themselves in
a state where major public works projects are scant and transparency
is high. But even proudly independent New Hampshire officials,
Sununu figured, wouldn't be immune to the temptations of one particular window into the rarefied world of the locally rich and famous:
a low-numbered license plate.

In a state where hoodies and jeans constitute semi-formal attire,
Sununu found, one of the few areas of life in which vanity was considered acceptable was in the pursuit of one of the low-numbered license plates that were personally handed out by the sitting governor
through the DMV. The odd tradition persists to this day. In the 2016
campaign, it was common to see low-numbered plates parked outside every major presidential candidate's events. New Hampshire politicos have always coveted low-numbered license plates for the same
reason that Hollywood B-listers try to score invites to the Oscars
after-parties: it makes them feel like they're among the cool kids.

The catch then, as it remains now, was that there was a limited
supply of low-numbered license plates to go around at any given time.
But thanks to the wonders of human mortality, they tend to become
available again at fairly regular intervals. When Sununu first took office in 1983, he decided to exercise his despotic prerogative by letting
the low-numbered license plates accumulate in his office's possession.
Then, when Bush and Dole were scrambling for endorsements five
years later, he made his move. If a particular state senator, let's say,
were on the fence over whom to endorse, Sununu would swoop in to
play political Santa Claus, perhaps scratching his chin pensively and

saying something to the tune of, "Would a number twelve license plate help you to see the vice president's attributes with clearer eyes?" The ploy worked to a remarkable degree, as Bush accumulated a huge endorsement advantage over Dole in New Hampshire.

Meanwhile, while the two front-runners were slugging it out, New York congressman Jack Kemp, former Delaware governor Pete du Pont, and Pat Robertson settled in for a heated three-way battle for the bronze medal. It was a prize that seemed worth winning, as whoever finished third in New Hampshire would have a path forward to compete in future states as the outsider alternative to the establishment-friendly Bush and Dole. Things got interesting— really interesting, in fact—as two young staffers who worked for Kemp that year recalled in separate conversations I had with them nearly three decades later.

If you can't win in politics, the next-best option is to have a good time at your opponents' expense. And in 1988, no one had a better time in New Hampshire than the consultants and operatives who ran Jack Kemp's statewide campaign. Kemp's New Hampshire team reveled in trolling their opponents at every turn. Case in point: when du Pont—the Phillips Exeter, Princeton, and Harvard Law School–educated scion of one of the nation's moneyed families— arrived at a multicandidate event one day at the Mall of New Hampshire, awaiting his arrival was a Rolls-Royce decked out in du Pont stickers, parked illegally in a handicapped zone. The du Pont campaign alleged that a dirty trick had been committed, but they had no proof as to the identity of the culprits (it was the Kemp campaign).

Members of Kemp's New Hampshire operation pulled off similar stunts at some of Bush's events around the state. Kemp volunteers would dress up as Arab sheikhs, in an effort to highlight some of the former Texas oilman's international ties that some considered unsavory. The Bush campaign responded to this particular stunt, however, on the day that Kemp flew in to appear at what had been billed as a major press conference to announce details of his new tax plan. When it came time for the event to begin, there was a problem:

no members of the media had shown up to cover it. Kemp was furious. He had taken an entire day out of his schedule to fly into New Hampshire for this one event, and it was all for naught. Were reporters really writing him off to such an extent that they weren't even willing to cover him? Not exactly. It was about a week later that the Kemp campaign heard through the grapevine that Bush aides had quietly spread word in the hours before Kemp's arrival that the press conference had been canceled.

The most impressive act of 1988 Republican political sabotage in New Hampshire was also the most difficult for me to believe when it was first related to me. But I've since had the details confirmed by its main conspirator, Scott Royce, who was then a twenty-four-year-old Kemp staffer. On February 8, Kemp had finished in a disappointing fourth place in the Iowa caucuses with just a week to recover before New Hampshire. The Kemp campaign had expected to do better in Iowa among evangelical caucus-goers and was unsure why he had faltered so badly. Then, a rumor made its way back to Kemp headquarters in New Hampshire that on the Sunday before the caucuses, operatives working for Pat Robertson's campaign had put out fliers suggesting dishonestly that Kemp's two daughters—both of whom were in their twenties at the time—had each had abortions.

Royce was primarily charged with leading Kemp's advance team in the months leading up to the New Hampshire primary—a job that involved putting thousands of miles on his Volkswagen to set up events and drive people around the state. But when he heard the rumor about the Robertson campaign's actions in Iowa, he became infuriated and determined that he would take it upon himself to respond. Royce found his opportunity on one of his daily drives from his home in nearby Bedford into Manchester when he discovered that the Robertson campaign was setting up a large phone-bank operation inside a previously abandoned building. Without telling any of his overseers in the campaign, Royce decided to take matters into his own hands. He stopped by a local hardware store and purchased a pair of heavy-duty cable-cutting pliers and size 12 rubber boots.

Royce actually wore a size 9 and figured the disparity would provide evidence to help exonerate him, if he became a suspect.

Aside from the possibility that he might electrocute himself, the other potential complication for Royce was the risk of getting caught—an outcome that would, at minimum, publicly humiliate him and ruin his career. The worst-case scenario was quite a bit worse: an extended trip to federal prison. The young Royce decided to go for it anyway. He fancied himself to be something of an amateur secret agent. In fact, shortly after college, he interviewed for a job with the CIA and was offered a position as an analyst. He turned the agency down, however, as he had wanted to be a field operative. Shortly after midnight after a long day of advance work, Royce drove to the site of the Robertson phone-banking operation and isolated the box. He made quick work of cutting the cables, thereby rendering the Robertson campaign's phone-bank operation useless. The plan went off without a hitch.

Shortly thereafter, the real fun began. In taking the position that the most obvious suspect was probably the culprit, the Robertson camp quietly began complaining to reporters and other campaigns' staffers that members of the Bush team must have been responsible for the act of treachery. It wasn't enough to create any damage, however, as Bush bested Dole for a critical ten-point Primary Day victory on his way to the nomination. Kemp did end up finishing in a distant third place in New Hampshire, edging out du Pont and Robertson for the prize. This immoral victory was short-lived though, as Kemp dropped out of the race less than a month later after failing to generate much buzz. Kemp's punchy young band of committed—if ethically questionable—New Hampshire staffers left the campaign with stories to tell for the rest of their lives. In presidential politics, sometimes the losers really do have more fun.

CHAPTER 13

B Y EARLY JUNE 2015, I had already made almost two dozen trips to the Granite State over the previous year and was fully immersed in the campaign—too immersed, in fact. In my world, the New Hampshire primary was the biggest story there was. In just about everyone else's world, however, it was not. I was reminded of this when I arrived by train in Boston and made my way to the Avis counter, where three employees were gathered around a single cell phone. It was the day of Caitlyn Jenner's big unveiling on the cover of *Vanity Fair*, and they were staring at the now iconic photo of the world's most famous transgendered person.

"Oh. My. Gawd," a male employee said in summing up the general mood of the powwow.

"Charlie is gonna flip out when he sees this," a female employee in her red Avis polo shirt added.

I waved my arms to get their attention. Finally, the woman offered a meek, "kennah-helpyou," but the two men couldn't be pulled away from the phone they were still gawking at with mouths agape.

This, I remembered with sudden clarity, was the kind of thing that most people actually cared about with the first voting still eight months away. Celebrity news continued to take precedence, and without a truly dynamic, can't-look-away candidate in the race, politics just couldn't match a sex-change celebrity for drama. Yet.

I got on the road and suffered through a driving rainstorm before I arrived for a late solo dinner at Martha's Exchange—a cozy microbrewery and restaurant in Nashua. Now that I was safely within the confines of New Hampshire's politically obsessed borders, I thought that I'd be able to turn my attention back to the campaign. I was again mistaken. It was mere moments after I put in my order for gorgonzola-stuffed chicken and an IPA that the bartender began raving to one of the servers about her reaction to the Caitlyn Jenner news. "I look up on CNN, and it's 'Call Me Caitlyn,'" she said, as if she could scarcely understand how a real news outlet could be reporting on such a trivial matter, which also happened to be the only thing she wanted to talk about. "I don't care what people do with their lives. But that's your news?"

"No, it's *your* news," is what I wanted to say. There was plenty of other news out there, just waiting for this bartender to consume, if she wanted to find it. News about the world. News about the local community. Hard news. Business news. News you can use. Whatever. It had never been easier to access any of it, via the wonderful series of tubes known as the World Wide Web. But Caitlyn Jenner was a story that people who consumed their news passively and in small doses could understand and pay attention to for a few nanoseconds, and so it was perfect for cable.

This internal rant got me thinking about the campaign again. What if there was a candidate who could do what Caitlyn Jenner was doing? Someone who had the ability to grab instantaneously the attention of the majority of people who were just going about their lives and not paying much attention to the election overall? As it turned out, we'd all find out soon enough. In the meantime, one candidate who definitely did *not* fit that profile was former Florida governor Jeb Bush. The son and brother of ex-presidents was the favorite candidate of the professional political and donor class, even as his early polling numbers among actual voters (the people who weren't paying attention much) were historically weak for a so-called front-runner.

Bush still wasn't even a candidate yet, not officially at least. He wouldn't make his announcement for another couple of weeks, and his relatively late entry into the race had everything to do with funds. Jeb Bush was good at raising money. Very good at it, in fact. But he wasn't satisfied with merely being the fund-raising leader in the Republican field. No, he wanted to be the political Scrooge McDuck with enough gold to fill a virtual-lap pool. And he was perfectly content to swim the backstroke in that pool while the other suckers in the race begged for whatever nickels on the dollar remained available to them. Bush's entire focus throughout the first half of 2015 was not to introduce himself to as many voters in early states as possible but instead to keep hitting up millionaires for more donations to his super PAC—Right to Rise.

Campaign-finance law prohibited presidential candidates from coordinating directly with their super PACs. So from the moment that Jeb Bush said the words, "I am running for President of the United States," his direct fund-raising appeals would thenceforth be confined to the $2,700 per election limit for individual donations to a candidate. (During a May 2015 non-campaign stop in Nevada, Bush accidentally let slip at a press conference that he was "running for president in 2016" before quickly correcting himself and adding the requisite "if I run" disclaimer.) But as long as Bush continued to act merely as a Definitely Running Non-Candidate and not "a candidate," he was unfettered in his drive to raise unlimited funds directly through the super PAC. Once he uttered the magic words (and didn't immediately correct them), he'd have to cut off coordination with Right to Rise, even as some of his most trusted aides would go on to run the super PAC. This was the kind of farce that the post–Citizens United campaign-finance landscape allowed, and Bush was eager to take full advantage of it. You couldn't blame him and his advisers for pushing the limits. He didn't make the rules.

He was just exploiting them for all they were worth—always with a straight face.

During an election in which just about every real contender was testing the outer reaches of the campaign-finance system, Bush was the pioneer who had ventured deepest into this previously un-explored jungle of cynically pretending that he was still trying to make up his mind about whether to run months after it had become clear that he was already running. From his perspective, he had no choice. Money, and unprecedented amounts of it, was the one thing that might save him from a tricky conundrum: GOP primary voters didn't like him all that much. Big donors, on the other hand, were smitten. Bush's theory of the case was that he could "shock and awe" his rivals with his fund-raising prowess and then pick off a victory in one of the first four voting states—most likely New Hampshire. The first part of the plan was coming together swimmingly. The second? Not so much.

I set out to cover Bush's latest New Hampshire visit as a not-yet-official candidate the day after my last visit with the New Hampshire Rebellion's leaders, and campaign finance was on my mind. I wanted to ask him about whether his decision to remain, for the time being, a Definitely Running Non-Candidate might back-fire and feed into perceptions that he was the candidate most tapped into playing the rigged game. It was a loaded question and perhaps a bit unfair. In theory, every candidate starts the race as a Definitely Running Non-Candidate—someone who is, as all future presiden-tial contenders like to say, "testing the waters." Bush wasn't the only one who was still technically exploring. But what set apart the pure-bred Definitely Running Non-Candidate (Bush) from the plain-vanilla "potential presidential hopefuls" was the far-beyond-belief amount of time Bush had been willing to spend to perpetuate the obvious charade that he had not yet decided whether to enter the race. He was not a sitting governor or other official. Bush's full-time job, for more than half a year at that point, had been to raise money for his technically nonexistent campaign. Was he just going to give it all back if he decided not to run? Bush raised over $100 million for

Right to Rise and hired a large team of campaign operatives who moved to Miami to join his not-in-any-way-official campaign headquarters. Meanwhile, he continued to maintain with a straight face that he might well wake up one morning and say, "Nah, never mind."

It was not lost on anyone that this posturing was ridiculous, and Bush himself didn't do much to keep the ruse going behind closed doors. One potential Bush campaign hire, who was coveted by several Republican presidential contenders but ended up sitting out the primary campaign, told me that when he asked Bush during his job interview about his vision for how the campaign would transpire, the Definitely Running Non-Candidate replied with a curt, "Me winning." Not that he'd already decided to get into the race or anything like that. Could go either way.

On the first day I followed him around the state, Bush began at an invitation-only business roundtable in Portsmouth. As is typically the case for business "roundtables," the table where he and the local businesspeople who came out on the middle of a workday to see him was actually rectangular in shape. The discussion, though, was collaborative, as many of the attendees were keen on giving the Definitely Running Non-Candidate some advice on how to run his non-campaign. "I think the Bush family is an asset that you have," one man told him. "You have a great story to tell, and your family does, and I hope you put that as part of your way of doing business in the campaign."

I found this pressing concern over how Bush could get past the burden of his family name to be somewhat amusing. I mean, sure, Americans don't tend to be huge fans of hereditary monarchies, and Bush's elder brother was about as popular as scurvy when he left office. But Jeb Bush would not *be* Jeb Bush had he not won the Mega Millions lifetime lottery ticket that was being born into that particular family. Sure, he was undoubtedly smart, hardworking, and charismatic enough, and a generally capable guy who accomplished a lot in his two terms and had some pretty reasonable ideas about how to expand the Republican tent. But let's not pretend that if he'd been born Joey Jefferson from Orlando, he would have been likely to find himself in a position to become governor of Florida—or, for that matter, risen to the ranks of a presidential front-runner, pulling in nine-figure sums in a matter of a few months. Yes, his family name was now a burden to him in some respects, but it was also a central reason he'd gotten this far.

After Bush took a few more questions at the square round-table, his communications director, Tim Miller—a quick-witted and sharp-tongued rascal who happened to be a friend of mine—announced that the candidate would be doing an "avail" downstairs. An avail, as it's typically called in campaign parlance, is the most common way that reporters on the campaign trail interact directly with candidates. It's shorthand for media "availability," that is, a press conference, but one that takes place on the fly with whomever happens to be on hand. On the freewheeling campaign trail in New Hampshire, in particular, avails typically have all the calm and civility of a four-year-old's birthday party. This one was no different, and even Bush—who had already participated in many of these things, appeared taken aback when the most zealous of the reporters on hand stuck their microphones so close to his face that it looked like they were trying to feed him. After taking just three questions, Miller issued the time-honored campaign flack's version of the bartender's "last call" by doling out an emphatic, "Last question!" My chance to ask about campaign finance would have to come later that night at the invitation-only house party that Bush was attending in the wealthy, Republican-heavy town of Bedford, which lies just to the southwest of Manchester.

It was still light out when I arrived at Rich and Lori Ashooh's Bedford residence. I pulled my rental car to the side of the street where I found Jason—a young, bearded tracker for the liberal group American Bridge standing just on the edge of the yard, safely within the realm of public property. Trackers try to make as insignificant an impression on the people around them as possible, while shooting video of every moment that they can, in case the candidate they are following around commits a gaffe that can later be exploited for political gain. Although it must be a wearisome existence to travel from campaign event to campaign event, shooting hundreds of hours of video among people who don't want you there, trackers often make a significant impact on campaigns. It was perhaps George Allen, the former governor of Virginia, who ushered in the "YouTube era" of politics in 2006 when he famously pointed out to his audience the Democratic tracker who was following his campaign, introducing him as "Macaca?" As soon as the strange word left his lips, Allen morphed from surefire Senate winner and potential 2008 Republican presidential front-runner into a soon-to-be-defeated political trivia question.

You'd think that anyone blessed with more than a half-dozen brain cells would recognize that it's probably best not to antagonize a person whose entire job is to get you into trouble—especially while his camera is set on "Record" and aimed directly at you. But the previous week, Rand Paul's New Hampshire state director, David Chesley, had made news by approaching Jason's camera at an event and licking the lens. The moment was duly posted on the Internet. When that kind of thing happens, it's a good day for the tracker.

I had gotten to know Jason a bit over the previous months, and he was always helpful when I arrived at events, as he was usually early and I usually wasn't. So after getting through the important stuff first—asking him about the details of Lick-gate—I asked if Bush had arrived yet. He had not, Jason told me. I thanked him and headed down the driveway toward the colonial New England home below. Trackers were never allowed inside invitation-only events. Instead, they had to stand on the margins in solitude, hoping to get a quick glimpse of the candidate on his way out of the party.

Former businessman Rich Ashooh was a local Republican power player who had run for Congress in 2010. He would go on to announce another campaign for the same seat in early 2016, taking on scandal-plagued Republican congressman Frank Giunta. In New Hampshire, there are few better ways to provide a boost to one's own political aspirations than by providing a boost to someone else's political aspirations, and so here he was lending the Ashoohs' sparkling colonial-style home to Jeb Bush for the evening. Their spacious living room, dining room, and kitchen were packed shoulder to shoulder by the time I made it inside, but a few minutes of small talk with some of the guests revealed that few people there were avowed Bush supporters. All of them had previously met either his brother or father in New Hampshire, and they wanted to learn more about the next Bush in line, but they were far from sold on Jeb.

Bush entered the kitchen from the backyard and began making his way around the ground floor, methodically engaging with the crowd. There were at least a hundred people inside, all of whom were looking up at the Definitely Running Non-Candidate's six-foot-four frame. I noticed that one of Bush's advance staffers had carved out a little space in front of the fireplace, and I figured that was where Bush would address the crowd. I positioned myself directly in front of the space. Sure enough, after he had finished with the meet-and-greet segment of the program, he made his way over to the anointed spot. He muttered something about asking members of the media to move back to allow New Hampshire voters to get a better view, but I decided that I was quite comfortable where I was, and no one protested.

Next, the Definitely Running Non-Candidate launched into his non-stump speech, complete with the requisite, non-résumé boosting anecdote about how they used to call him "Veto Corleone" back in Florida. It was all boilerplate stuff for anyone who'd seen Bush speak on TV in recent months. Nonetheless, I started thinking about what a rare opportunity this was to get close to Bush in the early stages of the campaign—a time when it would typically cost you a hundred grand or so for the privilege.

Bush took eight questions from the audience, some of them predictable and easy to answer (Q: How are you different than your brother? . . . A: I'm better looking.) and some that led him into trickier territory (Q: Is climate change a national security threat? . . . A: The climate is warming, but it's "intellectual arrogance" to suggest that the science is settled about the extent to which it's man-made.). I was intrigued by the way the questions were being framed. Almost every time someone in the crowd asked him something basic about his policy views, he or she began with the ridiculous preface, "If you should decide to become a candidate. . . . " It was the prospective supporters' way of telling the Definitely Running Non-Candidate that they were in on the joke, too, and were more than willing to play along.

As soon as Bush wrapped up the Q-and-A session and accepted the requisite burst of applause that followed, I took a step forward. Certain that even a brief opening exchange of pleasantries would give him the opportunity to escape politely, I let the reporter's note-book and tape recorder in my hand serve as my introduction and jumped right into it. "Governor," I said. "Do you think there's some-thing kind of absurd about a campaign-finance system in which you have to always say you're not officially a candidate, you're not run-ning yet, and yet you have a big paid infrastructure, you're raising millions of dollars—"

I thought there was a legitimate shot that he would let his guard down a bit and acknowledge, in some way, what was obvious. Yes, it *was* absurd. I wasn't expecting a wink and a nod. But maybe a smile or a subtle eye roll.

Nothing. He didn't even let me finish the question.

"It's not a campaign," Bush said flatly.

Right, it was a Definitely Running Non-Campaign. I already knew that. I shifted course and decided to play it straight.

"So you might not run?" I asked.

"I might not run," he replied, refusing to break character.

At this point, Bush started looking around the room for an escape route. He found one in my friend Tim, who arrived on the scene to help his boss out with a terse, "Come on, Scott."

I ignored Tim.

"What would cause you not to run?" I asked Bush.

"I don't know," the Definitely Running Non-Candidate said, still searching for a way to answer the question without outright lying. "I hope I get to the point where I make my decision relatively soon, and it would be—I don't know what it would be, but I haven't made up my mind completely."

I suppose it's possible that Bush might have passed a lie detector test in this moment. If he contracted a terminal disease the next day, for example, Bush probably wouldn't have run for president after all. But barring that remote prospect, the idea that he was raising enough money to fund a small country for a few months and still hadn't made up his mind about his intent remained absurd. I tried again.

"Do you have an idea of what you'd do with that money if you didn't run?" I asked.

Bush definitely had enough of me at that point.

"No," he replied. And then he turned away.

I headed back to my car a few minutes later, and my phone buzzed with a text message from Tim, the content of which was more or less exactly what I'd been expecting: "You had to be a prick."

No, I didn't *have* to be, I replied in obnoxious fashion. It was, I had to admit, kind of fun to put Bush on the spot over something so preposterous. Still, it didn't change a thing about the absurd non-candidacy that a Non-Candidate was now permitted to get away with. I'd had enough of this particular charade for the time being. I wanted to spend some time with a different kind of candidate: one who had absolutely no chance of winning but knew how to lose the right way.

At lunchtime the next day, I pulled into MaryAnn's diner in Derry, a large (by New Hampshire standards) middle-class town of about 35,000 people southeast of Manchester. Sporting an expansive dining room and brightly lit walls adorned with Americana kitsch, including a wide array of muscle-car photos and Betty Boop cartoons, MaryAnn's was up there with Manchester's Red Arrow Diner as one of the most frequented drop-by locales for presidential candidates in the state.

MaryAnn's had enjoyed a strange moment in the national spotlight four years earlier when a run-of-the-mill visit by Mitt Romney took a hard turn into the deeply uncomfortable. It went down when Romney, while posing for a photo with a group of waitresses, decided that it would be a good idea to pretend that one of them had grabbed his butt. "Oh!" the Republican front-runner shouted, jumping up suddenly and flashing a practical jokester's accusatory glance at the assailant he was attempting to frame good-naturedly, as the cameras rolled. "Ha. Ha. Ha. Ha," Romney added. It had been both hard to watch and impossible to look away.

By the time I entered MaryAnn's on this particular day, South Carolina senator Lindsey Graham was already making the rounds inside. Dressed in what I would come to know as his standard campaign-trail attire of baggy khakis fit for a junior cotillion and a loose-fitting, navy-blue dress shirt and sport coat, Graham was accompanied by no discernible staff contingent. As easygoing and composed as Romney had been self-conscious and anxious, Graham approached diners one by one to hit them with his unique brand of positively enchanting militarism. "Some people don't care about Benghazi," he explained to a woman in his syrupy drawl, as he leaned over her table like an old friend might. "I do."

Graham had an energy about him that was different than any other presidential candidate I'd encountered in person. In short, he was supremely accessible and utterly without pretension. He was also smart, charming, and genuinely funny. I could tell right away that this was a politician who truly enjoyed the give-and-take of campaigning in New Hampshire. When a diminutive woman with short-cropped hair approached him with her question, her cellphone camera was already rolling to capture his response. "Finance reform," she demanded. "Campaign-finance reform." She elaborated no further. I leaned in closely to make sure I picked up every word of Graham's answer.

"So after Citizens United, it's probably going to take a constitutional amendment—maybe you can do it statutorily—to reign in the unlimited giving to super PACs," Graham said.

I'd known that Graham was an advocate for a constitutional amendment to overturn the momentous Supreme Court decision, but it was kind of wild to hear him say so in person. The "solution" that almost all of the other GOP contenders were proposing was for a system that allowed unlimited individual giving, combined with immediate, full disclosure of the benefactors' identities. The idea behind that concept was that the First Amendment protects financial contributions as speech (as the Supreme Court had determined) but that any political candidate who is being bought should have to let the whole world know about it right away, so that voters could take the information into account.

The concept had some merit. It would at least co-opt the absurd maze of outside groups and reporting gimmicks that had allowed donors to retain their anonymity through contributions to so-called social welfare organizations, many of which were nothing more than front groups for certain candidates. Still, it was hard to see how a system that allowed a single individual to deposit, let's say, $100 million directly into one particular candidate's bank account would do much to mitigate the broader problem concerning the outsized influence of money in politics. Graham's constitutional amendment proposal may have been as much of a long shot as his own candidacy was, but it was inarguably bold. My fellow walkers in the New Hampshire Rebellion, I was sure, would have been impressed by the wispy-haired South Carolinian.

But then the woman had to ruin everything by asking Graham a follow-up.

"Are you for a constitutional amendment?" she asked, still shooting the exchange on video. At first blush, I thought the question an odd one. Graham had literally just finished saying that he was indeed for it. But the woman, it turned out, knew exactly what she was doing.

"If you write it in the right way," Graham said. And then he added the ultimate hedge: "The other alternative is to say, 'Unlimited giving. Your name's disclosed, but just give it to the party to ensure its intent. That's George Will's idea, and it has some attraction to me.'"

Graham—who had just finished elucidating a bold proposal to fix a shattered system—suddenly was sounding not much different than every other Republican candidate. Was he really going to let me down this quickly—on the very first day of his candidacy in New Hampshire, no less? I wanted to ask him myself. And so a couple of hours later, I arrived at another of southern New Hampshire's most revered casual dining institutions—MoeJoe's Family Restaurant in Manchester. When I walked in, Graham was already waiting inside with his press secretary, Brittany Bramell, in an otherwise empty dining room. This was a man, I would come to learn over the next few months, who never acted like his time was more valuable than anyone else's.

Although it was his first day in the state as a 2016 candidate, Graham was well acquainted with New Hampshire and its idiosyncrasies. He had spent the months leading up to the 2000 and 2008 primaries as an unofficial New Hampshire sidekick to John McCain, going just about everywhere that the Arizona senator—who sometimes referred to Graham as his "illegitimate son"—went around the state. And now he made it abundantly clear that he was tickled to be back, even as he showed off his McCain-esque penchant for dark humor, as he launched into the story about the time he'd declined an invitation to go see the famous Old Man of the Mountain rock formation that adorns New Hampshire license plates. "It's not like it's gonna fall down if I don't see it today," Graham recalled saying. It fell down a couple of months later.

I started to ask him some questions, but Graham kept looking for opportunities to get sidetracked and take in his surroundings. He loved this.

"Hey, Moe!" he said at one point, summoning the restaurant's female proprietor and cutting himself off in the middle of a story about what it was like to grow up in the back of the bar and pool hall that his parents owned in rural South Carolina. Graham explained our conversation to Moe: "I was telling Scott that anyone who can run a restaurant or bar can be a good politician because you want 'em to come in, have a good time, laugh, keep drinking, and come back." After spending most of my time in New Hampshire up until that point around politicians who wanted to win more than anything else, it was refreshing to be in this kind of low-key environment with one who was really just in it to enjoy the ride.

After he ordered two lobster rolls, I decided to hit him with the big question. "Is New Hampshire still New Hampshire?" I asked.

"And can the little guy come here—" Graham cut me off. He didn't need to hear another word. "After Citizens United, where you can have unlimited giving from unknown donors, the question is, Can New Hampshire survive?" he said, his tone now acutely serious. "If they go to national polling as an entry requirement [for debates], does that hurt New Hampshire? I think it does. My hope is that New Hampshire does survive because if it doesn't, then it changes the way you nominate people to become president of the United States pretty dramatically because if it were Florida, California, or New York, I wouldn't have a chance . . . this is a candidate-centric state, and that's the antidote to big money."

I thought that summed up the case for New Hampshire pretty succinctly, but Graham wasn't finished just yet.

"I think it is the last line of defense," he added with a flourish. "If big money is able to overcome the process in New Hampshire, then that's a big blow to democracy." I told Graham about the New Hampshire Rebellion and asked him what he thought of it. "Here's the deal," he said. "I think it's about disenfranchisement. Campaign-finance reform is basically sort of just one of several issues where people feel like they're losing control of their government and their voice. So after Citizens United, probably the only way to change the super PAC structure is to do a constitutional amendment. That'd be difficult. But at the end of the day, complete disclosure, even if you had unlimited giving, would go a long way."

Moe brought out the lobster rolls. I declined Graham's offer to take one, having already eaten lunch, and he began picking out the meat of one of the rolls with a fork, noting that he was "trying" to stick to a low-carb diet. Between chews, he shouted praise for the lobster back at Moe. I asked him whether his call for complete disclosure alone "at the end of the day" was a hedge on his support for a constitutional amendment overturning Citizens United (it was, of course, but I wanted to hear him say so).

"If somebody could write one that I thought would work, I'd be open to it, but I don't think it's going to work," he said, all but shooting down his own proposal again. "I don't want to tell people in this Rebellion group that that's a viable option." I left the interview feeling a bit perplexed but convinced that there was something different about Lindsey Graham—something that was tremendously agreeable.

When I next heard from Graham later that night, it was immediately after a round of gunfire broke out. Upon the first unexpected volley, I resisted the instinct to duck. The salvo reverberated around the steep hills surrounding Beverly Bruce's well-appointed property, which consisted of a sprawling country home sandwiched between two sizable barns. The shots had come without warning, but none of the several dozen guests who were mingling in the backyard showed any sign of concern. We were gathered in the wealthy solitude-seeker's paradise of Center Tuftonboro—a little slice of no-man's-land between the White Mountains vacation region and the northern edge of Lake Winnipesaukee. It was one of the swaths of rural New Hampshire where firearms outnumber people by a significant margin and "Private Property: No Trespassing" signs at the end of long dirt roads are best regarded as serious warnings rather than friendly suggestions. If the members of this upper-crust Republican crowd, literally sipping wine and eating cheese, had been entirely unperturbed by the unexpected artillery barrage, I figured that I should pretend to be unmoved by the outbreak of gunfire I'd just experienced.

As I waited calmly for the event to begin, I took a self-guided tour of one of Bruce's barns—"the game room," as I later learned she referred to it. The game room revealed the New Hampshire Republican activist's love of firearms not by way of a gun rack, but rather through the unfortunate victims of her and her husband's trigger-happy lifestyle, which were on display. There was a thick-maned lion presiding in the corner where a foosball table might have been in the game rooms that I was more accustomed to visiting in my youth. A few feet above a plush leather couch, a cheetah rested as comfortably as a dead animal can on a wooden beam, its long and spotted tail descending toward the heads of some of the guests in the room who continued to sip their wine. Others nibbled on brie and crackers, as they admired the zebra and hippo heads that protruded from the walls, flanking what appeared to be some sort of warthog petting zoo.

After a few minutes of perusing this makeshift natural-history museum or shrine to human savagery, depending on your personal views, I reemerged into the backyard. There in front of me was Bruce, the bespectacled homeowner and hunter of wild beasts. She wore a fur-and-animal-hide vest and an expression that said, "This is all perfectly normal."

"My husband shot the sable, and we made a vest out of it," she explained matter-of-factly to a guest who complimented her outfit.

Following closely behind Bruce and holding a generously poured glass of red wine came none other than the man of the hour, Lindsey Graham. My new favorite Republican presidential candidate wore the wide smile of a man who'd just experienced a big adrenaline rush, but I wasn't entirely sure why. I asked Bruce about the gunshots.

"I greeted him at the door with my rifle," she told me of her first encounter of the evening with the candidate standing by her side. "He said, 'Can I shoot it?' I said, 'Of course.' He said, 'What can I shoot?' So I had him shoot at a stump."

As I chatted with Bruce, Graham was greeting guests one by one with one "how y'all doin'" after another, mixed in with laughter and sips of his wine. I was dumbfounded—not because I couldn't believe that Graham could handle a firearm (although his slight frame and ill-fitting sport coat didn't suggest a particularly intimidating presence on the firing range). I was just blown away that the long-shot Republican White House contender who had declared his candidacy on the previous day had already broken one of the cardinal rules of running for president: if you're going to shoot a gun in New Hampshire, always invite the press to watch you do it.

It was precisely this strategic oversight that led me back to a strange and inescapable thought from earlier that day: I really liked Lindsey Graham. By that, I mean that I *legitimately* liked him as a person—not just in comparison to Ted Cruz or Rand Paul. I liked that Graham had shot Bruce's gun with no one looking because he thought it'd be fun, not because he wanted to do a photo-op. I liked that he talked to people, as if they were actual human beings, unlike the 95 percent of political candidates—even the ones who are "good at retail politics." I liked that he didn't take himself too seriously, even as he was deadly earnest about his policy views. And I liked that he was willing to buck his party on key issues, in a manner that was unlikely to help him politically but made it abundantly clear that he actually stood for a principle or two. Also, I have to admit, I kind of liked that he had very little chance of actually becoming president. It mitigated some of the guilt I felt over openly admiring a candidate who was a bit of a saber-rattler when it came to his foreign policy views.

Even in a typical election, Graham wouldn't have had much of a shot. In this race, he was dead in the water on Day One. Yes, he was an experienced third-term senator, a strong communicator, and a leading voice among Republican foreign-policy hawks. But as a five-foot-seven bachelor, he didn't exactly look the part, and it didn't help that he had a penchant for pissing off other conservatives. Among his apostasies: he believed that humans contribute to climate change, he thought the idea of deporting 15 million illegal immigrants was unwise and impractical, and—wouldn't you know it—he considered the campaign-finance system to be such a disaster that a constitutional amendment overturning the Supreme Court's Citizens United decision might be required.

Although he had been a fixture of TV news green rooms for decades and never had a problem coming up with memorable one-liners, Graham's biggest problem of all was his lack of visibility. When Fox News and CNN announced that they would limit their marquee nationally televised debates to just the top ten candidates, as determined by national polling, Graham tried to put on a brave face. "OK, so you're on the stage with ten people," he told me. "You get, like, what—three or four minutes, if you're lucky. Maybe you get a good sound bite. I'm going to be at a house party tonight for two hours. If you do enough of it, that puts you on the map in New Hampshire."

If he was looking to history as his barometer in making that case, Graham wasn't entirely delusional. When the 1984 campaign began, for instance, Gary Hart hadn't been any more of a blip on the radar than Graham was. But this was 2015, and the national media narrative, especially as determined by the debates, was clearly taking precedence over making connections at house parties. Considering that he would never have a realistic shot of making the main debate stage, Graham's role in the campaign had transformed from "extreme long-shot" to "Hey, we're all gonna die anyway, right? Let's have some fun with this thing!" And Graham knew how to have fun.

After he polished off his glass of wine, Graham retreated to the game room, chuckling as he read one of the "Do Not Feed the Animals" signs that were scattered around the premises. At one point, in the midst of Beverly Bruce's personally guided tour, she pointed him to the hippo head, its thick white teeth hanging just a few inches above Graham's own head.

"I shot that," Bruce said.

"Was it self-defense?" the candidate fired back.

Graham was still just getting warmed up. When it was time for him to address the crowd of about one hundred people who had turned out for the event, Bruce introduced him to her guests as a "national security hawk."

"There's no hawks on the wall, and let's keep it that way," Graham replied.

As he stepped onto the elevated fireplace that would serve as his stage for the evening, Graham nearly impaled his arm on what appeared to be a long-horned antelope. He barely flinched before warning the audience not to "get gored." As the laughs continued to spread around the room, Graham looked up at the adornments hanging above him on the wall and offered a friendly nod to the mounted water buffalo's head and other horned creature beside it, whose species escaped my knowledge base.

"Bill, Hillary, how y'all doing?" he said with a friendly wave. He wasn't finished yet.

"If I say anything to piss Beverly off, I apologize. I thought the worst thing that could happen to you in politics is losing. Until I came here."

Throughout this performance, Graham's comedic timing was impeccable. It even inspired one member of the audience to try his own hand at amateur night stand-up. As Graham was still talking, this particular gentleman turned to the man standing to his right and offered up a gag about Hillary Clinton and Osama bin Laden. The recipient of the distasteful and decidedly unfunny joke laughed harder at this than he did at any of the truly entertaining things Graham had said, reminding me that as much as Graham wanted to be on the cutting edge of a revamped, sophisticated, inclusive GOP, the party itself wasn't there with him. The Republican electorate wasn't much interested in outreach. That membership wanted to be outraged. And Lindsey Graham wasn't going to be the one to scratch that itch.

About an hour into the event, as people's attention started to drift visibly, Graham went on an extended riff on how the Republican Party's losses of the popular vote in five of the last six elections could be chalked up to its failure to appeal to minorities—Hispanics in particular. Only about half of the room applauded. But that didn't dissuade the candidate from emphasizing his support for comprehensive immigration reform, as he put the joke-telling on hiatus to make a serious point. "I think we're losing market share over the largest-growing demographic because of the way we've handled this issue," Graham said. "And I still can't figure out why we're losing the Asian vote, other than to say this: If you seem to be mean and intolerant to one group, it bleeds over to the other." All jokes aside, this was a powerful thing for a Republican presidential candidate to say. Graham was never going to succeed with the "burn it all down" crowd, but this was a message, I thought, that could resonate among some serious Republican voters in New Hampshire who wanted to win again. He was never going to win, I was still quite sure, but maybe he could work his way into the mix after all.

A couple of hours after the event, I was back at my hotel when I received a phone call from Brittany Bramell, who said that the senator would like to have a word with me. I figured that Graham wanted to emphasize one of the points he'd made during our conversation earlier in the day about promoting a more inclusive Republican Party. Or maybe, I thought, he was calling to clarify some facet of his public remarks.

As it turned out, Graham—a proud Luddite who had recently boasted of never having sent an e-mail in his life—had been scrolling through Twitter and saw a couple of photos I'd posted from Beverly Bruce's house of horrors with some accompanying commentary relating to the indignities of running for president. "Listen," he said, upon taking the phone from his press secretary. "If you really want to help get me elected president, keep putting up pictures of me posing with wild animals. And make sure as many Republican voters in New Hampshire see them as possible." He let loose an avalanche of laughter and then hung up the phone.

CHAPTER 14

ONE THING THAT BILL Clinton almost never did as a presidential wannabe was read from prepared statements. On the campaign trail, prewritten remarks were anathema to the improvised jazz that made the Arkansas governor click with his audiences. The stories were legendary about his compulsive need to listen intently to everyone's question, shake every hand in the room, and commit each day's new names and faces to memory. Here was someone who was so engaging and comfortable in his own skin, he made even his most seasoned rivals for the 1992 Democratic nomination look like bumbling neophytes in comparison. Working from a script was an amateur move—a crutch for those poor souls running for president who didn't have "It." Bill Clinton had it. And Bill Clinton did not read from prepared statements.

But on a snowy sidewalk in Nashua, Clinton found himself with paper in hand, reciting the words that his vaunted team of so-called "gurus" had penned that previous weekend during an emergency powwow in Little Rock. The move was born of desperation.

Clinton's lifelong dream of becoming president of the United States was fading away. No one had any doubt about that. With just eight days to go before the New Hampshire primary, the double-digit lead he had built against his Democratic rivals had long ago vanished amid the double-whammy of allegations that he had dodged the Vietnam draft and had engaged in a twelve-year-long extramarital affair with Gennifer Flowers. Three weeks earlier, Clinton and his wife, Hillary, had appeared together on a post–Super Bowl edition of *60 Minutes* to deny the charges that Flowers had levied in *Star* magazine. Flowers came right back at the Democratic front-runner the following day in a press conference, in which taped phone conversations appeared to show Clinton coaching her in how to fend off questions about their trysts. But it was the draft-dodging charge, which Clinton also denied, that was really killing his hopes of winning late converts in veteran-heavy New Hampshire.

And so he read from the prepared statement, intent on making sure that he made every point that he needed to make with his political life on the line. "Let's face it," Clinton read to the assembled press pack, encircling the distressed candidate like ravenous lions ready to pounce on a wounded gazelle, "for too much of the last couple of weeks, this election has been about me, or rather, some false and twisted tabloid version of me." He sounded rehearsed, uninspired, and nearly defeated. It went on like this for a while longer. The mood among Clinton's staff was grim.

After Clinton finished his statement, he climbed into the front seat of a three-row SUV. In the middle row behind him sat Hillary and John Broderick—Clinton's New Hampshire co-chairman. In the back row were James Carville and George Stephanopoulos— who held to his ear one of the first clamshell cell phones that anyone in the group had seen. As the driver shepherded them to the next event at Stonyfield Yogurt in Londonderry, no one spoke for about five minutes. What was there to say? Finally, Broderick decided it was time to lay down a marker.

"Governor," he began. "Can I ask you a question?"

"Sure," Clinton replied.

"Why'd you do that?" Broderick said. "That was sad. If you're gonna run the campaign like that, you might as well go back to Arkansas now because it's all over."

At that, Carville and Stephanopoulos perked up. The dual-engine powerhouse of Clinton's national political machine was not used to state-level operatives dressing down their candidate like that. But Broderick wasn't relenting.

"Do you want to be president of the United States?" he asked. "Or do you want to let that guy who wears the pocket protector be president?" Broderick was referring to Paul Tsongas—the wonky former Massachusetts senator who had overtaken Clinton in the polls.

"Well," Clinton finally replied after his New Hampshire aide came up for air. "What would you have me do?"

Broderick reached into his pocket and pulled out a piece of paper. But this wasn't another prepared statement. It was a two-page memo that he and Terry Shumaker—Clinton's other New Hampshire co-chairman—had drafted to make their case to the candidate for how he should approach the last week of the campaign in New Hampshire. Neither Broderick nor Shumaker had been invited to the strategy session in Little Rock. Although they lacked the larger-than-life personality of the Ragin' Cajun and the golden-boy glow of Stephanopoulos, the two veterans of New Hampshire politics had plenty of their own ideas about how Clinton could make his comeback in the state that they knew best. At the top of the list: Get out of the bubble. Early on in the campaign, Shumaker had helped convince Clinton not to ask for Secret Service protection, knowing that added security would prove an obstacle to him getting up close and personal with crowds. Still, up until this point, Clinton had stood behind too many rope lines and was generally reluctant to dive full-bore into the swarms of people who came out to see him. He had to change that reticence and do it the New Hampshire way. His only shot now was to act like the underdog he'd become.

As the van rumbled north along Route 102, Clinton ingested the memo and then passed it back to Broderick. "Goddamn it, George,"

Clinton snapped to Stephanopoulos. "Why do we keep doing this stuff?" Broderick and Shumaker took the candidate's displeasure as a full-fledged endorsement of the new plan.

When they arrived in Londonderry, a newly emboldened Broderick offered some guidance for the still-disheartened team. "Nobody leaves this van unless they're smiling," he said. For the benefit of the gathered cameras, everyone did as they were told. As the junk-food-loving governor entered the yogurt shop, Stephanopoulos and Carville approached Broderick, who worried that he was about to be told his services were no longer required by the campaign. Instead, the duo offered a tepid acknowledgment that maybe the New Hampshire guys' ideas weren't so bad after all. It was a good start, but when he entered the venue himself, Broderick noted with frustration that another constrictive rope line had already been set up inside. It looked like change wasn't going to come easily.

As the event was coming to an end, Clinton and his team were walking out the back door when the governor turned to Broderick. "How'd you think that went?" the candidate asked. "I thought it was terrible, sir," Broderick replied. "Terrible. You're like a caged lion in there with all of the ropes. You've got to break out of the ropes."

Clinton made clear that he understood now. As he and the rest of the group made their way back out to the SUV, which was parked behind the yogurt store, they encountered a woman and her young son standing alone. Out of range of the press pack that was still assembled inside, the woman asked Clinton if she could speak with him privately for a moment. Clinton turned to his wife and aides. "Why don't you get back in the van," he said. "I'll be there in a minute."

Clinton chatted with the woman for about five minutes. Meanwhile, his aides inside the van were becoming increasingly agitated. They had a schedule to keep, and they were running well behind as usual. But Clinton was still talking, and now he had his arms around the woman and her son. A few moments later, he finally wrapped it up and climbed into the van. That's when someone made the mistake of telling the candidate about how they were now running even further behind schedule. "That woman just lost her husband," Clinton snapped. "And she said her son admires me, and she asked if I would speak to him. I thought that was pretty important to do."

From that day forward, there were no rope lines to be found at Bill Clinton's events in New Hampshire. Clinton frequented diners. He went to the Mall of New Hampshire, where shoppers approached him one by one and told him not to give up and that they were rooting for him. He famously told voters at an Elks Club meeting in Dover that if they'd give him a second chance, he'd be there for them "until the last dog dies."

After a solid week of campaigning in the manner in which Broderick and Shumaker suggested, Clinton's spirits remained down nonetheless. The reason for his consternation was known only to a small group of people within the campaign: their internal poll numbers showed Clinton finishing all the way back in third place, behind both Tsongas and Nebraska senator Bob Kerrey. A third-place finish in New Hampshire would kill Clinton's campaign. With the Democratic candidates all ceding the Iowa caucuses to hometown senator Tom Harkin that year, New Hampshire was the very first testing ground of the nominating contest, and Clinton just could not afford to win the bronze. Sure, he might *try* to spin it as a respectable showing that would allow him to continue on in the race, but there was no way that the broader public—and particularly the press—would buy it. This was the guy who had risen from relative obscurity to the top of the heap—the centrist who had been poised to lead the Democratic Party out of the wilderness and give it a real shot to win back the White House for the first time in sixteen years. A second-place finish behind Tsongas—who hailed from neighboring Massachusetts—now, that was something the Clinton campaign definitely could spin into a moral victory. But third? No, that wouldn't cut it.

Early on the night before the primary, after the latest round of bleak internal polling had come in, Clinton and his aides dined at the Puritan Backroom—a Manchester casual-dining institution since 1917 where the fried chicken fingers were almost as good as the barbecue back home in Arkansas and a single serving provided almost enough leftovers to feed a family of four for a week. After Clinton finished licking his fingers clean, he retreated to the kitchen to greet the staff and thank them for the meal. He was antsy. When he had no one else to talk to in the back of the restaurant, he came back out front again and shot the breeze with the few diners who were finishing their meals on this late Monday night. And then Bill Clinton decided that he wanted to go bowling. A few staffers and members of the press accompanied him to the local candlepin spot, where he bowled a couple of strings and chitchatted with some locals who had expected a low-key night at the lanes but instead found themselves hanging out with the future president of the United States.

On Primary Day, Clinton surprised even himself by taking second place in the New Hampshire primary, losing to Tsongas by 8 percent but comfortably beating Harkin, Kerrey, and former California governor Jerry Brown. It was a result that would have been perceived as a significant blow to Clinton only a month earlier. Up until that point, no one had ever lost the New Hampshire primary and gone on to become the president of the United States. But after nearly collapsing, Clinton now had something more important on his side than history: momentum. By exceeding his own hopes in New Hampshire, he didn't have to fake a happy expression when he addressed his cheering supporters at a hotel in Merrimack and issued one of the most famous lines in the history of presidential politics. "While the evening is young, and we don't know yet what the final tally will be, I think we know enough to say with some certainty that New Hampshire tonight has made Bill Clinton the Comeback Kid."

Broderick went on to become chief justice of the New Hampshire Supreme Court, and Shumaker was appointed US ambassador to Trinidad during Bill Clinton's second term. Shumaker remained especially active in state-level Democratic politics and was a prominent backer of Hillary Clinton's 2016 presidential campaign in New Hampshire. Soon after the former secretary of state launched her second White House bid, I sat down for a conversation with Shumaker in his Manchester office. As we started talking about the current political landscape, my eyes began wandering around the room. I noticed that among the campaign paraphernalia on display was a framed poster with various missives scrolled in Sharpie from members of Clinton's 1992 New Hampshire team. One particular message stood out: "Terry—What, me worry? Thanks, Bill Clinton."

CHAPTER 15

T HROUGHOUT THE SPRING OF 2015, the Democratic and Republican races both nationally and in New Hampshire remained firmly ensconced within two tidy media narratives. The first was that Hillary Clinton was a shoe-in for the Democratic nomination, roughly as likely to lose her party's nod as she was to succumb to an asteroid landing directly on her head. On the Republican side, all of the smart people were pretty sure, the last man standing would almost definitely be Wisconsin governor Scott Walker, former Florida governor Jeb Bush, or Florida senator Marco Rubio. Donald Trump's candidacy, meanwhile, was regarded as a delightful and utterly harmless joke.

For decades, Trump had been charming television audiences and his famous friends alike by playing with unflinching earnestness the role of a deranged New York City billionaire with Narcissistic Personality Disorder, implementing a fourth-grade vocabulary to dole out his endless series of farcically hyperbolic boasts and insults against everyone from Ronald Reagan to Rosie O'Donnell.

Although he had teased potential White House bids in 1987, 1999, and 2011, Trump was best known in the political world for his months-long crusade to prove that the first black president of the United States was not really an American. This racially charged P. T. Barnum act had made him a part of the presidential conversation four years earlier until Obama dressed him down at the White House Correspondents Dinner with impressively savage precision, as Trump sat stone-faced and powerless a few rows in front of him. For Republicans, Trump had been a useful idiot, donating to the RNC and other national GOP causes, remaining harmlessly at his gold-plated kids' table while the adults in the room mapped out the party's path forward. Almost no one thought he was serious when he began rambling on about his 2016 ambitions.

I figured Trump would continue the ruse for as long as he could get away with it before coming up with an excuse for remaining on the sidelines and was as surprised as anyone when he actually got into the race. From the moment in his announcement speech when he decried undocumented Mexican immigrants, in general, as "rapists"—small pools of spittle accumulating on the corners of his mouth, as he fulminated in the modern-day Mussolini style that became his calling card—it seemed indisputable to me that he was an earnestly unhinged person. Even though I knew that people were "mad as fuck," as Ted had put it to me at Fagin's pub, I didn't fully appreciate just how mad they really were, and I thought he had no chance at all of actually winning.

Although I saw no path to the nomination, I did believe that Trump might become a bigger factor in the race than most people assumed. Trump had a lot of assets as a candidate, including his singular ability to attract free media, his personal wealth, and his unparalleled skill at exploiting people's fears and grievances. "You're getting ripped off, and it's someone else's fault" was a powerful message in wide swaths of America where you used to be able to get by with a high school education and a steady blue-collar job. His core supporters, disproportionately white and male—like Ted from the bar in Berlin—weren't ideological by nature and didn't have much time to follow politics closely but were pretty sure that they were getting screwed. Even Trump's most passionate backers, I would come to discover, typically recognized that he was in many ways a buffoon. But he was *their* buffoon. In their minds, would the election of Donald Trump really make things any worse? I mean, hey, at least he wasn't another Clinton or a Bush. Maybe it was time to try something really different. "I wonder what will happen if I press this red button." That was the line of reasoning that made possible the once unthinkable.

The most significant factor working in Trump's favor was that he had absolutely no compunctions about appealing to such people's worst instincts rather than trying to lift them up with a hopeful message. The man was utterly without shame—a personal characteristic that is among the most valuable for a national politician to possess. He was also precisely the kind of candidate that the New Hampshire primary was designed to safeguard against, wasn't he? Trump was an obscene demagogue who had achieved tremendous (a favorite Trump word) success (another) via a combination of inherited wealth (not a phrase you hear pass from his lips) and Darwinian instincts.

When Trump immediately began receiving more media interest than the rest of the Republican field combined, I did not share the budding sense of alarm that it was ignoble or unprofessional for journalists to give him so much attention. There was nothing wrong with covering Trump, in my view, as long as media outlets did so with a heavy nod to the incontrovertible fact that the man was a comic character. In many ways, I believed strongly that he was exactly the candidate that America deserved, though I wasn't enough of a masochist to go the extra step and say he was the *president* we had coming to us. But I did think the broadcast media dropped the ball when they covered Trump so uncritically—showing so many of his rallies on cable TV unedited and in their entirety, not delving deeply enough into his at best uneven business record, and basically treating him as just another candidate instead of the threat to the republic that he actually was. That turned out to be one of the primary derelictions of duty that allowed the Trump phenomenon—which started as a natural outcome of the Republican Party's own malpractice—to snowball into something truly out of control. With the arrival of summer, I looked forward to seeing Trump in New Hampshire, live and in person, so that I could get a better handle on the extent of his appeal and his staying power. I had no idea of the experience that would soon be in store for me.

The other major development in the campaign that transpired around this time—and not entirely unrelated—was Bernie Sanders's emergence from nonentity to a somewhat credible nuisance to the unassailable Clinton juggernaut in Iowa, and especially in New Hampshire. The media by and large had been even slower in picking up on the extent of Bernie's appeal than they had in appreciating Trump's staying power. But no one in the race was getting bigger crowds than Bernie Sanders. His earliest campaign rallies—in Burlington, Vermont; Madison, Wisconsin; and Portland, Maine—looked more like general election rallies than the modest crowds that a traditional long-shot contender might draw. In spite of his lack of media coverage, there was no doubt that the curmudgeonly democratic socialist was hitting a similar populist nerve that Trump had struck with full force.

In many ways, Sanders's initial rise in New Hampshire was even more surprising than Trump's was. Yes, Sanders hailed from neighboring Vermont and was a particularly familiar figure to many of New Hampshire's most active progressives in the crunchy hamlets that dot the Connecticut River Valley along the shared border. But a seventy-three-year-old charisma-deficient white guy with a Brooklyn patois wasn't exactly the kind of poll-tested Clinton challenger that a political consultant would have created in a lab, in order to try to take her down. As it turned out, all of the characteristics that made the political class dismiss Sanders were the same ones that voters seemed to like about him. It wasn't just the unvarnished economic populism that resonated—the promises of free public college tuition and higher taxes on the millionaires and billionaires who'd had it too good for too long. It was his indisputable authenticity. Nothing about the guy was calculating. He was the anti-Clinton in just about every way.

A CNN/WMUR poll released in the last week of June 2015 showed Sanders trailing Clinton by just eight points in New Hampshire (43 percent to 35 percent). It was an astounding number for Clinton, who had essentially the entire New Hampshire Democratic leadership at her side and was widely considered to be the inevitable victor in the state. The morning after that poll came out, I had coffee in downtown Manchester with an aggressively on-message Clinton aide who sought to convince me that Sanders's support in the state had topped out. "I'm pretty sure that poll is his ceiling," the Clinton aide said. But considering that earlier in the year, Clinton's lead over Sanders in New Hampshire had been consistently within the range of 30 to 55 percent, you didn't have to be great with numbers to come to the conclusion that Bernie was on the rise.

To try to get a better handle on the overall dynamics at play behind the scenes, particularly in the Democratic race, I drove up from New York City on a Tuesday in July. When I got to Concord in the late afternoon, I decided to drop by Sanders's state campaign headquarters unannounced to see what I could see. I considered briefly the idea of changing out of my summer driving attire (shorts, T-shirt, and sandals) but decided against it. I looked the part.

The place had opened the previous week, and it was still Sanders's only office in the state. Based on how well he was doing in the polls, I expected a flurry of activity—legions of eager young volunteers working the phones, as part of an effort to make a difference for the next Eugene McCarthy who was about to turn the Democratic establishment upside down. What I found instead was an almost complete lack of activity around the strip mall storefront, which was plastered with a half-dozen "Bernie For President" signs. The place where Bernie Sanders intended to launch his New Hampshire revolution was next door to a Cash For Gold joint and a beauty salon called Shear Magic. The parking spot I steered my rental car into was adorned with a sign that read, "Reserved for Good Sense Financial Services, Inc."

The lights inside the campaign headquarters were off, but through the windows I could see the outline of a bearded man who appeared to be in his fifties. He was only slightly better dressed than I was and sat hunched over a notepad, jabbering into his cell phone. This was Kurt Ehrenberg, Sanders's New Hampshire state political director and a longtime Sierra Club activist, who had previously led a months-long draft effort to try to convince Massachusetts senator Elizabeth Warren to enter the race. He wore the frazzled, drained expression that I'd come to know from years of experience covering campaigns, an expression that belonged to a man who had spent more hours on conference calls in recent weeks than he had sleeping in his bed. But he was nonetheless gracious enough to chat.

Ehrenberg told me that he and four other people composed the entirety of Sanders's official New Hampshire team: two field staffers, an operations manager, and an unpaid intern. They had all just arrived back in the state the previous day from the candidate's most recent rally in Portland, Maine. Although New Hampshire was the priority, Sanders was speaking to huge crowds around the country, in order to keep the early excitement levels high and prod the national media into paying attention. Sanders had also been generating the biggest crowds of any candidate in New Hampshire during his previous visits to the state. I asked Ehrenberg if he'd expected this level of interest when he first got involved with the campaign in May.

"I had an inkling," he said. "You know, he's something special. He really is authentic. He's been singing the same tune for thirty years. He doesn't care about focus groups or polls. He knows what he believes, and he's going to get out there and talk about it. I think there's a real hunger for that in American politics right now." Ehrenberg said that the campaign had already signed up 14,000 people in New Hampshire who were interested in volunteering for the Sanders campaign.

I noted that several candidates from neighboring Massachusetts had found success in recent New Hampshire primaries (Mitt Romney, John Kerry, Michael Dukakis) and asked Ehrenberg whether the same principle, to a somewhat lesser degree, might apply to a Vermonter. "It doesn't hurt," he said. Ehrenberg noted that the pro-Sanders movement in the state was particularly strong around the western New Hampshire college town of Keene—a hippie haven near the Vermont border that boasted a head shop called Phat Stuff and an oddball reputation (a state Supreme Court decision the previous month had ruled that a "Robin Hood" group could continue to feed strangers' expired parking meters in Keene, sparing unknowing drivers the expense of $5 tickets). Ehrenberg acknowledged that Sanders had a long way to go in competing with Clinton in areas where blue-collar Democrats dominated, like Manchester. "We need to do really well with the people who are going to benefit most from [Sanders's] policies," he said. "Our job is to prove that he can win and to give people who don't know Bernie a chance to get to know him."

As challenging as the fundamental parameters of the race remained for Sanders in New Hampshire, none of what Ehrenberg was telling me sounded inconceivable. Clinton's institutional strength was unparalleled in recent political history, but she clearly was a flawed candidate who had some fundamental problems with conveying trustworthiness and excitement. I asked Ehrenberg one final question: Did he expect to win? Before answering, he looked out at the horizon for a moment to reflect, before he offered his prediction. "I think we're going to win New Hampshire," he said. Few "serious" people would have believed him.

Ehrenberg offered to give me a brief tour of the dark headquarters where the rest of Sanders's bare-bones New Hampshire campaign staffers were now gathered in a windowless room, all four of them sitting on folding chairs set up around a small table. On my way out the door, he handed me one of the empty envelopes that Sanders's team handed out to supporters after each event, so that they might contribute whatever spare cash they have in their pockets to the campaign. This was the Sanders campaign's version of a super PAC. At that very moment, Clinton might well have been in a meeting to discuss ways to prod another of her campaign's multimillionaire donors, in order to build on the $45 million war chest she had raised between the mid-April launch and the end of June. Ehrenberg, I thought to myself, better be damned smart about the way he invested the crinkled-up bills that he and his team had been collecting from its own donors. I had no idea at the time how quickly that spare change would add up.

The next morning, I drove to downtown Manchester to get some work done at Café la Reine—a cozy coffee shop on Elm Street. I rejoiced silently when I pulled up on Bridge Street at the intersection of Elm just as another car was leaving a parking spot. You wouldn't think so, but scoring a space in downtown Manchester on a weekday can be difficult. As I was withdrawing my wallet to fish out my credit card and slide it through the automated parking meter in triumph, I was bombarded by a well-dressed, friendly looking kid in his early twenties, who looked like he might have been on his way to a Coldplay concert. "I couldn't figure out how to work those things when I first moved here, either," he said with a missionary's smile, by way of introduction. I actually knew how to work the thing just fine but didn't say so. I gave him a little nod.

"Hey, are you registered to vote?" he asked, as if he were trying to make the obviously premeditated question seem like an afterthought.

That was when I noticed the clipboard that he had until then been concealing behind his back and the red-and-blue sticker with the familiar "H" logo on his T-shirt. I told him that I wasn't a New Hampshire resident, so he was wasting his time on me. At first, he seemed a bit unsure about whether to press the matter further, but when I started to walk away, he offered a warm farewell.

I hadn't taken thirty steps across the street toward Café la Reine before I was approached by a young woman wearing the same "H" sticker and carrying the same clipboard. "Clinton fellow?" I asked her. "Fellow" was a euphemism in Clinton campaign parlance for "unpaid summer intern." She said that she was. This time, I introduced myself to her as a reporter and asked her if I could take a look at her sign-up sheet. She reacted as if I'd asked her to please hand over all of the credit cards in her wallet. These kids were pretty well trained. And there were lots of them, I now noticed, all up and down Elm Street. They were approaching people at random to add their contact information to the Clinton campaign's list. It wasn't exactly precision micro-targeting, but this was a campaign that had almost limitless resources and a talent pool of striving youngsters who were willing to work for free.

I approached one of the Clinton fellows, who were all now swarming passersby on Elm Street like eager mosquitoes, and asked for directions to the campaign headquarters. It turned out that the Clinton nerve center was just down the block on the north end of Elm Street. When I arrived at the large brick building, there were no yard signs or any other indications that this was the site of the largest political operation in the state. I checked the directory but discovered that the Clinton campaign was not listed as a tenant in the building. The idea was to make it purposely difficult for trespassers like me to find.

Another young Clinton fellow directed me to the appropriate floor, where once again there was no sign that one of the world's most famous women was operating her New Hampshire campaign out of this building. I turned to my left and walked the length of the hallway. No dice, so I tried the other direction. There, tucked at the end of the corridor, was a window leading into a separate room that looked like the waiting area of a dentist office. Painted on the back wall was the telltale "H" with the red arrow pointed right, but other than that, I could see no signs of activity. There was a small, windowless reception area to the left and then a second door with a code lock visible over the handle, which led into the main area. The sterile, strictly off-limits confines of Hillary Clinton's New Hampshire campaign office presented a stark contrast to the wide-open, "come on in!" setup of Sanders's office. Yes, it was only office space. But it said a lot about the images that the two leading Democratic campaigns were projecting heading into the summer. Team Sanders was figuring it out on the fly, while the Clinton campaign was playing not to lose.

CHAPTER 16

O N MARCH 20, 1995, Pat Buchanan had one of the worst
rollouts in the history of presidential politics. The location
of Buchanan's announcement of his campaign—the Manchester Institute of the Arts and Sciences—was in keeping with the
conservative culture warrior's plan to once again make New Hampshire the lynchpin of his early state strategy. Buchanan had taken the
same tack during his first White House run four years earlier when
he'd put a minor scare into the incumbent President George H. W.
Bush's campaign (and wounded Bush heading into the general election) by managing to corral 38 percent of the vote in the Republican primary. Although his overt religiosity wasn't an ideal fit for
the state, large swaths of the New Hampshire Republican electorate
suited Buchanan's profile quite nicely: feisty, allergic to big government, and unafraid to be a little outlandish. In some ways a precursor
to the Donald Trump phenomenon, Buchanan knew how to court
controversy. The anti-NAFTA, anti-immigration, anti-feminist,

anti-affirmative action, populist crusader often attracted detractors who were every bit as passionate as his supporters.

Seconds after Buchanan began his remarks on that March day in Manchester, flanked by his wife and sister, three protesters jumped from their seats in the front row and rushed up onto the stage. Before anyone could react, one of the protesters was standing directly in front of Buchanan's face, holding a homemade sign up for the cameras that read, "Pat Buchanan Is a Racist!" A second protester, holding a different sign, got even closer to the candidate than the first one. Buchanan, who'd been suspended for a year as an undergraduate at Georgetown after picking a fight with two cops, grabbed the interloper's collar to keep him at bay. With news photographers standing just a few feet away from the melee, members of Buchanan's staff dragged the protesters off the stage with at least as much aggressive force as the instigators had used to disrupt the event. As the situation began to subside, a female voice could still be heard shouting, "You're a fascist!"

Buchanan took it all in stride, to the extent that anyone in his situation could have, maintaining his composure and extending his arms to his sides in the manner of his former boss, Richard Nixon, but giving the "thumbs up" rather than the "V" for victory sign. As the audience began to settle down after what had been a scary situation, Buchanan used the chaos as an opportunity. "Now you know what we're fighting against in this country, my friends," he said.

The protesters had been unusually committed to their cause of ruining Buchanan's rollout. They'd arrived on site early that morning and told members of the candidate's staff that they wanted to volunteer for the campaign. No one suspected a ruse, as the three strangers said and did all the right things, even helping the advance crew set up the stage. For their efforts, they had been rewarded with front row seats. Oops.

The violent disruption inevitably became a focal point of much of the media coverage that followed—an impending fate that Buchanan seemed to anticipate. About halfway through his announcement speech, he once more returned to the men who'd instigated the melee. "So like our visitors this morning, the custodians of political correctness do not frighten me," Buchanan said. "And I will do what is needed to defend the borders of my country, if it means putting the National Guard all along our southern frontier." The room loved it. But for much of the country, the scene served only to highlight the most negative perceptions of Buchanan as a resentment-driven extremist who had said some nice things about Hitler in the past, referred to gay people as "sodomites," and now had his very own team of brown shirts to rough up his enemies.

The opening day of Buchanan's campaign cemented the impression that he had little chance in New Hampshire, or anywhere else for that matter. Buchanan began his 1996 run as a significant underdog against Senate majority leader Bob Dole, the GOP front-runner, and Senator Phil Gramm of Texas, who was a fund-raising dynamo. Buchanan also had a slew of other plausible contenders to deal with, ranging from publishing executive Steve Forbes, who had a personal fortune at his disposal, to former Tennessee governor Lamar Alexander, who wore a snazzy checkered shirt and liked to go on long walks when he was campaigning.

During the next few months, the outlook didn't appear much brighter for Buchanan, but he did have two key factors quietly working in his favor. The first was that all of the other Republican candidates underestimated him. The second was that he genuinely enjoyed being on the trail and was totally at ease on the stump. Buchanan loved picnics and barbecues and delivering his stump speech to the passionate supporters who would chant, "Go, Pat, go!" He loved learning about the people who lived in the far-flung mill towns that he frequented and about the products that workers made in the factories he toured. He loved sitting in the passenger seat of vans as he was shuttled between events—time that he'd often spend interrogating his volunteer drivers about their own lives. And most of all, he loved the intellectual give-and-take of running for president in New Hampshire. Buchanan marveled at how the questions he received from voters at town hall meetings would often be far tougher than the ones he was asked by the national media—a card-carrying member of which he'd been as a host of CNN's *Crossfire* and of his own radio show.

Peter Robbio, who ran Buchanan's New Hampshire campaign, remembers that one of the candidate's favorite activities was to stop by the various headquarters of the state's still-powerful local newspapers. When he sat down for meetings with the often left-leaning editors, Buchanan would be presented with what he referred to as "golden oldies"—binders filled with some of the most incendiary pronouncements that he'd made over the decades. "Without fail, they'd throw those quotes at him, and he'd say, 'I didn't exactly say that, and here's why,'" Robbio recalls. "They'd get into a little contentious debate, then the editor's manner would change a bit and you'd realize they were thinking, 'I really hate what this guy's saying, but I really like the guy.' He'd win people over that way all the time."

By mid-autumn, Buchanan's momentum was becoming evident to many of the same people who'd once discounted him, and it wasn't just confined to New Hampshire. Two states—Alaska and Louisiana—had scheduled contests of questionable relevance ahead of Iowa in 1996 (they managed to avoid triggering the requisite leap-frogging response from Bill Gardner, because neither contest was a primary election and thus did not infringe upon New Hampshire state law). On January 29, after campaigning in the forty-ninth state, Buchanan edged out Forbes in Alaska's nonbinding straw poll. Fewer than 10,000 Alaskans participated in a vote that generated minimal national press coverage, but Buchanan was soon able to piggyback on that victory with a more meaningful upset win in the Louisiana caucuses. In doing so, he terminated the campaign of Phil Gramm, who hailed from neighboring Texas and had been widely expected to win. Gramm was so confident of victory in Louisiana that he'd mostly ignored the state until right before Caucus Day. He dropped out of the race a week later.

The Republican establishment was suddenly bordering on collective panic, determined to do whatever it took to stop Buchanan, whose momentum continued to build. Meanwhile, Buchanan's rivals began pushing negative stories to the press. The week before the New Hampshire primary, the Center for Public Integrity—a Washington-based interest group—published a damning report that linked the Buchanan campaign's co-chairman, Larry Pratt, to meetings that had been organized by white supremacist and militia groups. This was just about the last kind of scandal that Buchanan needed, as he sought to make his closing argument. Internally, Buchanan aides discussed whether to throw Pratt overboard and dismiss him from the campaign. The pugnacious Buchanan, however, had other ideas.

At the final Republican presidential debate before Primary Day, Buchanan used his closing statement to lambaste what he called the "savage attack" against Pratt. "Larry Pratt is a devout Christian," Buchanan said, as he karate chopped the air in characteristic fashion. "He's being attacked because he supports me. He's being attacked because he's defended Second Amendment rights his whole life. And that's why they're going after him."

Inside the WMUR green room where they were watching the debate, a small contingent of Buchanan aides could not believe what they were seeing. Buchanan hadn't told any of them that he intended to defend Pratt, and they were in a collective panic that the move would backfire—one step too far for the unapologetic populist. The *New York Times* and other national media outlets rendered their own verdicts in scathing editorials that denounced Buchanan for his defense of Pratt. The next week, the Republican primary voters of New Hampshire rendered their own verdict. Buchanan won the primary, edging out Dole by a single point. His supporters in New Hampshire, it turned out, didn't much care what the *New York Times* thought.

CHAPTER 17

MY FIRST FACE-TO-FACE EXPERIENCE with Donald Trump came in mid-July 2015 at the Weirs Community Center along the shores of Lake Winnipesaukee in Laconia. At the time, Trump was still a week away from ascending to the top spot in the New Hampshire polls—a position he wouldn't relinquish in a single public survey all the way through the February primary— but he had already become the candidate of the summer. It was an unofficial status that just about everyone in the know assumed would fade by the time the first cool breezes of autumn arrived, and yet the phenomenon was undoubtedly real. Trump was drawing massive crowds at rallies around the country and had recently taken the lead from Jeb Bush in national polls.

The morning of the Trump rally, I first swung by Wisconsin governor Scott Walker's inaugural New Hampshire event. After impressing party activists and the national media at an Iowa Republican confab early in the year, Walker was still leading in the polls in Iowa, the neighboring early state where a victory was most important to his campaign, and he appeared to be well positioned in New Hampshire, too. Walker offered the option of a young, deeply conservative man who wasn't scary to the establishment and had the political skills required to go the distance. But he was also burdened by a couple of fundamental handicaps that would ultimately amount to his rapid undoing. Although he had spent more than two decades in the trenches of Wisconsin politics, he wasn't quite up to snuff on national policy, and it showed. He just didn't come across as particularly prepared to run for president—a problem that exacerbated his second critical flaw as a White House hopeful: stature. Basically, it boiled down to this: Could voters imagine this man addressing the country in a crisis as president of the United States? Walker may have been a street fighter in the conservative movement and a second-term governor of an important state, but for many, he didn't pass the Oval Office test.

I wrote down somewhere in my reporter's notebook that the Walker event that morning had taken place at Joey's Diner in Amherst, and I'm glad that I did because it was instantly forgettable. About the most interesting thing that happened came when the Wisconsin governor jumped up onto the bed of a red pickup truck to address the overflow crowd outside the event. But even that manufactured moment was rather lame, as he delivered from his elevated perch the same carefully crafted stump speech, just about word for word, that he would repeat a few minutes later inside the diner. I decided to skip his second event of the day so that I could make sure I'd get to Laconia on time for Trump. Why attend another glorified photo-op when I had an invitation to a fifty-car pileup?

Before setting out on the hour drive to Laconia, I made a pit stop at A&E Coffee Roastery—Amherst's finest caffeine dispensary—where I set to work on filing my brief and tedious story on the Walker event. As I settled into an armchair with my large iced regular and began my Twitter-scrolling, writing-avoidance ritual, I received a phone call from Sam Stein, senior politics editor for the *Huffington Post* in Washington. Sam told me about a decision that our site's founder and editor-in-chief, Arianna Huffington, had announced to editors earlier in the day: although we would continue to cover his campaign, all future HuffPost stories that featured Donald Trump would appear in the site's entertainment section, rather than in the politics section. The reason provided for the change was that Trump's campaign was nothing more than a media-driven sideshow, fit for Kardashian-level scrutiny, rather than the earnest inspection required to scrutinize a real contender for the presidency. Trump would soon fall as quickly as he'd risen, the expectation went, and we would get out ahead of the rest of the media in treating his candidacy as the overt joke that it was. My own mandate in covering Trump would not change, Sam assured me. From now on, I'd just have to check the box next to "Entertainment" rather than "Politics" when I filed my stories about him. I didn't have any input on this decision, and so my opinion about its merits didn't much matter, but I figured correctly that it would inevitably have an impact on my own access to Trump.

I made it to Laconia as the summer afternoon was at its shimmering peak. The traffic was fairly substantial by the time I caught my first glimpse of Lake Winnipesaukee—New Hampshire's largest body of water and a major tourist destination—but not even that could sour my mood. The only thing missing was ice cream. One of the best things about New Hampshire in the summertime is that you're never more than a few miles away from an ice cream shop. One might assume it's all lobster rolls and clam chowder, but for reasons I can't explain, ice cream is as integral a part of New Hampshire comfort food as those other staples are. I pulled into the Happy Cow Ice Cream Shop just north of bustling downtown Laconia and ordered a mint chocolate chip in a waffle cone. As I sat on the park bench eating my pre-dinner dessert, enjoying the warmth of the now fading sunlight and the faint breeze that topped it all off, I thought about what a shame it was that this confluence of tranquillity was all about to be upended by an air horn in a suit, whose taste in home decor would have made Louis XIV snicker.

I arrived at the event site around 5:30 p.m.—an hour before Trump was set to kick things off inside the Weirs Community

Center. A crowd of several hundred people had already lined up out-side the doors leading into the small building. I flashed my "media credential" (a *Huffington Post* business card) to the cops who stood outside the back entrance to the building and entered the packed house along the left side of the stage. Like many public buildings in New Hampshire, the community center had no air conditioning. It felt like the temperature inside was easily into the triple digits, and a quick scan of the room revealed that several of the older Trump fans who had already been waiting for hours appeared to be on the verge of passing out. Anxious volunteers handed out free water bottles at a steady clip. As I looked outside the window onto the beautiful and temperate summer evening, I wondered if Trump's advance team had *preferred* the cramped, sweaty indoor venue to the expansive outdoor setting that the pier offered. Red meat tastes best, after all, when the stove's cranked up. The extra heat gives it a nice, crisp char.

While waiting for the program to start, I began approaching people at random, asking them what they liked about Trump. The answers were fairly consistent. "What he says, he means," Cecil Baldwin, who was in town from Arizona with his wife, told me, adding, "We need someone like him." Marge Dahla, who had made the trip from the North Country hamlet of East Dalton, said that she "loves how he speaks" and that Trump's personal fortune insu-lated him from the special interests that had taken hold of career politicians. "He's not beholden to people," she reiterated.

The general sentiment—that Trump was a truth-telling out-sider—was more or less what I'd expected. It wasn't just that he was a celebrity. These people *liked* that Trump was a plutocratic blowhard who caused members of the establishment to wrinkle their noses. My most memorable conversation was with a Mexican American mother and her adult son—Delilah Rodriguez and Alex Chapa of Laconia and Manchester—who were most effusive in singing the praises of the man who had launched his high-flying presidential campaign by declaring undocumented immigrants from Mexico to be rapists. Dressed in a shiny blue button-down shirt and red tie, his hair spiked with gel, Chapa looked a decade younger than his thirty-nine years. An Iraq War veteran who signed up for the army ten days after 9/11, he told me that his grandparents on his father's side had immigrated to the United States from Mexico legally in the 1940s. He was in general agreement with Trump on border security but would go a step further than the candidate by closing the border "for like ten years."

"American Hispanics don't want all the illegals taking our tax money for free rights," he said, standing next to his mother. Chapa clearly understood how this sentiment might come across as pulling the ladder up behind him, depriving others who wanted a better life in the United States from achieving that goal, but he didn't care. "We're Mexican and we're saying this!" he added, as if he were a bit taken aback by the words that were coming out of his mouth.

As I started to chat with him, it soon became clear that while he supported Trump's position on immigration, it wasn't the main attraction for Chapa. To him, Trump was a role model, a guy who "knows how to make money," as Chapa put it, and a man's man, who said and did whatever he wanted without worrying about consequences like public ridicule that tend to hold other people back. "I like him because he's a billionaire," Chapa said. "And he's powerful, and he's international, yet when he talks, he says it straight up, like how real Americans talk in a bar or at home. I love it."

What struck me the most about Trump supporters like Chapa was their universal sincerity. They really believed in the guy with every fiber of their beings, and they didn't sound like people who might change their allegiances. Unlike the people who'd come out to catch a glimpse of Scott Walker that morning and make some early judgments about him, these Trump fans had already rendered their verdict about the campaign.

Showtime finally arrived when the introductory speaker welcomed "the next president of the United States, Donald Trump."

"There's his hair!" someone shouted, as the legendary nest of golden locks shimmered toward the stage under the direction of a huge contingent of dark-suited and stern-faced private security guards. Trump himself was dressed in his typical uniform: a bright-red power tie, white shirt, and slimming, navy-blue suit. True to form, his first task of the speech was to marvel aloud about the size of his crowd, the hugeness of which he could scarcely find words to describe adequately while staying within the restrictive confines of the English language. "There's a massive group of people outside that the press won't report, by the way," Trump shouted into the microphone. "They won't talk about it. They're not going to talk about the hundreds—literally—I would say four times the size of this crowd!" Many in the crowd—small and sedate by Trumpian standards—oohed in response to Trump's estimation of their numbers.

As he meandered his way into something approximating a stump speech, Trump railed in typical fashion about how "the last thing we need is another Bush" and how the United States was getting "screwed" by a duplicitous but savvy country called "Chee-EYE-nah."

"I beat China. I beat them!" he added.

Trump even led his own distinctive version of the call and response.

"How much money do I have?" the candidate called out to his flock.

"Ten billion!" the faithful shouted in unison.

Like countless politicians before him, Trump sought to turn one of his most glaring weaknesses—his standing among Hispanic voters—into a strength. "I have so many Hispanics, and they love me," he said, using syntax that only he could dream up. "And interestingly, we just got from the state of Nevada a poll [that] just came out, and Trump won with a tremendous amount. And the second line was, 'Takes Hispanic vote in a landslide,' and I've been saying that. I'm going to win the Hispanic vote."

The survey he was referring to was conducted by a notoriously unreliable polling company, and it only showed him with a lead among *Republican* Hispanics in Nevada. But Delilah Rodriguez, Chapa's mother, was fully convinced. "Yes, you are!" she shouted back at the candidate.

As minutes ticked away, the heat continued to take effect on the increasingly red-faced and sweating candidate. Later on in the campaign, the sight of hundreds of disinterested people walking out in the middle of Trump's rallies would become commonplace. But at this one, I saw just one person make for the exits while Trump was still on stage. "I've heard enough," a middle-aged man said aloud, as he headed for the parking lot. Just about everyone else in the crowd continued to hang on his every utterance, no matter how nonsensical. Still, there was a collective sense that pretty much everyone in the room was in on the joke. I even noticed a couple of Trump's security guards chuckling to themselves.

Many of his fans, however, remained visibly starstruck, scarcely able to keep it together in Trump's presence. When the candidate called on one man in his thirties to ask a question, the lucky guy's facial reaction was akin to what you'd expect from a fifteen-year-old girl right after she's asked to come up onto the stage to be serenaded by Justin Bieber. But the highlight of the event came during the very first exchange of the Q-and-A when a man rose from his chair, accepted the microphone from an aide, and announced by way of introduction that he was a Vietnam veteran. Never inclined to sit back and let a stranger one-up him, Trump shot back immediately, "I did the Vietnam Veterans memorial in New York. Did you know I'm responsible for that?"

Trump didn't mention the four student deferments he'd received in avoiding the Vietnam-era draft, nor did he bring up the separate medical deferment he was granted at the time for a "foot thing," as he'd later put it. The guy had put up some cash to build a memorial in New York, which—in his severely warped perspective—was more impressive than actually fighting in the war.

As soon as the rally ended, I made my way out the back door as quickly as possible in an effort to beat the crowd. A few minutes later, I pulled my rental car to the side of the road and searched on my phone for a nearby coffee shop to file a brief story. An approaching police siren caused me to look in my rearview mirror, where I saw a motorcade approaching rapidly. Trump and his entourage were being led out of town by police escort—one last spectacle to put a punctuation mark on the evening. I found myself wondering where they were going. I knew that at this stage of the campaign, Trump returned home every night to Manhattan to sleep in his own bed. The nearest major airport was in Manchester, which was a solid hour away, and I couldn't imagine that he would subject himself to that level of inconvenience. I figured that Trump was probably heading to a private airfield somewhere nearby. A quick search on Google Maps revealed that Laconia Municipal Airport was just down the road, so without giving it much further thought, I headed in that direction.

A few minutes later, I pulled into the small airport and noticed that a couple of dozen gawkers had gotten there first. They were gathered outside the waiting area at the private terminal, peering into the windows. That was odd, I thought. Why didn't they just go inside? There was nothing preventing them—or anyone else, for that matter—from entering the fixed-based operator (FBO) waiting area. But it was as if they assumed that they'd be breaking some sort of law if they got too close to Trump, who did not have Secret Service protection at this point in the campaign. Without giving it any additional thought, I walked right into the small building where I assumed Trump was holed up.

Upon entering, the very first person I laid eyes on was lounging on one of the two leather chairs that were positioned in front of a wall-mounted flat-screen TV tuned to Fox News. It was Trump, fully engaged in his favorite activity: watching himself. Surrounding him was a small contingent of aides, bodyguards, and airport employees, all of whom dared not get closer than about a ten-foot radius from the impulsive agitator to whom they each referred to in both public and private as "Mr. Trump." It was as if such a holy figure required a buffer zone, room for the enormity of his presence. I knew that this might prove to be my one and only chance to talk to Trump, especially considering my news organization's new policy, which had not yet been announced, but I hadn't prepared any questions in advance and wasn't sure of the best way to approach him.

I spotted Trump's campaign manager, Corey Lewandowski, whom I'd known previously in his role as a New Hampshire–based conservative political activist. Lewandowski was an intense, energy-drink-pounding operative with a tidy buzz cut and the disposition of a man who has something to prove. I had been to his home to interview him during the 2012 campaign and had always found him to be someone I could work with. After exchanging pleasantries and complimenting him for the sizable crowd his candidate had attracted that evening, I asked Lewandowski if I might have a few minutes of Trump's time. He told me to hold on for a moment and then approached the candidate, whispering something into his ear. Trump answered his minion with a kingly nod and then motioned for me to sit in the leather chair next to him.

"The *Huffington Post* has been very fair to me," was the first thing Trump said to me after shaking my hand. I knew that he kept extremely close score of who had written and said what about him. This was, after all, a man who was famous in journalistic circles for scrolling handwritten nasty notes on unflattering reporters' articles and then mailing them to the offenders. I was therefore relieved that he couldn't place my name beyond my employer. In truth, I had been pretty hostile and dismissive of Trump in my reporting to that point and knew that I probably would not have been granted this opportunity had he been aware of that.

I started out by asking him about some recent comments that Rick Perry had made, in which the former Texas governor had called Trump a "cancer on conservatism," among other things. At that point in the race, Perry was the only Republican candidate who was even attempting to lay a finger on Trump. The others, it seemed, had all bought into the idea that he'd go away naturally, like a bout of the flu. True to form, Trump asked why I would bother asking him about a GOP rival who was merely polling in the low single digits. But in a departure from the character he played on TV, he refused to get too personal, adding that he believed Perry to be "a nice person." This was the tenor that Trump would maintain throughout our brief conversation—a watered-down version of the character he portrayed on television.

Trump couldn't resist boasting that earlier in the night, his driver had told him he'd been in New Hampshire for a quarter century and had never seen a crowd so large. When I asked him how much of his own money he'd be willing to put into the campaign, he replied that he'd "do what I have to do" and did not dismiss out of hand the idea when I asked him if he'd eventually be willing to drop $1 billion on it. We were still at a point in the race when it wasn't entirely clear the extent to which Trump would benefit from the unprecedented level of free media he was already receiving. In the time left until Primary Day, as it turned out, he would scarcely need to spend a dime of his own money to win in New Hampshire.

Next, I threw him what I thought would be a tricky little curve ball: "Do you think Sarah Palin was ready to be president?" Much of Trump's success up to that point in the race had stemmed from his ability to tap into the disaffected, economically struggling voters who were some of Palin's strongest supporters in 2008 and beyond. If he said something detrimental about the former Alaska governor, he risked offending his own base. But if he was too kind, he could turn off the vast majority of GOP voters who'd long ago accepted the reality that Palin had been dangerously unqualified for the office that John McCain had chosen her to seek. "Uuuuuhh," Trump replied, hesitating for the first time. "Well, you know, she's a friend of mine, and I think she's a terrific person." I waited for him to elaborate. "She's a terrific person," he repeated, adding, "Go ahead."

It was just the kind of noncommittal answer you typically hear from a skilled politician, not a passing fad. My god, I thought. He's adapting! Shortly thereafter, Trump ended the short interview, as some of his braver admirers had moved in closer to the unofficial no-fly zone that surrounded him, and they wanted pictures. Before obliging their requests and doing some last-minute preparation for his impending phone interview with Bill O'Reilly, Trump took his turn at asking me a question.

"Are you going back to New York?"

I was. "You got room for me?" I asked, motioning toward his private plane that was parked in the airfield. It wasn't the 757 that Trump usually flew in but rather a more modest aircraft that was small enough to land at the Laconia airport.

Trump turned to Lewandowski. "The problem is if we put him on the plane, he'll write a bad story," the candidate speculated accurately. "I don't think they have a seat. I would love to." Alas, I'd have to take my decidedly non-gold-encrusted rental car back to New York.

After he finished his phone interview with O'Reilly, I watched Trump's plane take off and then headed back out on the road. The next morning, the *Huffington Post* announced publicly our new policy of only covering Trump in the entertainment section, where a story based on my interview had been posted overnight. Trump's campaign wasn't happy. The first call I received was from his press secretary, former model turned Mr. Trump-devotee Hope Hicks. She argued that Trump could be "both" an entertainer and a politician and genuinely seemed unable to understand why we didn't see it that way. I explained to Hicks that I had not devised the policy and still planned to cover Trump the same way I had been previously. Her answer to that particular assertion was that it would be difficult for the campaign to work with me from here on out. I'm sure it would be, I thought. It was tough to argue with her on that front.

Next, I received a call from Lewandowski, who attempted to project calm. "It's nothing personal," he said. "But if you guys are going to do this, I don't see how I can credential the *Huffington Post* for events going forward."

The following day, the Trump campaign took me off their e-mail distribution list for press releases. The day after that, Trump told an audience in Iowa that John McCain was "not a war hero," adding that he liked "the people who don't get captured" in wars. The day after that, his poll numbers went up again.

CHAPTER 18

I T WAS EARLY ON a Sunday morning in October 2015, and the weekend crowd at the Manchester Hilton Garden Inn was just starting to file into the breakfast area for the buffet. The special of the day was the frankly daunting potato pancakes topped with barbecue sauce and bacon. I took a seat at a table for four in front of the bar, ordered a cup of coffee, and watched a few minutes later as John McCain emerged from the elevator. Before I could get up, the seventy-nine-year-old Arizona senator was greeted in the hallway by Brittany Bramell, who worked on his 2008 presidential campaign. McCain ducked behind the fireplace for a few moments of privacy with Bramell. I didn't know what was happening but assumed she was briefing him before the interview we had scheduled. A few minutes later, McCain reemerged and made a beeline for the buffet. Meanwhile, Bramell came over to say hi.

"What was going on back there?" I asked her.

"Oh, I have to comb his hair every morning," she said.

Oh, right. The man whose military service Donald Trump had famously denigrated couldn't comb his own hair because he couldn't lift his arms to his head. And he couldn't lift his arms to his head because of the broken bones he'd suffered upon being shot down over North Vietnam, landing in a lake, and then enduring unspeakable torture during his five-and-a-half-year stint at the Hanoi Hilton. McCain had been living with his physical handicap for almost half a century, but the senator wasn't one to talk about his own courage unprompted. He much preferred to regale audiences with profane and evocative stories from his more than three decades of government service. There was no topic he liked to discuss more than New Hampshire—the state that became like a second home to him during his two victorious primary campaigns in 2000 and 2008. The reverence that McCain had for the people, process, and history of the New Hampshire primary was deep, and the feeling mutual. No person, living or dead—excluding, perhaps, Bill Gardner—better captured the essence of the primary at its best than John McCain.

He sat down at my table with a bowl of cereal and a blueberry scone in hand and offered a "Good morning." When I asked him about his current endeavors on the trail, McCain acknowledged that it had been tough sledding trying to drum up support for his buddy Lindsey Graham, for whom he was preparing to set out on another day by his side, crisscrossing the state. It was like old times, only without the receptive audiences. "I wish it was better," McCain said, adding unconvincingly that there was still a lot of time left for Graham to turn things around.

He was eager to get out of the present and start talking about the past, and I was happy to listen. McCain's memory for details of campaigning in New Hampshire had faded a bit, but his delight in it was contagious. He was wearing on his right wrist a replica of a bracelet that was given to him at a town hall meeting in Wolfeboro, New Hampshire, in August 2007 (the original one broke, and he had it replaced) by the mother of Matthew Stanley, who was killed in combat outside of Baghdad. She had asked McCain to wear it under the condition that the candidate promise to do everything in his power as president to make sure that her son's death wasn't in vain. It was a story that McCain retold often on the 2008 campaign trail and one that left few dry eyes in the room, no matter how many times people had heard it.

Despite there being no scarcity of poignant memories like that one from his 2008 run, most veterans of McCain's two presidential campaigns will tell you that the 2000 one was their favorite. That year, he found himself as a true underdog from the beginning—a position that allowed him to run exactly the way he wanted to and probably have more fun than any presidential candidate has had in New Hampshire before or since.

The enduring love affair between McCain and New Hampshire began in Peterborough, a postcard-perfect town nestled into the mostly rural stretch of rolling hills between Keene and Manchester. All across this prototypically New England small town, American flags flutter in front of colonial-style homes, and the Worcester Lunch Car–style diner has remained mostly unchanged since it opened in 1949. The street sign that welcomes visitors calls it "a good town to live in," and for McCain, Peterborough proved to be a good town to campaign in. In particular, the two-story Peterborough Town House at the center of town proved to be McCain's favorite venue in all of New Hampshire. With its white pilasters and octagonal tower perched at the summit and Old Glory flanking the lantern-lit entrance, the building practically bled Americana through its red bricks.

In the summer of 1999, McCain was a relatively obscure senator who had not yet formally launched his long-shot presidential campaign. The legendary days of the freewheeling Straight Talk Express and passionate throngs of New Hampshire supporters dubbed "McCainiacs" were still in the future. At the time, McCain was facing down the prospect of competing not only against the George W. Bush juggernaut and all of the front-runner's financial might but also the largely forgotten—but at the time formidable-seeming— candidacy of Elizabeth Dole (not to mention a handful of other middling competitors, including Steve Forbes, Lamar Alexander, and John Kasich). Barely registering in the polls and with almost no money, McCain's small New Hampshire staff attempted to promote his first town-hall meeting in Peterborough by sending out a direct-mail barrage to thousands of local voters, which enticed them with an "ice cream social" that would feature the Arizona senator.

Among those who were there, estimates of the crowd count for the event have tended to decrease steadily over time, but the body of evidence suggests that somewhere between a dozen and thirty people showed up. The campaign had planned to hold the event in the expansive, balcony-equipped auditorium but because of the lack of interest, they moved it to the basement. "There wasn't one person under age seventy," according to McCain. And most of the retirees who did make the trip were more interested in the free hot-fudge sundaes than they were in hearing McCain's arid pitch about the importance of campaign-finance reform.

It was an inauspicious beginning. Still, the upstart candidate didn't try to change his message to appeal to a bigger audience. Instead, he vowed to out-hustle every other candidate in the race, especially Bush, who campaigned in New Hampshire infrequently and with his motorcades and large contingent of Texas rangers keeping him at an imperial distance from voters. Eventually, people started to notice. As McCain slowly built momentum in the coming months, his 2000 campaign became the quintessential example of a candidate using New Hampshire to propel himself from afterthought to legitimate presidential contender. McCain more or less perfected the art of the New Hampshire town-hall meeting format, not as a stage to get some nice photos and footage for the evening news crews on hand to use, but rather as a setting by which he would earnestly attempt to win over voters a few at a time. Curious New Hampshirites who saw him at small venues around the state and came away impressed would then convey their favorable impressions to friends and family, and interest grew by word of mouth. It was social media for the dial-up age. There couldn't have been a more old-fashioned manner of campaigning, and it suited McCain perfectly.

One of the key factors that made New Hampshire voters—particularly independents—start paying attention to McCain was that he talked about things Republicans didn't normally talk about, especially his quest to rid government of "big money" influences. According to polling, campaign-finance reform was not among the most pressing concerns for most people, but McCain spoke about the issue in such a passionate and genuine way that his interest in doing something significant to upend the system began to rub off on a sizable swath of the electorate. He ended up holding 114 New Hampshire town-hall meetings leading up to the 2000 primary. The state couldn't seem to get enough of the man who embodied its unflinching, sarcastic, and hard-to-please character.

The media liked him, too, and McCain would often joke that the smitten journalists who tagged along with him were his "base." As they rode with him on the bus, they enjoyed the kind of give-and-take with the candidate that became much harder to replicate in later presidential campaigns when the Internet really took hold. Sometimes reporters would run out of questions and start talking to McCain about their own families and life in general. It was all pretty cozy (probably a little too cozy), but around-the-clock was just the way McCain liked to operate. "We started getting up early in the morning and having early morning town-hall meetings before people went to work," he recalled to me with wistful delight. "That way, if you start early, you can do four or five a day."

There were plenty of times when McCain said something that he shouldn't have said to a reporter. But there weren't many "gaffes," in the way we think of them today. Little of what he uttered stuck out in a negative way, in part because he was saying so much that the media would quickly move on to something else. More than anything, McCain liked to get out into the hinterlands—away from the Manchester area and the seacoast to musty, long-neglected VFW halls in the state's sleepy midsection and far-flung North Country outposts where he could take in the natural elements that energized him, while also getting more media bang for his buck. "Another aspect of the small towns is that they appreciated you coming,"

McCain told me. "And what my opponents didn't understand, even if you were in a small town, the national media by the thousands are looking for anything. So they'd show up and join on the bus. Later in the campaign there would be almost as many reporters as people at the town halls."

One of McCain's most memorable bus trips of the 2000 campaign began in Dixville Notch, the wooded hamlet just south of the Canadian border where Neil Tillotson—the inventor of latex gloves, who was then one hundred years old—first organized and continued to carry out the midnight vote at the Balsams resort. McCain was pleased to get a meeting with the local legend. Here was a man, he knew, who would be happy to indulge in McCain's favorite pastime: extensive conversation about the good old days.

"Tell me something, Mr. Tillotson," McCain asked him in a story that he would recall time and again over the years. "Out of all these candidates who come up here every four years, who has been your favorite?"

"Roosevelt!" Tillotson replied.

"Wow, Franklin Roosevelt. A four-term president—"

"No," Tillotson said, cutting McCain off. "Teddy!"

The day before the primary and with momentum now clearly on his side, McCain wisely declined to attend a Bisquick-sponsored pancake breakfast at the Army National Guard Armory in Manchester. The two Republican candidates who did take part in the festivities were Bush and Gary Bauer—a prominent Christian conservative activist. Arnie Arnesen, a liberal state-level operative turned talk-radio host, had been asked to emcee a pancake-flipping contest between the two GOP contenders, who were both struggling to keep up with McCain in New Hampshire.

First up, the Texas governor approached the task with his characteristic swagger. Escorted by Tom Rath, his top New Hampshire political consultant, Bush moseyed onto the stage, delivered a few remarks, and flipped a pancake. But not only did he flip it, he flipped it *high*—too high for most anyone who doesn't practice flipping pancakes on a regular basis to catch. But Bush *did* catch it—and not in the expansive pan with which the pancake was made. No, he landed the thing on the small spatula that he used to flip it, while the pan rested on the stove—a daring method that added several degrees of difficulty to the feat. Perhaps knowing that it would be the last victory his candidate would have in New Hampshire that winter, as the pancake landed dead in the middle of Bush's spatula, Rath raised both of his hands in the air in triumph. Not done yet, Bush then flipped the pancake into his free hand with a casual flick of his wrist. Then he winked and pointed at a couple of members of the audience before leaving the stage with the strut of a rock guitarist who'd just shredded the final notes of "Free Bird."

"I want you to know that was not a rigged event," a clearly impressed Arnesen told the crowd. "He actually caught it with the flipper, not with the pan!"

Next, it was Bauer's turn. As he approached the stage, Arnesen decided to needle the far more diminutive of the two Republican candidates. "I just want Gary to know that Tom Rath suggested to me that Gary might show his proficiency with short stacks," she said into the microphone.

The joke didn't totally make sense, but Arnesen's playful jab seemed to rattle the physically timid Bauer, who—it was now already clear—was not a man who was up to the task of flipping a pancake in front of a crowd with the ease that Bush conveyed. And yet he had nothing to lose. With McCain absent, Bauer had to at least try to beat Bush at something—even if that something was the act of tossing solidified batter into the sky and then catching it with a tool that was ill-equipped for the task.

And so Bauer flipped his pancake. He flipped it high—dangerously high—higher than Bush had. Too high, as it turned out. High enough and with enough backward momentum that when gravity began taking its hold, the pancake drifted well behind Bauer's head. It was out of reach. But Bauer didn't give up. The presidency was on the line here! He backpedaled a bit like a baby deer trying to gain its footing, and then he shifted his body to the left. For Gary Bauer, time must have seemed to slow down at this point. He surely realized that it would have taken a miracle for him to catch the pancake on the spatula—a miracle even more spectacular than the act of God that would have allowed his flagging campaign to remain afloat after New Hampshire's voters had their say. And so, Bauer gave up on trying to catch the pancake with his spatula. But he had a backup plan. He reached out his left hand at the very last moment and caught the pancake with the frying pan. Wow, good enough! Bauer could now settle for a respectable second-place showing in the pancake flip, as long as he could finish securing the pancake in his pan and prevent it from hitting the floor. He just had to stick the landing.

He didn't. In a jaw-dropping instant, Gary Bauer began to stumble off the stage. As he tumbled backward, his legs shuffled under him in place in the manner of Wile E. Coyote when the cartoon character has already fallen off the cliff but hasn't realized it yet. And then, Bauer plummeted over the edge, careening into a blue curtain and landing out of sight of the dozens of video cameras that were trained on him. Arnesen provided the play-by-play: "Whooah . . . Ooooooh. Oh, no. Oh, no. Candidate missing in action!"

To his credit, Bauer was resilient. He licked his wounds and then sprang back onto his feet within seconds. Then he leaped back onto the stage and gave the crowd a double-thumbs up, trying to put on his best game face. "I'm a fighter, folks!" he said with an accompanying, machine-gun burst of nervous laughter. Arnesen, meanwhile, pronounced his performance worthy of a Perfect Ten: "And who said this wasn't going to be an exciting event?"

As Bauer was recovering from his wounded ego, and with a big snowstorm blanketing the state, McCain finished his final New Hampshire sprint with a series of outdoor events in Keene, Hanover, and Concord, ending the day in Portsmouth. His campaign had conducted some late polling, and the Arizona senator knew that the race was breaking his way—though he remained oblivious to the extent that he was dominating Bush. It was snowing hard as McCain delivered his closing remarks on the Portsmouth waterfront. The captain of a passing merchant ship kept blasting the vessel's horn, sending the crowd into a frenzy with the racket, which at times drowned out the candidate's words. The New Hampshire primary had found its icon.

With New Hampshirites shoveling out after the snowstorm on Primary Day, February 1, 2000, it was clear that McCain was likely to win. The most recent polls showed him beating Bush—who had won Iowa easily—by a margin of eight to ten points. But one final concerning moment for the famously superstitious McCain came when he visited a polling station that morning in Concord. A woman who was running the voting operation there was none too pleased when the candidate appeared unannounced with his wife, Cindy, and the accompanying media entourage in tow. "Senator Mc-Cain, you're disturbing the right of the people of New Hampshire to cast a vote!" she shouted at him. "I want you out of here now. That means you too, media!"

"Shit," McCain thought to himself. "This isn't exactly what we wanted!"

That theoretically bad omen, however, proved to be without merit. McCain went on to defeat George W. Bush by nineteen points, capping off the most unlikely blowout in the history of the New Hampshire primary. Bauer, meanwhile, earned the support of 1,640 New Hampshire voters—good enough for just shy of 0.7 percent of the vote. Bisquick didn't even offer him an endorsement deal.

CHAPTER 19

I N August 2015, my wife and I were married in Whitefield at the
Mountain View Grand Resort, a beautiful 150-year-old hotel.
The place boasted New Hampshire's oldest hand-operated elevator and had a distinct *The Shining* vibe. We had met on the campaign trail in New Hampshire four years earlier (where we were both
covering a Jon Huntsman event at the Salem-Derry Elks Lodge).
Although weather reports called for rain, it turned into the kind of
sparkling summer evening you don't allow yourself to hope for leading up to your wedding day. To ensure that the New Hampshire
theme was thoroughly beaten to death, we even cajoled an initially
reluctant Secretary of State Bill Gardner to break with decades of
self-imposed wedding ceremony exile to preside as our justice of the
peace.

I was excited to spend an extended weekend with friends and
family in one of the most beautiful corners of the state without
thinking one bit about the primary. And as Whitefield is a town
of fewer than 2,500 people and is located in a rather inconvenient

stretch of wilderness just north of the White Mountains, I was reasonably certain that I wouldn't encounter anything that was directly related to the campaign. On a morning jog the day before the wedding, however, two of the three cars that I passed on the road were adorned with Carly Fiorina bumper stickers. "Huh," I thought. "Maybe Fiorina's really starting to resonate."

The former Hewlett-Packard CEO's profile had risen substantially since the previous month's so-called kids' table debate in Cleveland that featured all of the GOP presidential candidates who didn't make the cut for the main event. Fiorina had thoroughly dominated the JV game, and her poll numbers had been rising a bit in New Hampshire. If the hard-to-reach denizens of Whitefield were leading indicators of how she was resonating in the hinterlands, maybe she was about to become a more significant factor in the race than anyone realized.

Or maybe not. When I got back to the hotel, a friend told me that she had run into Carly Fiorina in the gym that morning. It turned out she had held an event in the area on the previous day and had spent the night at the hotel. Carly-mentum in Whitefield had been confined to a couple of her own staffers' vehicles, and I was reminded why it's a very bad idea to read too much into anecdotal evidence.

In trying to assess the strength of a presidential candidate, just about the only method worse than assessing bumper-sticker sightings is to give serious consideration to the media narrative of the moment. As August turned to September, the new narrative on the Republican race was that Trump's supporters were responding to his "authenticity." What? There were a lot of adjectives I could think of to describe a man who would unflinchingly use words like "greatest," "biggest," and "best" to describe everything from his buildings to his bowel movements, but "authentic" wasn't one of them.

To me, Trump's appeal was pretty clear. He wasn't authentic. He was just different than every politician who'd come before him. He said whatever the hell he wanted to say, whenever he wanted to say it, but not because he was *authentic*. Trump was skillful in his ability to deliver an entertaining if mindless performance for people who wanted to escape the drudgery and hardships in their own lives. Like any great illusionist, he knew how to make them believe that something much better was magically awaiting them just around the corner, if only they'd *trust* him.

In every presidential campaign in recent memory, voters have made abundantly clear that they detested Washington, but in the end, they've always turned to someone who pretty much embodies its prevailing ethos. But no presidential campaign preceding this one had ever featured a character so wildly over-the-top as Trump. At this point in the race—before he turned to inciting violence, as well as lying even more aggressively and regularly—Trump was still widely perceived in the broader media narrative as something of a novelty. In retrospect, that collective misjudgment was a big part of what ultimately allowed him to become so dangerous.

Another media narrative that proved equally flawed was the assumption that Jeb Bush would ultimately find a way to compete seriously for the nomination and should continue to be covered as a front-runner. There was simply no way that a candidate who boasted as many inherent advantages as Bush did could continue to languish far behind in the polls. With the arrival of September—that pivotal month when voters tend to "get serious," according to unsubstantiated legend—the man with the most money to play with and the presidential pedigree to cull from would surely get another look. I believed it, too. The voters, it turned out, were unimpressed by this subjective assessment of how they would behave.

On the Thursday after Labor Day, I hit the road from New York City and drove five hours through a drenching rainstorm to a Jeb Bush town-hall event at an elementary school in Salem, New Hampshire, a Boston commuter town just across the Massachusetts border. There were about 150 people there—not a great turnout for a supposed front-runner at this point and downright miniscule by Sanders's and Trump's standards. The candidate was fine—reasonably engaging and sharp on policy—but the lack of energy in

the room was noticeable. In his defense, Bush was justifiably preoc-
cupied by the clock, with the Patriots set to take the field that night
in Foxborough for the first game of their Super Bowl title defense.
Even when he was talking about football, Bush sounded defeated.
He admitted that he was a Dolphins fan, but he didn't sound much
like one. "Once again, we'll get crushed by the Patriots—that's our
tradition, and we'll stick to it, I'm sure," the somewhat gloomy candidate predicted. "I actually went to high school with [Patriots head
coach] Bill Belichick, and he was an incredibly smart kid. He's the
best coach in the NFL. And you've got the best quarterback."

Bush stopped short of noting that former Dolphins star Dan
Marino had never won a Super Bowl and didn't point out that Patriots quarterback Tom Brady had an exceptionally beautiful wife, but
his attempts to ingratiate himself with Patriots fans while denigrat-
ing his own team came across as a bit off-putting. Bush assured the
crowd that he'd provide them a buffer before the 8:30 p.m. kickoff.
"Gotta get in a brewski, too," he said. "Don't know about everyone
else, but I do." OK, so he drank beer. That was one agreeable way
in which he was different from his older brother. But I saw no signs
that this particular Bush, who was far less charismatic than the previous one, would do any better in New Hampshire.

That Saturday morning, I got out of bed at the Manchester
Radisson and headed downstairs to retrieve my first cup of coffee
of the day. I was greeted in the elevator by a man in his thirties
dressed in a black mask who looked like Batman but wasn't quite.
"Morning," he said as the elevator door closed behind us with a thud
that sounded more emphatic than usual. I'm not normally inclined
to verbally interact with *anyone* before ingesting caffeine, and I immediately began pulling out all the stops to avoid speaking a word
to this particular gentleman. I gave him a friendly nod and looked
him up and down. As much as I didn't want to talk to him, it was
too early for me to avoid staring at something like this. He could
tell that I was impressed. "Wait until I get my armor on," he said
with the sigh of a man who had a long day of work ahead of him. "It
weighs like seventy pounds."

As I made my way to the parking lot, past throngs of adults who were lining up for Granite State Comic Con, some of them dressed in full robot suits and makeup that must have taken at least two hours to apply, it occurred to me that Donald Trump was running his campaign a bit like a comic-book superhero. It didn't matter that almost none of what he said was based in reality. He'd created a world in which every aspect of American life was under attack from nefarious, shape-shifting evildoers. Fortunately, he, Donald Trump, was the only one who could save the day. With the stroke of a pen, he'd end the trade deals that sold out the common man; by sheer force of his will and strength, he'd build a magical wall to keep the grotesque Mexican hordes out; and he'd outflank the Chinese using his most famous superpower of all: his deal-making skills. This was a world that was easy for people to understand.

John Kasich, on the other hand, was most definitely not a superhero. A plain-vanilla Ohioan (albeit with an infamous temper), Kasich built his political career on his reputation as a no-frills Midwesterner who knows how to get the job done and doesn't have time to deal with any of the nonsense, OK? Kasich also had a distinct oddball side—the kind that only people who are supremely comfortable in their own skin are willing to show off in public. Kasich liked to play the role of life coach, and in spite of his penchant for snapping at people who displeased him, he often came across as supremely human in a profession where that quality can be glaringly absent. The most notable thing that happened during Kasich's brief run for president in 2000 took place one morning in Amherst, New Hampshire, where a woman who was planning a house party for the then Ohio congressman later in the day, accidentally ran over and killed her dog while backing out of her driveway. It must have been horrible, but the woman held the event anyway, and when it ended, Kasich grabbed a shovel and helped dig the unfortunate canine's grave. Suffice it to say that you wouldn't see Donald Trump doing something like that.

I wanted to catch Kasich's speech at the New Hampshire Institute of Politics, where he was addressing a regional college

Republicans conference. When I entered the main ballroom a few minutes before the Ohio governor was slated to begin his remarks, I spotted my friend Robert Draper, who was working on a profile of Kasich for the *New York Times Magazine* and had flown in with Kasich from Columbus that morning. I started catching up with Draper when a slightly built, middle-aged man in a black polo shirt, black slacks, and chunky black shoes stepped in front of us. At first glance, he looked like a golf pro or a lawnmower salesman from Tampa. He stood there for a moment, admiring the historic New Hampshire primary photographs that adorned the wall, and I turned my attention back to Draper.

"Have you two met?" Draper asked, signaling to me that I should approach the man who was dressed to revel in the weekend to its fullest extent. Now I figured that the stranger was perhaps a facilities manager at the school whom Draper had gotten to know— or maybe a mid-level campaign staffer. But as I got a closer look at his face, it suddenly dawned on me in a flash of embarrassment that I was looking at John Kasich himself. As I shook hands with him, the candidate flashed a sly smile that seemed to confirm the strange joy that he took in being aggressively anonymous.

Like Lindsey Graham, Kasich was focused almost entirely on New Hampshire, and with a senior staff led by John McCain 2000 veteran John Weaver, his model was clear. Unlike Graham, however, Kasich was actually making some inroads. In addition to his frequent visits to the state after declaring his candidacy in July, an aligned super PAC spent $5 million on a summer advertising blitz at a time when the Ohio governor had the airwaves almost entirely to himself, as the other candidates conserved resources. The early efforts to introduce Kasich were paying dividends, as he had broken into the double digits in some recent polls, besting such better-known candidates as Bush and Marco Rubio.

Why was he starting to resonate? In short, Kasich refused to be anything but himself. He was sanctimonious, goofy, capable, snippy, thoughtful, patronizing, and smart—sometimes all at the same time.

And he didn't sugarcoat anything. During this particular address to the college Republicans, for instance, he talked about how his own mom and dad had been killed by a drunk driver and how a friend of his in Columbus had recently found her son dead in their basement, a victim of a drug overdose. "I look at religion as a foundation from which I can build my life," he said. "Because there's no solace when the big things come that aren't great." The anecdote didn't match the mood of the young audience on a nice late-summer day. That Kasich didn't particularly care was central to his appeal and his ultimate limitations as a candidate.

As authentically religious as he was, Kasich was far from a Ted Cruz or Ben Carson–style Bible-banger. Almost in the same breath as he spoke about his own faith, Kasich praised as equally valid a secular humanist's desire to change the world for the better. He also waxed poetic about why doctors, PhDs, and wealthy people sometimes end up joining terrorist groups because of the universal human desire to find meaning in life. "I would maintain that you do not find happiness searching for happiness," he said. "You find happiness and satisfaction when you live a life bigger than yourself." The whole thing was like a therapy session, and that was exactly how Kasich ran his campaign every day.

When he finally got around to reciting his own résumé—the tax cuts and economic expansion in Ohio, as well as the leading role he had played as House budget chairman in balancing the federal budget in 1997, I remembered that Kasich was, in fact, trying to get these people to vote for him, not purchase his self-help book. But without saying so directly, for that would sound way too much like a typical politician, he was conveying with his every fiber that his campaign was not about him—a sentiment that politicians often express but rarely mean. He didn't have to wear a baseball cap with a slogan to tell people that he was going to Make America Great Again. Kasich was putting to the test the idea that voters would discover on their own that he was capable of doing just that. It didn't seem like a great bet to me, but it was certainly interesting. "You'll have a great time if you help us—I promise you that," Kasich said before closing out his remarkably soft pitch with a bold, kind of obnoxious, prediction that was in keeping with his inimitable self-assuredness. "And guess what else?" he added. "I kind of think I'm going to become president."

Kasich's next event was a town-hall meeting inside a middle-school classroom in Raymond, fifteen miles east of Manchester. Just before it was set to begin, the candidate, still dressed in his casual weekend attire, pulled up a chair among the few dozen people who had turned out, as if he were there as a spectator. As he later told it to the crowd, most of whom initially recognized him about as well as I had earlier in the day in Manchester, he leaned into the ear of the woman sitting next to him and said with cynical dismissiveness, "I hear the guy's really boring."

That's the kind of person John Kasich was: weird but refreshing in that he truly did not give a shit about trying to impress anyone. He was only trying to please himself, and at that, he usually succeeded. After an introductory speaker listed some of his achievements in government, Kasich jumped up from his seat in the crowd and immediately recounted the oddball shtick he had just performed for his own benefit. "Did you know it was me?" he asked the woman who'd been sitting next to him. She hadn't. "Yeah, so much fun," he added.

At a time when it appeared that the Republican presidential campaign might reach Peak Insanity at any moment, Kasich oozed with rationality. He talked about how he believed unequivocally that humans contributed to climate change, for example, and made clear that he did not want to engage in "nation building" on the international stage. "I may not be pounding the desk and all this flash and dash, ripping into Obama," Kasich said, fully embracing his role as the Reasonable Republican—an archetype that has had many variants over the years in New Hampshire presidential politics. "That's not why I'm doing this. I want to fix the country."

One of Kasich's fundamental problems was that for every compelling point he made, he'd let fly a throwaway line that would come across as completely off-putting. "Who doesn't exercise?" he asked his audience in Raymond, scanning the room to see what fat slobs might raise their hands. "Why aren't you exercising?" he then scolded no one in particular. During the Q-and-A session, a college-aged woman asked Kasich about his plan for promoting clean energy. Her question was reasonable and well-articulated, but Kasich dismissed it as if she'd asked him about time travel. "The problem is, young lady, you can't just make things happen," he said.

I cringed. "Young lady" wasn't exactly the preferred nomenclature for college-aged women in the second decade of the twenty-first century. I later heard that on the ride to the next event, one of Kasich's young staffers gently chided the candidate for talking to this New Hampshire primary voter as if she were his fifteen-year-old daughter who had been caught staying out past her curfew. This, to me, seemed to be the most imposing hazard for Kasich's candidacy—not his relative anonymity or center-right inclinations, but rather his tendency to come off as a sermonizing old-fogy-in-training, liable to dispense a homily at any moment.

That afternoon, Kasich and Carly Fiorina were both slated to speak at Scamman Farm in Stratham. With its bales of hay, corn maze, and pumpkin patch, the farm looked more like it belonged in Iowa than New Hampshire. The owners of the place—former state House Speaker Doug Scamman and his wife, Stella, a former state representative—have been fixtures of the local Republican scene for about as long as anyone could remember. And as it had for decades, the American Gothic–style backdrop that their property boasted made for a particularly pretty picture on sunny days like this one. George W. Bush had drawn thousands of people at the Scammans' property in his 2000 and 2004 campaigns, and the farm's most recent claim to fame was that it was the site that Mitt Romney's campaign chose to launch his second presidential bid in June 2011.

In an apparent attempt to convey the impression that he was actually running for president and not trying to sell them a new sprinkler, Kasich had changed out of his short-sleeved golf shirt into a far more civilized button-down and slacks. Whiffs of not-very-spicy chili fit for the typical New Hampshirite palate permeated the air, as Kasich took to a makeshift stage that was about three feet long and three feet wide in front of an oversized-American-flag-adorned barn. His stream-of-consciousness stump speech was unmemorable, but what happened next was not.

Doug Scamman, who was serving as the event's emcee, first announced to the crowd that the Seacoast Republican Women had invited all of the GOP presidential candidates to the event, though only three of them had accepted. Then he said this: "The next person I'm going to introduce was not invited, as far as I know, but many of you probably know Joe Sandman [*sic*]. He's at the MSNBC *Morning Joe* show. So it gives me a great deal of pleasure to introduce Joe Scarborough."

The crowd clapped hesitantly, as the self-possessed cable news host and former Republican congressman—clearly annoyed at having been introduced as something of a party crasher—took the stage. "Well, of all the introductions I've ever had, that was the most interesting because I guarantee you I would not be here today if I were not invited," Scarborough said. "I would be with my children back in Connecticut enduring high taxes and maybe even cooler weather." OK, then.

Scarborough went on to explain that he had made the trip to "vouch" for Kasich, his former colleague in the US Congress, though he stopped short of endorsing him formally. Just in case anyone was wondering—and it was unclear that anyone was—Scarborough assured the crowd that he himself wasn't running for president. It dawned on me, however, that we were in an environment in which it was entirely feasible for a politician-turned-TV-commentator to decide on a whim that he was going to announce a presidential bid. Mike Huckabee had done just that a couple of months earlier. And Scarborough, after all, had served almost six years in the US Congress—almost six years more experience in office than Donald Trump, Ben Carson, or Carly Fiorina had under their belts. He was as unflappable and charismatic as any of the candidates other than Trump, and wasn't that just about all you needed to be successful on the presidential stage these days?

After Scarborough finished up his speech on Kasich's behalf, Fiorina arrived on site, decked out in her New Hampshire every-gal uniform: a flannel shirt with the requisite American flag pin, faded jeans, and cowboy boots. In her normal life outside of the campaign trail, Fiorina, who boasted a net worth of about $60 million, would be about as likely to attend a chili cook-off on a farm in New Hampshire as she would an Insane Clown Posse concert. But Fiorina had built her business career on her skill as a salesperson, and she was more adept than many of the career politicians in the race at selling her image to great effect. Sure enough, "She wears cowboy boots!" was what one woman shouted to her friend after getting an up-close glimpse at the lone female Republican candidate's footwear. "I like her even more now."

Fiorina's stump speech was as harsh, unyielding, and meticulously scripted as Kasich's was freewheeling and conversational. She spoke without notes, but it was almost as if you could see the prewritten attacks on an imaginary page in front of her, as she hit Hillary Clinton for her "lies" and Donald Trump—carefully avoiding any mention of his name—for equating leadership effectiveness "with how big your helicopter is." The crowd ate it up.

"Now there's a line," one woman in the crowd next to me cooed.

"It's perfect," another acclaimed.

A third woman just stood there with her mouth ajar, unable to convey in words the rapturous feeling that she was apparently experiencing from watching the stone-faced Fiorina lay into her opponents one by one. "She just—" the woman said, shaking her head in awe, unable to finish the thought.

As it turned out, I was witnessing Peak Fiorina—the pinnacle of her popularity in the race. It was nonetheless impressive that she'd managed to elbow her way into the realm of viability at all. Frankly, I found her appeal as a presidential candidate entirely baffling. There was no doubt that Fiorina knew how to give a speech and would shine even brighter in the upcoming debate when she would share a stage with ten less rhetorically gifted men. But this was a woman who, by most accounts, was notable in the business world because of the unusually high level of ineptitude she had brought to the corner office at Hewlett-Packard. In that position, she'd carried out a merger with Compaq in 2001 that went about as well for HP as the decision to sell Babe Ruth to the New York Yankees had for the Boston Red Sox. After her subsequent move to lay off 30,000 employees did nothing to stem the tide of the company's growing misfortunes, Fiorina was fired in 2005, but not without the nice little parting gift of a $21 million golden parachute. For her second act, Fiorina ran for a US Senate seat in California in 2010, losing by double digits to incumbent democrat Barbara Boxer. So naturally, her next move was to run for president of the United States. The idea of seeking the world's most powerful office on the heels of being fired from one job and failing to win another would strike most people as a bit presumptuous (yet just look at how far the seemingly ridiculous candidacy of Donald Trump had already gotten). Here was Fiorina, running somewhat successfully for the nation's highest office, once again as an "outsider"—a claim she could make only because of her failure to win her first political race. What a country.

On this particular day, however, it seemed like I was the only one on hand who felt this way. The crowd was in the mood for a fight, and Fiorina was bringing it. They cheered every time she mentioned "Benghazi," "e-mails," and "lies," saving their biggest reaction for when she asked them to "admit that in your hearts of hearts, every one of you wants to see me debate Hillary Clinton." Fiorina knew how to hit the crowd with a buzzword barrage every bit as well as Trump did. And that skill, more than any line on her résumé, was what mattered to these Republican voters—most of them women— who flocked to her in droves.

After Fiorina spoke, well-wishers lined up to greet her, many of them dressed in bright-red "Team Carly" T-shirts. "We're going to come down and help you," promised one woman from Maine, who attended the event with her ninety-nine-year-old friend. "Cancel everything and put her in the White House today."

Even Joe Scarborough, who was there to support Kasich, appeared to offer Fiorina some encouragement. That, at least, is what it looked like he was doing when he leaned in closely to whisper some unknown wisdom into her ear, cameras all around to capture the cinematic moment. Just about the only New Hampshire Republican at the event who wasn't ready to anoint her as a major threat to Hillary Clinton's chances was the delightfully cranky John H. Sununu, who was on hand to hawk copies of his new book, *The Quiet Man*—about George H. W. Bush's presidency.

"Hey, Carly," the unimpressed former governor shouted as the candidate passed by his booth. "Have you read the book? It teaches you how to be president!"

Nothing tops off a chili cook-off quite like a barbecue-and-beer bash, and so Kasich and Fiorina headed next to the Strafford County Republicans–hosted outdoor gathering just down the road in Dover. The official sanctioning of alcohol inevitably inserts a wild card in any political event, particularly one that takes place on a Saturday evening on a nice late-summer day. Fiorina, however, did not change her tenor—not one bit—to match the mood of this well-lubricated crowd. In fact, she delivered her lines almost word for word and dramatic pause for dramatic pause. Political professionals call this "message discipline." I call it "soul-sucking."

After Fiorina completed this latest performance of her script, the candidate's traveling press secretary announced that she would be doing a short media "gaggle," another word for an "avail," in which the assembled press would be allowed to ask her questions. Unsurprisingly, most of the subsequent queries contained the word "Trump"—an obvious source of frustration for Fiorina, who noted with exasperation that none of the voters she had encountered throughout the day had asked her about the front-runner. That wasn't true. I'd actually heard firsthand more than one voter in Stratham offering her encouragement for fending off Trump's misogynistic attacks. Still, it offered Fiorina a nice opportunity to play the role of sanctimonious media critic. "You should really think about that," she admonished the assembled press, as if she were trying to do them a favor. In her most self-righteous moments, I'd noticed that Fiorina had a tendency to swivel her head in an abrupt, circular motion, as though she were trying to keep an invisible hula hoop in orbit around her neck. She was doing that as she chastised us for focusing so much on Trump.

Fiorina's contemptuous posturing was making the mood miserable, but then Lindsey Graham arrived, and everything changed in an instant. He wasn't holding a big glass of red wine this time, but the South Carolina senator was accompanied by an even more invigorating social lubricant: John McCain. In typical fashion, the Arizona senator regaled well-wishers with his usual cocktail of friendly banter, Irish jokes, and faintly uncomfortable references to acquaintances who "just returned from the Betty Ford Clinic." Although he'd heard all of the gags hundreds of times before, no one laughed harder than his sidekick, Graham. The political Laurel and Hardy made their way on foot through the parking lot, huge smiles on each of their faces, as old friends from previous campaigns mostly surged past Graham toward the two-time primary New Hampshire primary winner, whom they called, "John."

Invariably, whenever the focus remained on him for too long, the dutiful McCain tried to change the subject. "Meet Lindsey Graham—he's a fellow veteran!" he told each of them, eager to pass the attention onto the man who was actually a candidate in 2016. In spite of his noble efforts, it couldn't have been clearer that he still relished his own role as honorary New Hampshire candidate-for-life. Peter Hamby, the head of news at Snapchat, asked McCain to record a ten-second video message for the popular millennial-centric app. The Arizona senator didn't flinch in accepting the challenge. "The geezer is here again, this time to support Lindsey Graham," he said in perfect social-media rhythm.

After they took the stage together, McCain kept his introductory remarks short, and Graham's stump speech was what it always was: filled with charming, lighthearted jokes and calls for bloody combat on the international stage. "The more you drink, the better I sound!" Graham said correctly and to much laughter, right before the part about how we need to send ground troops back into Iraq. Graham may have been going nowhere in this race, but McCain was happy to come along for the ride, even as he remained realistic. "He's getting better every time," was all that McCain could muster after the speech, when someone asked him how he thought Graham was doing in New Hampshire.

When the event concluded, the two made their way back to the parking lot slowly, greeting McCain's old friends one at a time. I happened to be standing next to Ben Carson's wife, Candy, who was representing her husband at the event, when she asked an aide, "Where's Lindsey Graham?"

The aide pointed him out. "He's in the red," he told her.

An embarrassed expression suddenly passed over Mrs. Carson's face. "Oh, God," she said. "I saw him before, and I didn't know who he was."

CHAPTER 20

ON NOVEMBER 12, 2003, Massachusetts senator John Kerry took a walk through the woods along the Merrimack River in Litchfield, New Hampshire. The air was misty and the leaf-strewn ground soggy as Kerry strode with his hands in his jacket pockets, a pack of campaign reporters following closely behind. The intent of the arboreal photo-op was to provide an evocative background for the Democratic presidential candidate, in order to highlight his strong record on the environment, but there was a problem: all that any of the reporters wanted to ask him about was his sinking campaign.

Kerry's presidential hopes were in free fall. Unable to find his footing in a race that had been his to lose at the outset, he had fired his campaign manager four days earlier, and then two of his senior aides had quit in protest. Meanwhile, Howard Dean was cruising. On the strength of his full-throated opposition to the Iraq War, his passionate support base of "Deaniacs," and his revolutionary online fund-raising juggernaut, the former Vermont governor had surged from an afterthought to the top of the Democratic pack in Iowa and New Hampshire and had become an unlikely phenomenon.

As Kerry trudged along the sodden branches and dead leaves in his rain boots, he criticized the Bush administration for ushering in tax cuts for the wealthiest Americans while at the same time providing giveaways to some of the nation's worst polluters. A few feet away, Andy Hiller—a political reporter for Boston station WHDH—was taping his prerecorded tease for a segment that would air later that night. With the candidate close enough to hear every word, Hiller delivered his memorable line: "Howard Dean . . . surging in the polls. And John Kerry . . . lost in the woods."

As far behind as he had fallen, Kerry did have a couple of factors working in his favor in New Hampshire. First of all, he was from neighboring Massachusetts, which was worth more politically than any advantage that Dean might gain by way of hailing from just across the western border (the Boston media markets reached far more New Hampshire voters than the Burlington, Vermont, media did). Second, two months earlier, Kerry had won the endorsement of former governor Jeanne Shaheen after her husband, Bill, had signed on as chairman of his New Hampshire campaign, and he had gained the backing of the International Association of Fire Fighters (IAFF), which was the first union to endorse a Democratic candidate that year other than Congressman Dick Gephardt. These weren't token endorsements. Shaheen was on the ground in New Hampshire working on Kerry's behalf nearly around the clock, and almost every day when he was campaigning in the state, Kerry would attend multiple IAFF "firehouse chili feeds." The events gave the blue-blooded candidate some blue-collar cred, and he always made sure to eat some chili (appreciative, no doubt, that it was low-carb).

Two days after his "lost in the woods" ignominy, the worst appeared to be over for Kerry's campaign when he brought the house down with a resounding speech at the Democratic candidates' big Jefferson-Jackson dinner in Iowa. It was at that event where Kerry revealed his campaign's new slogan, "The Real Deal." The context of the phrase was an implied warning to Democratic voters as they made their decision on who was best positioned to take on George W. Bush, a wartime president, in November. This was no time to nominate an untested wild card like Dean, Kerry was arguing. As a Vietnam War hero and an experienced Washington hand, he was the far safer bet.

When Kerry returned to New Hampshire after a triumphant night in Des Moines, his campaign rolled out what it called "The Real Deal Express"—an homage to the Straight Talk Express that Kerry's buddy John McCain had driven to victory in New Hampshire four years earlier. Then, just as the Real Deal Express was about to set out for its inaugural New Hampshire stop, there was WHDH's Andy Hiller standing nearby in front of a camera. Once again, the local TV reporter was ready to shoot another tease, and Hiller still wasn't impressed. "How many times," he asked his audience, "can you kick off a deflated football?"

It may have been a wiseass question, but it was also a fair one. Not only was Kerry still well behind Dean in the polls, but the anecdotal evidence suggested that the Massachusetts senator would continue to have an uphill struggle to catch him. On the stump, the sixty-year-old candidate was good at connecting with people from his own generation, bantering easily about Peter, Paul, and Mary; Vietnam; and LBJ. But he was awkward with people who had been born after Woodstock. When an eight-year-old boy asked Kerry at one New Hampshire town-hall meeting what the candidate planned to do about Iraq, Kerry, in an effort to come off as personable, replied by asking the kid what *he* would do about it.

Once voters got past the easily lampooned facets of Kerry's personality, however, they often found that they liked him. The firefighters helped with that, and so did Kerry himself. During a January visit to the Timberland company headquarters in Stratham, Kerry, a multimillionaire, purchased a discounted coat that he wore every day on the campaign trail from there on out. The crowds and energy on the trail picked up noticeably, as the winds now seemed to be shifting in Kerry's direction.

Dean, however, was still in the lead. Although he may have been an unconventional candidate, the campaign that the Vermonter's team was running in New Hampshire was utterly conventional. Since the day he began to actively explore a long-shot candidacy all the way back in May 2002, the populist firebrand had been solidifying his online fund-raising prowess with a slowly building, solid structural foundation in New Hampshire. Like many successful New Hampshire underdogs before him, Dean had begun speaking at house parties with only a couple of dozen people in attendance and, mostly through word of mouth, the crowds had gotten bigger and bigger, until he finally outgrew the house-party format altogether and had to move his events to larger venues.

Dean appeared to be just as strong in Iowa as he was in New Hampshire. But amid all the excitement of his massive crowds of fired-up young people, the other major Democratic candidates in the race began training their fire almost exclusively on the now established front-runner throughout the fall. The attacks, in turn, began to have an impact. By December, Dean's numbers started to slip noticeably, and he began referring to himself in speeches as "a human pin cushion."

Then in early January, *NBC News* aired a report on comments that Dean had made on Canadian television four years earlier, in which he'd disparaged the Iowa caucuses, noting that the event was "dominated by special interests." The timing couldn't have been worse. Dean was still leading in the state at the time, but the bottom quickly dropped out of his Iowa campaign. In a misguided effort to rally his troops upon Kerry's massive victory and his own devastating third-place finish on Caucus Night, Dean screamed the scream heard 'round the world, and his standing heading into New Hampshire became desperate.

For Kerry, on the other hand, everything was now going right. Straight from his victory in Iowa, he flew overnight and landed in Manchester early the next morning, where several hundred cheering supporters were at the airport waiting to greet him. His bounce coming out of the first voting state was dramatic, and he quickly overtook Dean in the New Hampshire polls. An alarming number of Dean's New Hampshire precinct captains, meanwhile, were calling their candidate to let them know that they were abandoning ship. All the signs were there that it was just about over for Dean, and yet the former Vermont governor remained largely oblivious of the extent to which the already infamous shriek had devastated his chances. "We were trying to help him understand how damaging it was, and he just wouldn't buy it," recalls Karen Hicks, who was Dean's New Hampshire state director. "He was so cranky after Iowa and really feeling mistrustful of people on his campaign."

Shortly before a rally in Peterborough, Hicks and a group of other aides pulled Dean aside and told him that he needed to acknowledge the effect that the scream was having on people's perceptions of him and to try to turn it to his advantage. The right move, they suggested, would be to hold up the moment as an example of how he was not just another scripted, blow-dried politician. Dean agreed to do it, but he didn't follow through.

Not that it would have mattered much anyway, as Kerry ended up winning New Hampshire by a comfortable twelve-point margin. In the general election, he struggled painfully to connect, but for those couple of months leading into Iowa and New Hampshire, Kerry was at the top of his game. Right when he appeared to be down and out, everything started clicking for him. Nearly a decade later, just before he was confirmed as secretary of state, John Kerry was still wearing in public the coat that he purchased at the Timberland headquarters in Stratham—a reminder of his halcyon days as a presidential candidate who was at his best when he was almost vanquished.

CHAPTER 21

S INCE VOTERS STARTED SELECTING candidates directly, no Republican or Democratic presidential nominee has finished worse than second place in the New Hampshire primary. By 2016, however, even the primary's most spirited defenders had to concede an inconvenient fact: since 1992, no New Hampshire primary victor had gone on to win the presidency. The most common rebuttal to charges of New Hampshire's fading relevance was that the primary's real value is not in predicting who would become president but rather in "winnowing the field." It was a fair point. But in order to keep its good name in that regard, I believed strongly, New Hampshire's voters would have to do something about making sure that Ben Carson didn't get anywhere near the silver medal in the 2016 primary.

Carson had earned his own page in the annals of conservative folklore after dressing down President Obama at a National Prayer Breakfast in 2013. His up-from-nothing life story was so compelling, his credentials as a world-renowned brain surgeon so unimpeachable, and his demeanor so unassuming that his instant appeal as a candidate in the year of the outsider was self-evident. But upon spending some time with him on the trail and actually listening carefully to what he was saying, my conclusion became inescapable: the idea of a "President Ben Carson" was disturbing enough to lose sleep over, no matter how remote the possibility.

At first blush, many of Carson's more unhinged pronouncements about basic scientific principles sounded suspiciously like cynical attempts to mitigate his own rarefied professional accomplishments, as part of an effort to appeal to the more academically modest crowd that composed his political base. No Yale-educated director of pediatric neurosurgery at Johns Hopkins could really believe, as Carson had stated, that the big bang theory was a "fairy tale" concocted by "highfalutin scientists" or that Darwin's theory of evolution was a clever trick perpetuated by "the adversary" (Carson's highfalutin term for the Devil). No student of American history could really believe that Obamacare was "the worst thing that has happened in this nation since slavery," as Carson had declared it. No presidential candidate of sound mind could earnestly be concerned, as Carson had said he was, that impending national anarchy might prevent the 2016 election from taking place at all. Carson apparently did believe all of these things, which is why he kept outdoing his own rhetoric, even as some of his advisers at times appeared to be conducting public interventions to get him to stop. Carson seemed like a nice guy, but he was objectively out to lunch. And for months, that was A-ok with a large swath of Republican primary voters, who elevated the nutty brain surgeon into second place in the national polls.

After spending some time with him in New Hampshire, I started to realize the full extent to which Carson's paranoid know-nothing act wasn't an act at all. I'd long found that some of the smartest people I knew were also the most eccentric. But at this level of politics, I'd never seen real-deal madness quite like Carson offered. I caught up with him on the last day of September, when he had three events scheduled around the seacoast region. He had been in the race officially for five months but previously had made only a couple of trips to New Hampshire. On the way up through southern New England and into New Hampshire, I had to drive through an inundating rainstorm, which turned out to be an appropriate setup for the apocalyptical pronouncements to which I would soon be subjected.

When I arrived at Carson's first event of the day in Exeter, I sought reprieve from the elements under my cherished oversized umbrella—the kind that tends to catch passersby in the face when used on a crowded sidewalk—and still, I was soaked. Standing in a damp shirt, wet pants, and flooded shoes, I arrived inside the crowded retirement facility's ballroom just after Carson had taken the stage and begun his lecture. As I stood in the back of the room, I had to strain to hear what he was saying, even though he was speaking into a microphone. The average audience member's age appeared to be well into the seventies, and there was a lot of wincing and headshaking going on in the back rows from people who couldn't hear a word he was saying. The emcee who had introduced the candidate picked up on this dynamic and butted in to ask Carson to hold the microphone closer to his mouth. "I couldn't get it any higher," the candidate replied in his peculiar near-whisper. "It'd be in my mouth."

Carson spoke with a particular kind of inflection that sounded a bit like a late-career Michael Jackson telling a particularly terrifying ghost story. I knew that he was a subdued man with a calm, physician's bearing, which had contrasted so nicely in the debates with the monster-truck rally in human form that was Donald Trump. Still, it was fascinating to see how lethargic Carson actually was in a room. I only had to wait about five minutes, however, before he doled out his first Nazi reference of the day. For Ben Carson, the compulsion to compare just about everything to Hitler's Germany was like hiccupping: once he got started, it was hard for him to stop. He'd gotten into trouble for this tendency many times before, but he wasn't going to change just because the politically correct crowd wasn't willing to acknowledge the Nazi-like menace that confronted the United States of America in 2016.

"You know, I think back to Nazi Germany," Carson said, earning my sudden and undivided attention. "And I know the P.C. police say you're not supposed to say, 'Nazi Germany,' but I'm saying it anyway because I don't care what they say."

The P.C. police put in their place and Carson's rhetorical bravery now firmly established, he was ready to go full-Führer. "In Nazi Germany, a lot of those people did not believe in what Hitler was doing," Carson continued. "But did they speak up? No. They kept their mouths shut, and they kept their heads down, and look what happened."

The crowd sat in silence. Carson wasn't done. "And some people say, 'Oh, nothing like that could ever happen in America,'" the man who would go on to become one of Donald Trump's most active surrogates said. "I beg to differ."

Carson's lack of self-awareness was so intense, his intellectual dishonesty so thorough, that he had no problem criticizing politicians who throw rhetorical "hand grenades," while in the same breath warning that the stock market crash, which helped lead to the Great Depression in 1929, would be a "walk in the park" compared to the economic collapse that was impending, if the United States did not return to the gold standard. After the inimitable prophet of doom wrapped up his mild-mannered soliloquy on the impending annihilation of everything that was good in the world, I approached Sandra McKay—an undecided independent voter who lived at the retirement facility. When I asked her what she thought of Carson, she seemed to be struggling to find a way to sound polite when discussing the very nice crazy man who'd come to ask for her vote. "He's very certain of what's going on, and I don't know if he has any reason to be that certain," she said. "I love his [personal] story . . . but I don't know." That was reassuring to hear, at least.

At the media avail following his speech, I decided to press Carson to elaborate on his view that people who kept their mouths shut in the United States might soon find themselves unknowingly paving the way for the Fourth Reich. He didn't back down an inch, turning the tables on me, as if I had been the unreasonable one for asking the question.

"I mean, if people don't speak up for what they believe, then other people will change things without them having a voice," Carson replied.

"What does that have to do with Nazi Germany?" I asked.

"Well," Carson said matter-of-factly. "Hitler changed things there, and nobody protested. Nobody provided any opposition to him, and that's what facilitated his rise."

Yes, I supposed that it was true that "Hitler changed things" and that some people in the United States today also wanted to "change things," but it didn't take a brain surgeon to realize this argument was the equivalent of contending that because fire trucks and apples both are red, fire trucks and apples are essentially the same thing. Just for kicks, I asked Carson who in America today was most like Hitler. The implied answer, of course, was President Obama. I didn't expect him to say it, but I wanted to see if he might come close.

"I'm not going to go into that," Carson said, showing the restraint of a burglar who has stolen everything in the house but decided to leave the carpet intact. "I think the example is pretty clear."

Actually, the example wasn't clear at all. It was absurd, and so was the idea that this man—who was a member of the medical team that performed the first-ever successful separation of twins conjoined at the head—could actually believe what he was saying. But he *did* seem to believe it. That was made clearer when Carson's own campaign manager that week told ABC News that he was trying to wean the candidate off his penchant to equate everything that was bad with history's most infamous regime. It was the kind of public intervention that you just didn't ever see a campaign staffer make on behalf of a candidate (again, this was months before Trump's daily antics ratcheted up the lunacy dial to eleven). Yet if Carson really was spinning out of control, his poll numbers hadn't started to fall. There could be no doubt that a significant portion of Republican primary voters really liked the subdued brand of apocalyptic Hitler Tourette's that Carson was offering them. To me, it was both illuminating and scary.

The Nazi babble wasn't even the most memorable part of Carson's press conference. That particular highlight didn't come until the last question, when Carson—who looked as though he might fall asleep at any moment—was asked what he would do as president, in order to address Tropical Storm Joaquin, a weather disturbance that was at the time menacing the East Coast of the United States.

Now here was the kind of question that any two-bit candidate would be able to answer without the slightest problem. Try it yourself. If you were in Carson's position, what would you say about how you'd prepare the country for a hurricane? Maybe you'd call the governors of threatened states. Perhaps you'd check in with the Federal Emergency Management Agency to get an assessment of how it was preparing for the storm. Or perhaps you'd merely "monitor the situation closely." That would be a fine answer, too!

Here's what Carson said: "Uh, I don't know." And then he smiled just a little, giggled, and made his way for the exit. Ladies and gentlemen, the next president of the United States!

Later in the afternoon, Carson more or less repeated his screwball stump speech during an appearance at the cavernous Huddleston Hall Ballroom at the University of New Hampshire in Durham. The crowd there, however, was not as skeptical as the one at the retirement facility had been. These were Carson's people, and there were a lot of them. I counted about 300 who had made it inside the room and another 150 or so who were blocked from entering by fire regulations.

The highlight of this particular event came during the very first question of the Q-and-A portion of the festivities when an older man near the stage rose from his seat. "Doctor Carson," he said. "I can't believe the amount of things that you and I agree on, and I think that you probably recall that you and I had a short talk in Washington on Saturday. And I'm in the health-care field, and the reason why I'm running for president along with you is I'm an outsider, too."

Oh, good! Someone who was off his rocker as much as Carson! It only got more entertaining from there, as this other presidential candidate in the room identified himself as a "private investigator for over thirty years, investigating wrongdoing in Washington" and began talking about nuclear power and nefarious plots in a manner that was impossible to follow. Many of the Carson faithful began groaning as the incoherent rambling continued. I was loving it. This sort of thing happened not infrequently in New Hampshire, and it's the reason most campaigns assign staffers to hold the microphones up to people in the audience, rather than handing them over, so that they can be taken away at any moment. But this particular gentleman had full control over his voice amplification device, and he was going to use it to full effect. The only thing that could stop him now was Carson himself, and just about any other candidate in this situation would have tried to pivot away from the lunacy as quickly as possible, while disavowing himself from it. Not Ben Carson.

"I'm happy to hear all of the things you have to say," Carson told the man. A kindred spirit!

After the event, Carson didn't spend more than a minute or two glad-handing inside the hall. His popularity rested largely on his best-selling books and cable-news hits, and he wasn't exactly a grind-it-out-one-handshake-at-a-time kind of candidate. But once he made it outside, the scene was one of minimally controlled chaos. There were the usual for-profit autograph seekers with their baseballs at the ready for the semi-celebrity candidate to sign, but most of the dozens of people who surrounded Carson as he made his way to the SUV parked on the street were dyed-in-the-wool believers. "There goes the next president of the United States," one man in a black windbreaker shouted. He was indeed talking about Ben Carson.

"I hope so," the woman next to him replied. "I just worry so much about all the negativity in Washington."

That's right. Her solution for ending the negativity in Washington was a man who'd just stopped a half-step short of calling his political opponents Nazis.

"It can't get any worse," the man said.

That night, Carson held a meet-and-greet with some fellow physicians at The Red Door just outside of Portsmouth—a snug, old meeting place on a small island connected to the mainland by a bridge. The venue was the kind of creaky New England

meetinghouse where you could easily imagine disheveled revolution-
aries hatching plans to take on the redcoats over candlelit pints of
strong ale. When I arrived, a big pot of clam chowder was heating
on the stove, as local doctors and their spouses stood in the expansive meeting-room area discussing more contemporary topics than
King George III, such as whether the football-playing Patriots' tendency to try to run up the score against their opponents might soon
backfire.

At this point in the evening, Carson looked as though he might
fall asleep at any moment, but in fairness to the man whose appeal as
a potential commander in chief continued to escape me, he sounded
much more well-versed in foreign policy than he had during the debates. Carson elucidated the differences between the various Kurdish
factions, for instance, in the manner of a man whose professional
training required mastery of the art of memorization. He even offered up some charm in the form of a revealing moment of self-dep-
recation when he told his fellow medical professionals on hand that
as a young child, he had dreamed of becoming a missionary physician and traveling to some of the world's poorest places, "until I
turned thirteen and decided I'd rather be rich."

That line got some knowing laughs from the doctors in the
room, some of whom had probably experienced a similar realization
themselves. Carson also received big applause when he boasted that
his training as a physician would help him make "decisions based
on evidence versus ideology." I thought back to all of the intensely
ideological drivel that Carson had been espousing throughout the
day and had to admire the guy's chutzpah. Was this the new reality
in New Hampshire? To the most audacious and delusional go the
rewards? Ben Carson and Donald Trump were at that moment the
top two Republican contenders in the state.

The next morning, I pondered the ramifications of Carson's
staying power at Popovers on the Square in Portsmouth—a casual-dining institution set among the quaint Irish gift shops and
wood-paneled bars and restaurants of New Hampshire's most
charming small city. If you've never had a popover, I recommend you

put this book down right away and get on the road to Portsmouth. Why they're not more readily available around the country, I can't tell you. I don't want to ruin the surprise, but suffice it to say that the popover combines all of the best attributes of the croissant, the muffin, and the scone. Served warm and flaky, directly out of the oven, this particular popover was the best I'd ever had. I could have eaten three more of them, but I still had Dr. Carson on my mind, and I worried that if he found out, I'd be giving him permission to add "a Hermann Göring–like tendency to overindulge in desserts" to his grievances against the liberal media.

So instead of ordering more popovers, I decided to feel the Bern. In an ascent that surprised just about everyone, including himself, the Vermont senator hadn't just caught up with Hillary Clinton, he had overtaken her in most of the New Hampshire polls conducted since August. That he was connecting with voters was now indisputable, but I wondered whether his campaign infrastructure had caught up with this unexpected groundswell. I knew that the Sanders campaign had recently expanded its footprint across the state, as part of an effort to provide some structure that would help the insurgent candidate sustain his charge. I searched online and found the street address for Sanders's relatively new Portsmouth campaign office. Once again, I dropped by unannounced and found that the place looked like a typical regional campaign outpost. It was located at the very end of an industrial park next to an active construction site and had Bernie signs plastered across the window, but although it was midmorning on a weekday, all of the lights were off. I knocked a couple of times.

No answer.

I knocked louder.

Still nothing.

Halfheartedly, I tried the door handle. It was unlocked.

Not sure what else to do, I walked right into the Portsmouth field office of the new front-runner to win the first Democratic presidential primary of 2016.

"Hello?"

There didn't appear to be anyone in there. Just to be sure, I walked into a second room behind the foyer. "Anybody home?" I shouted, as if I were a character in a lame horror movie who was seconds from being murdered.

Silence. I peeked into a third room, where several cell phones and a laptop rested on a table—all containing, no doubt, a trove of confidential information about the campaign. As I exited the building, I tried to imagine Hillary Clinton's New Hampshire staffers offering a similar opportunity to trespassers who might have had more nefarious intentions than I did. I couldn't do it. The Sanders campaign, for all of its efforts to expand into a well-oiled machine, was still just winging it—a bunch of democratic socialists who couldn't be bothered to lock the front door, and it didn't matter. Sanders was winning in New Hampshire, and Clinton was powerless to turn the tide. Considering the extent of her apparent invulnerability a few months before, it was a bit hard to believe. But all she could do now was try to mitigate what was looking increasingly like a severe embarrassment in the state that had rescued her husband's White House hopes a quarter-century earlier.

CHAPTER 22

I N LATE 2006, MITT Romney's top advisers gathered for a meeting in Boston to begin laying out a strategy for the 2008 presidential campaign that the outgoing Massachusetts governor
already had decided to launch. Tom Rath, who would become Romney's top New Hampshire adviser, suggested that he run as "Mr. Fix
It"—the competent manager and nonideological private-equity wiz-
ard who found a sensible way to provide nearly universal health care
in his state. That tact, Rath believed, would play particularly well
in the nation's first primary state, where voters in previous elections
had often awarded competence over flash. But when the room began
discussing Romney's likely Republican rivals, the consensus was that
it would be difficult for him to run successfully as Mr. Fix It when
Rudy Giuliani would widely be seen as the more dynamic leader.
Romney, who did rescue the 2002 Salt Lake City Winter Olympics,
would nonetheless have a hard time standing out in the management
department against the guy who helped turn around New York City
and rallied the entire country in the aftermath of one of the worst

days in its history. So the room settled on positioning Romney as the deeply *conservative* manager in the race.

In the summer of 2007, I began covering my first presidential campaign as an embedded off-air reporter for CBS News and was assigned to the Romney campaign. For as long as Romney remained in the race (five more months, as it turned out), I would trail him wherever he went. I was armed for the task with an array of video equipment and a dangerous combination of great enthusiasm and negligible expertise on how to cover a presidential campaign. In stark contrast to the popular image perpetuated by the top dogs of journalism who were the "Boys on the Bus" in the 1960s and 1970s, for more two decades prior to my own first campaign, all of the network news divisions had placed the onus of on-the-ground campaign coverage on young and wildly inexperienced reporters. This system provided the networks with cheap labor and a pool of available go-getters who were eager to work endless strings of sixteen-hour days on the road without seeing their own homes for weeks or months at a time. I'd never been more excited and less prepared to do anything in my life.

I hit the road with the candidate on Labor Day at a time when the decision to emphasize Romney's previously subdued conservatism appeared to be a sound one. Although he was less known nationally than three of his Republican rivals—Giuliani, McCain, and actor-turned-Tennessee-senator Fred Thompson—Romney looked on paper like a candidate who was capable of going the distance. He had the appearance, poise, and pedigree of a president, and he had used his fund-raising prowess and personal fortune to make a big commitment to advertising heavily in all of the early states. Although he was already fighting perceptions that he was a political chameleon—one who ran and governed as a moderate in Massachusetts before discovering just in time for the Republican nominating fight that he was, in fact, an arch-conservative—Romney's big push in the early states had been paying off, as he was leading in both Iowa and New Hampshire.

I was pretty confident that I could handle the editorial side of my new gig. But I was scared witless about the many technical aspects of acting as a one-man band. As an embed, I needed to be a camera person, sound person, producer, and satellite truck, all in the form of an overwhelmed twenty-four-year-old with a BlackBerry holster attached to his ill-fitting khakis. The campaign trail was tough sledding, for me and for Romney.

When I got to the Milford Labor Day parade that afternoon, I dutifully followed behind Romney as he lurched in mechanical, perpendicular movements to shake hands with parade-goers on both sides. "Hi, I'm Mitt Romney," he'd say upon approaching each person with the grace and ease of Herman Munster.

Four years later, Romney would take a lot of heat in his 2012 presidential campaign for coming across as stiff and preprogrammed. Generally forgotten is that in his first presidential run, these deficiencies were massively more pronounced.

"Goodtahseeya. Goodtahseeya," he'd repeat, like a parrot reprising something he'd once heard a human say.

"Ha. Ha. Ha. Oh, wouldjahlookatthat?"

"Hi, I'm Mitt Romney."

"How old are you, six? Oh, you're eleven? Wow!"

"Hi, I'm Mitt Romney."

For Romney—who happened to be an exceedingly nice and convivial man in private settings—the act of establishing even the most elemental form of connection with his fellow humans on the trail often felt like he was trying to solve an impossible riddle. It was as if I could hear the voice in his head, asking repeatedly, "Now, how might I attempt to form a bond with the earthlings in my midst?"

Although both states were critical to his overall strategy for winning the 2008 GOP nomination, Romney had deemed Iowa to be priority "1A" and New Hampshire priority "1B." The emphasis on Iowa would later prove to be a critical error. Iowa's socially conservative, evangelical voters—who compose a majority of the GOP caucus electorate—had not yet found their candidate and were at the time defaulting to Romney. But if ever there was a paper tiger in the Hawkeye State, it was the former Massachusetts governor. He may have been talking the talk of a traditional movement conservative, but he walked the walk unconvincingly. My fellow reporters covering Romney and I would exchange knowing glances every time we were in some tiny farm town with forty people in the crowd and he would get to one of the more absurd parts of his stump speech. It went like this: "And when I'm president, I'll make sure our kids know that before they have babies, they should get married."

It was an empty promise with no substantive policy proposal of any kind to back it up. And though it was a surefire applause line among the Iowa retirees who showed up for his events, if Romney's standing in Iowa looked too good to be true, that's because it was. When a deep-dimpled former Baptist minister turned downhome everyman politician named Mike Huckabee finished in second place in the Ames Straw Poll in August and emerged as a viable contender, the man from Massachusetts stood little chance. In retrospect, Romney should have stepped off the gas pedal in Iowa and turned his focus to New Hampshire—a state that was a much more natural fit for him. But Romney's "Iowa first" strategy remained in place, even as his New Hampshire team misjudged who his strongest competitor in the Granite State would turn out to be. Throughout the summer and fall of 2007, Romney directed the focus of his increasingly bitter primary fight in New Hampshire against Giuliani. Meanwhile, he mostly ignored McCain, whose standing among the ranks of the politically dead was generally regarded as a given.

When McCain launched his 2008 run, his plan from the outset had been to act the part of the Republican Party's heir apparent to his onetime rival George W. Bush. But the Arizona senator had turned out to be a front-runner in name only. His efforts to push through that year's comprehensive immigration reform bill in the Senate, combined with his unwavering support for the increasingly unpopular war in Iraq, proved a double-whammy against him.

The McCain campaign's bank account sank as quickly as his poll numbers. After his top advisers delivered one sanguine presentation in the early summer of 2007 on how McCain intended to steamroll all of his competitors, former Texas senator Phil Gramm—a McCain backer who had run for president unsuccessfully a dozen years

earlier—spoke up in a manner that presaged the campaign's imminent downfall. "This has all been really great," Gramm said in his
Texas twang. "But I've got one question. How much money do we
take in, and how much do we send out?" The answer to Gramm's
two-pronged question: way too little, and way too much.

"It's always darkest before it gets totally black." It was one of
McCain's favorite sayings, and from just about every vantage point,
it looked like an appropriately pessimistic view of the state of his
campaign. Hundreds of staffers were laid off, and McCain dramatically dialed back his ambitions. As bleak as things looked, however,
no one who was left on McCain's team was ready to give up just
yet. One of the few survivors of the staff purge, Charlie Black—a
longtime heavyweight in the Republican consulting world—warned
McCain, "You're going to have terrible press, and all you have to do
is endure." He was right about the terrible press. When McCain's
support in New Hampshire bottomed out at 10 percent in late July,
the narrative for the Republican nominating fight had turned almost
entirely to the battle between Romney and Giuliani. McCain had
become an afterthought, but that was kind of OK with him. Being
the front-runner appealed to McCain's disposition about as much as
expired milk did. He didn't mind that trips to New Hampshire now
meant commuting on Southwest Airlines flights from BWI Airport,
carrying his own bag, sometimes without a single aide in tow. It was
John McCain against the world now, and if anyone knew how to
endure that kind of odds, it was McCain.

With his campaign on life support, his reshuffled senior staff
had come up with the kind of last-ditch strategy that they knew
would appeal to McCain's "us against the world" mentality. They
called it "living off the land." Instead of the original, grandiose plans
for the kind of national field operation that would give him an air
of inevitability, McCain would now clear off the cobwebs from the
Straight Talk Express and bet it all on New Hampshire, as he had
done in 2000.

Over the ensuing four months, signs of progress were hard
to come by, as the surging candidacy of Mike Huckabee in Iowa

further relegated McCain into the ranks of the second-tier candidates. When McCain hosted a mid-July luncheon at the Chamber of Commerce in Concord, an event designed to demonstrate that his campaign was still functioning, he drew a massive contingent of national political reporters. They weren't there to see how the comeback was going. No, they'd showed up because they'd expected that the wounded candidate might announce that he was withdrawing from the race. "Are there any circumstances you could imagine in which you would drop out?" McCain was asked by one reporter.

"Contracting a fatal disease," he shot back.

Even as McCain was shaking as many hands as his seventy-one-year-old body could withstand in diners, coffee shops, and town halls up and down New Hampshire, he wasn't seeing much movement in the polls against Giuliani and Romney. Each time the Arizona senator would arrive late at night at the Manchester airport, his New Hampshire–based senior adviser Steve Duprey would pick him up in his Suburban and take him to the Courtyard by Marriott in Concord, where he'd stay for the discounted "candidate rate." Not even the perpetually upbeat Duprey, who called himself the Secretary of Fun, could realistically challenge perceptions that the thing was all but over.

There was no single moment when things suddenly started heading in the right direction. Instead, McCain's fortunes began to change slowly. In the weeks leading up to one particularly dreamy, snow-swept night in northern New Hampshire, everyone around him could begin to feel the familiar rumblings of a modest shift in momentum. Even if it wasn't registering in the polls just yet, the crowd sizes and responses that the candidate was beginning to get from audiences around the state told the story. McCain and his aides didn't need poll numbers to tell them that New Hampshirites were excited about him again. For that, all the evidence they needed was the "Mac is back!" chants that began greeting the candidate wherever he went and the feeling in the air that something was happening.

Although the troop surge in Iraq that he supported vocally and unequivocally remained widely unpopular, McCain continued to gain ground via the force of his personality and convictions. He campaigned around the state the only way he knew how: by persuading small groups of voters and hoping they'd convey their positive impressions of him to friends, family, and neighbors. For Romney, who was fading quickly in Iowa, McCain's rise in New Hampshire became a significant problem. It didn't help the former Massachusetts governor's standing that Giuliani's once-robust support in New Hampshire was collapsing, as the former New York City mayor gave up on a traditional early state strategy and decamped to Florida, where he planned to make an unrealistic last stand after reverting to the ranks of a campaign sideshow. The problem for Romney was that the vast majority of Giuliani's New Hampshire support had begun to move in McCain's direction.

By late December, Romney was still holding onto a narrow lead over McCain in New Hampshire, with Huckabee building a lead in Iowa. Suddenly, for Romney, New Hampshire was no longer 1B—it was, for all intents and purposes, a must-win for the former Massachusetts governor every bit as much as it was for McCain. As part of an effort to reverse this trajectory, Romney added a line or two to his stump speech about how McCain had "failed Reagan 101" in not having previously supported President Bush's tax-cut plans, but the struggling former governor still couldn't find his groove beyond that. The problem, in a nutshell, was that he couldn't stop talking about grackles and mashed potatoes.

The air temperature was seasonably face-numbing when I headed out for a pre-Christmas northern New Hampshire swing with Romney that included town-hall meetings in the Carroll County hamlets of North Conway and Tuftonboro. Romney had always begun these events with hit-or-miss jokes and little anecdotes about his family, but on this particular trip he added a drawn-out story to his set list that couldn't have been more tonally out of step with a campaign that was two weeks away from its make-or-break moment on Primary Day. It was a saccharine tale about how he and his five sons had once accidentally come upon a nest of young grackles, whose mother was nowhere to be found. In a turn of events fit for an episode of *The Brady Bunch*, the Romney brood subsequently devoted themselves to nurturing and raising the baby grackles. The highpoint of the story came when Romney demonstrated how his son Matt attempted to encourage the young birds to leave the nest by flapping his own arms in the manner of an oversized grackle. Many members of the audience—and all of us in the traveling press corps—would laugh each time Romney flapped his arms like a bird. But standing in the back of the room, the powerless operatives who composed Romney's New Hampshire brain trust weren't as amused. Their campaign was on the ropes, and here was the candidate, telling a long-winded story about grackles. When Romney and his wife, Ann, began regularly engaging in extensive public discourse about his proficiency at making mashed potatoes, they sensed that the campaign was at risk of spinning out of control.

On his final Iowa swing before the caucuses, Romney suddenly abandoned his strategy of attacking Huckabee at every opportunity and instead started focusing his attacks entirely McCain, who wasn't even really competing in the caucuses. It was confirmation that Iowa was all but lost, and though the Romney campaign still held out some hope, Huckabee won the caucuses the next day by a more comfortable than expected nine-point margin. At the moment when the checkmark next to Huckabee's name flashed onto the Fox News Channel screen at the West Des Moines Sheraton early in the night, I'd never felt the air go out of a room more suddenly and completely. As they looked in vain for a quiet spot in the hotel lobby to huddle, senior Romney aides looked like kids who had just been told their dog died. They had just four days to try to turn things around in New Hampshire.

A few hours later, we loaded into the press charter plane at the Des Moines airport with Portsmouth as our destination. The plane was carrying a large contingent of national media heavy-hitters who had booked their seats many weeks earlier, under the expectation that Romney would be the likely Republican victor in Iowa. As we sat on the plane waiting to pull back from the gate, I remember watching a replay of Barack Obama's historic "They said this day would never come" Iowa victory speech on my seatback TV and thinking for the first time that the Illinois senator might actually become president. Romney, with his grackle and mashed potatoes stories, looked small in comparison.

The sun had not yet risen when we landed in Portsmouth, but Romney's New Hampshire team had managed to assemble a couple of hundred sign-waving supporters to try to lift the downtrodden candidate's spirits. Tom Rath, who had found a twenty-four-hour Dunkin' Donuts in the area to provide the stimulants required for such an occasion, led the crowd in an ad hoc version of "Sweet Caroline." The song felt like a drill going through my head, as I was utterly exhausted and knew that I had about forty-five minutes of sleep to look forward to before I had to produce the live shot for Romney's round of morning show interviews. Romney, I had to admit, had it worse than I did. He had a full day of events ahead of him, for which he had to be "on" at every moment. The very idea of it was too miserable for me to contemplate.

Still, there was nothing fake about Romney's own humbled reaction to this vibrant New Hampshire welcoming reception, and he seemed to believe that he still had a shot. But with just four days to work with, he was going to have to come up with something better than grackle stories.

At a town-hall meeting in Derry the next day, Romney unveiled a new prop: an illuminated sign that hung on the wall that said, "Washington Is Broken." The gist of the slogan had been a part of his message since Day One of his candidacy—that he was the turnaround artist who could come in and fix what ailed DC—but had largely been lost in the haphazard mix of social issues. Finally, Romney had elucidated in just three words the premise of a candidacy that his aides had first batted around more than a year earlier before deciding against it: Washington was broken and Mr. Fix It was here to put it back together again.

Over that final weekend and on the Monday before Primary Day, Romney really did seem to be hitting his stride. Every political professional knows how dangerous it is to make determinations about a campaign's strength based solely on crowd size and perceived "energy," but it was difficult to ignore the sense of momentum—difficult, that is, for those of us who hadn't been attending McCain's events and didn't realize that the Arizona senator's crowds were even bigger and more energized than Romney's were.

On primary eve, Romney held his final New Hampshire town-hall meeting at McKelvie Intermediate School in Bedford. The place was packed, and it was rocking. A few minutes before he went out to deliver his final stump speech of the 2008 New Hampshire campaign, Romney stood backstage with some family and top members of his New Hampshire and national team. He allowed himself a few moments to wax nostalgic about the long journey that had led to this moment, and then he turned to the task at hand. "So what do you guys think I should start with tonight?" Romney asked. "Maybe the Olympics story? Something about the flag? Or how about the mashed potatoes?"

Romney's New Hampshire state director Jim Merrill was the first to pipe up.

"Governor," Merrill said. "No mashed potatoes story. You need to ask for their vote. This is it. This is not mashed potatoes."

Romney looked at Merrill for a moment with an expression that indicated he was a bit hurt. That mashed potatoes story *killed*! He was *good* at making mashed potatoes, gosh darnit!

Everyone was quiet for a moment. Then, to Merrill's great relief, former Missouri senator Jim Talent—a senior Romney adviser—stepped in. "You know, governor," Talent said. "I think Jim's right. Let's lose the mashed potatoes."

Romney lost the mashed potatoes. The next day, he lost New Hampshire to McCain by five points.

A little less than ten months later, his hopes of becoming president looking dimmer by the day, John McCain was losing to Barack Obama in New Hampshire by a double-digit margin. A desperation play for the state's four electoral votes was not exactly a savvy use of the candidate's time in the final hours of the general election, but McCain insisted on making a nostalgic trek to the Granite State on the Sunday night before Election Day. An airport rally in Manchester would have made far more sense logistically at this stage in the game, but the Republican nominee was not to be denied one final visit to his favorite spot in New Hampshire: Peterborough Town House.

The swelling crowd, swarms of Secret Service agents and dozens of TV cameras that showed up for McCain's final New Hampshire stop of 2008 made for quite a contrast from the gloomy, underattended ice cream social that had marked the beginning of his sordid love affair with the state more than nine years earlier. Many of the faces in the front row of the jam-packed event were familiar, and McCain gave them one of his most resounding performances in months. With the clock ticking, his staff practically had to drag him off the stage. McCain ended up losing New Hampshire to Obama by almost ten points, but in a strange way, he managed to go out on his own terms.

CHAPTER 23

IT'S AN UNPOPULAR POSITION, I know, but I don't like autumn. I've always been confused by the majority of people who take acute joy in digging their cozy sweaters out of the closet and ordering their first pumpkin-spiced latte of the season, as if they're new mothers finally able to enjoy their first glass of wine in nine months. To me, the defining characteristic of fall is that it heralds winter's imminent arrival. I like football, but I hate shorter days, cold nights, and all of the other elements that compose the elixir of sadness of the season. Fall sucks.

Yet, I will admit that if you have to tolerate the arrival of this seasonal harbinger of nature's death, New England is just about the best place to put on your plaid shirt and give it the full, crisp embrace. When October 2015 arrived in New Hampshire, it was time for me to start monitoring *Yankee Magazine*'s online peak-foliage forecast map of New England. My wife laughs at me for this, but I like to follow along with the daily changes in the leaves' colors, and I scoff at people who lower themselves to leaf-peeping in a "near-peak" area when a "peak" opportunity can be found just a twenty-minute drive northward.

It had been an unusually warm September in New Hampshire, which meant that the peak peeping time in each area of the state would be a couple of weeks later than usual. So at the end of the first week of October, there was still plenty of green mixed in with the psychedelic kaleidoscope of reds, oranges, and yellows that had begun to envelop southern New Hampshire.

Winter's arrival in New Hampshire typically marked the final stage of the campaign when "real people"—who didn't work in the state's political industrial complex—typically started to pay close attention. But this particular race, by just about every measure, had been decidedly atypical. If the polls were to believed, Donald Trump was now running away from the rest of the Republican field both in New Hampshire and just about everywhere else. It remained possible, I thought, that Trump's standing was mostly a function of low-information voters continuing to reward the loudest voice in the room because they didn't know what else was out there yet. With his lead widening, that prospect seemed increasingly unlikely, but I wanted to see for myself whether there might be another candidate who was quietly gaining steam in a manner similar to the way John McCain had snuck up on his competition in 2000 and 2008. If any lucid Republican was going to stop Trump from running away with victory in the nation's first primary, it looked like it'd have to be Chris Christie, Jeb Bush, or John Kasich, each of whom had been campaigning "the New Hampshire way" by trying to earn one vote at a time in diners, churches, businesses, and homes across the state. In my previous interactions with them, none of the three had struck me as particularly McCain-like, but they each also had their own unique strengths that might keep them in the game, if everything fell into place just the right way.

Trump's success, I thought, must have been particularly frustrating to the man who possessed the second-loudest voice in the race, Christie, whose own political prospects appeared to be plunging as steadily as the temperatures were. Still, I continued to be impressed by how well the New Jersey governor played in the rooms of New Hampshire. During one particularly poignant soliloquy on treating drug addiction, which he made at Shooter's Tavern in the lakes region outpost of Belmont, Christie was at his very best. First, he told the crowd that his mom had smoked cigarettes for most of her life, even long after she knew they were bad for her, and had failed time after time in her attempts to quit. When she was finally hospitalized for what would prove to be terminal lung cancer at the age of seventy-one, Christie said, no one suggested that it was her fault she'd gotten the disease. "Yet somehow," Christie said, pacing the bar with his confident stride. "If it's heroin or cocaine or alcohol, we say, 'Ah, they decided it. They're getting what they deserve.'"

Next, Christie moved on to relate the tear-jerking story of a high-achieving former law-school classmate who "had it all," until he hurt his back running one day and was prescribed Percocet to help with the pain. Christie's friend became addicted to the drug, initiating a downward spiral over the course of several years that led to the loss of his job, his home, his family, and eventually his life. "There but for the grace of God," Christie said. "It can happen to anyone."

The six and a half minutes of Christie's speech on the topic, which our HuffPost video team shot and edited, subsequently generated more than 8 million views on Facebook. I hadn't expected that kind of response, but maybe I should have. Christie, after all, had spoken in a deeply personal way about an issue that had taken precedence in the New Hampshire race but was still being under-covered by the national media. A poll conducted by WMUR—New Hampshire's only network-affiliated news station—showed that the drug epidemic was the number-one concern of New Hampshire voters. With the heroin crisis continuing to spiral out of control, voters in the state deemed drugs to be more pressing than the economy, education, health care, foreign policy, and everything else. If you spent any significant time in the state, it wasn't hard to see why. In Manchester, you could walk out of the Radisson Hotel on Elm Street on any given day and witness how bad the problem was. Homeless, strung-out people of all ages stumbled the streets in a daze, panhandling aggressively and discarding needles in public parking lots. And those were just the most visible addicts. The response to the Christie video captured the extent to which opioids had become a crisis among all races and in every American community—poor, middle class, and wealthy. That fall, Republican and Democratic presidential candidates alike had been talking about drug addiction with increasing regularity, but none had managed to capture the emerging consensus favoring treatment over incarceration better than Christie.

Two days after I got around to posting the clip of Christie's speech, on a Tuesday afternoon, Rachel Maddow played the whole thing on her primetime MSNBC show. At the time it was airing, I was having a beer with a Bernie Sanders campaign staffer at Republic—a coffee, wine, and locally sourced restaurant that is the closest you can find to Brooklyn in New Hampshire—when my cell phone started blowing up. Over the next few days, our video was featured by countless other media organizations. It was just the kind of emotional "moment" that had long propelled campaigns in the Granite State, and Christie's campaign knew it.

The New Jersey governor began talking about the video at the beginning of every appearance in the state. When I ran into him outside a debate in Milwaukee, Wisconsin, Christie told me about the parents of a child who had been battling addiction. They'd seen the video and decided to drive four and a half hours from their home in Connecticut to attend one of his events. He also mentioned another couple who had lost a son to an overdose just a week earlier and had come to Hanover to comfort their daughter, who was a student at Dartmouth. While on campus, they came upon Christie and thanked him profusely for raising awareness of the issue, even though it was too late for their own family.

From a personal standpoint, it was rewarding to hear that the video was having a meaningful impact on people's lives. It captured a moment that was deeply human and authentic, but would it make a lasting political difference for Christie? That was less clear. The New Jersey governor had been starting to tick up in the polls a bit in its aftermath, but he was still firmly planted in the single digits, while

Trump continued to dominate the field without even once setting foot inside a place like Shooter's Tavern, where campaigns in New Hampshire had traditionally been won.

The situation was at least as dire for Jeb Bush, who could no longer lay plausible claim to the front-runner status that had once been regarded as a near birthright. The week after attending Christie's event at Shooter's Tavern, I caught a midday Bush town-hall meeting at a medical supply center in Portsmouth, and the energy in that room was nonexistent. The event didn't get off to an especially promising start when the company manager who introduced the candidate provided a Wikipedia-style review of Bush's background, which included the bullet point that Bush played tennis while a student at Phillips Andover Academy and was the son and brother of former presidents. "Hey, he's just like us!" was probably not a thought that crossed many of the minds of the employees in attendance. Although Bush was working as hard and sleeping as little as any candidate in the race, Trump's portrayal of him as entitled and—more devastatingly—"low energy" had clearly resonated.

After his inauspicious introduction, the former Florida governor meandered his way into what passed as his stump speech, providing a laundry list of goals for a third Bush presidency that appeared more inconceivable by the second. As he told the crowd about his plans to embrace an energy revolution, decrease government regulations, and simplify the tax code, I saw more than a couple of people in the room fighting back a sudden bout of narcolepsy. I'm pretty sure that few would have noticed if he'd thrown in a "Yadda, yadda, yadda. You get the idea. I mean, whatever." The slow-motion car crash dragged on for another forty-five minutes or so: I watched three people rise from their chairs and leave the event and found myself wondering why more members of the audience weren't joining them. Bush, who often spoke about how "joyfully" he was campaigning, appeared to be entirely joyless. Not only did he fail to make clear his reasons that the people in the room should entrust him with the presidency, at no point throughout the entire event did he get around to asking them for their votes—a cardinal sin in New Hampshire, if there ever was one.

With neither Christie nor Bush appearing likely to coalesce the anti-Trump bloc—which still composed a clear majority of the New Hampshire Republican electorate—I decided to check in on an even more improbable savior for the GOP. What I found was not particularly encouraging. I linked up with John Kasich the next week on his newly minted campaign bus. Kasich, I had been assured by his staff, had been made aware of this arrangement, as the HuffPost video team waited for him to board. You wouldn't have known it. When he stepped onto the bus, I greeted the Ohio governor in the traditional manner: with a handshake and a friendly smile. He, however, wasn't interested in exchanging pleasantries. After offering his hand with the enthusiasm of someone who was about to have it chopped off, he brushed past me, ignored my crew entirely, sat down with a coffee in hand, and pulled out his iPad. Our cameras rolled for four minutes—during which Kasich said not a single word. Instead, he sat with his head in his hand and listened intently to a country tune that featured some hyper-literal lyrics about the love between a father and son.

Unsure of what else to do as the candidate continued his reverie, I began chatting quietly with his press secretary in the back of the bus. That was a mistake. The governor of Ohio glared at me as if I had screamed in his ear. "Shhhhh," he snapped. It had been quite a long time since another adult shushed me, but I'd heard stories about Kasich's legendary temper. I just hadn't expected to bear witness to it as a reporter covering his campaign.

The bus first rolled to Woodstock, New Hampshire, a tourist trap of a town, where Kasich's early morning crankiness was on display. As he strolled along the town's main drag, he encountered a couple from Ohio, who shouted out excitedly in the direction of their governor. Kasich, in turn, offered a meek reply, sounding generally unimpressed. He was equally disengaged when, during a stop inside one of the shops, the deeply religious candidate wondered aloud why it was that people in far-flung mountain towns such as this one seemed to be "more in touch with God" than they were elsewhere in New Hampshire. "It's because we're in the mountains and we're closer to him," a shopper offered in response. Considering the context, I thought that this was a great answer. Kasich didn't appear to agree. He barely acknowledged the woman's response—a strange unwillingness to engage from a man who could, when he felt like it, demonstrate an Oprah-like interest in the spiritual health of other people. That was the deal with Kasich: when he wasn't into it, he couldn't fake it.

The rest of the morning, Kasich tried on an array of silly hats, considered and decided against buying a pair of wool mittens for his teenage daughter, and donned a leather jacket at the American Police Motorcycle Museum in Meredith, where—by now in much more buoyant humor—he regaled the assembled press with stories from his own motorcycle-riding days. "Live free or die," the bad-to-the-bone governor said, recalling his own near-death misadventure. "That's kind of how it is with the motorcycle."

Through it all, Kasich was sometimes charming, often flippant, and always untroubled about the way he came across. When a local reporter asked him how he intended to distinguish himself from other Republican candidates in the race who had similar records and platforms, Kasich couldn't hide his disdain for the premise. "You know, I've never heard that question before," Kasich shot back, oozing with sarcasm.

"How about gun control?" another local reporter asked. This was a softball pitched right down the middle of the plate if there ever was one.

"Well, I'm not for it."

He would not elaborate further.

We ended the day back at Beverly Bruce's house in Center Tuftonboro—site of Lindsey Graham's impromptu stand-up comedy routine from a few months back. In the interim, a Minnesota dentist had gained intense notoriety for killing the beloved Cecil the Lion while on a hunting trip in Africa. In deference to the fallout from that scandal, Bruce hosted this particular event not in her game room but in a separate barn. It drew a decent turnout, and Kasich was now on his best behavior. Just about everyone there, it seemed to me, seemed supportive of his message.

A week and a half later, the latest CBS/YouGov survey of likely New Hampshire primary voters came out. Trump: 38, Carson: 12, Bush: 8, Kasich: 5, Christie: 2. Nothing, it seemed, that Christie, Bush, and Kasich were doing on the ground in New Hampshire had registered in the least bit.

CHAPTER 24

I N THE LEAD-UP TO the 2012 presidential campaign, Jon Huntsman was the potential Republican presidential candidate whom
President Obama's reelection team feared the most. Huntsman's
pedigree as an accomplished, attractive, reform-minded governor
of Utah was so compelling, in fact, that some observers wondered
whether Obama had been seeking to exile him from the American
political scene by choosing him to be ambassador to China in 2009.
That appointment, however, amounted to the addition of another
impressive credential on Huntsman's résumé when he decided to
enter the race in the spring of 2011. That his billionaire father, Jon
Huntsman Sr., was widely expected to bankroll his candidacy was
all the more evidence that he could be a serious contender.

John Weaver, who had been John McCain's top strategist during
the 2000 New Hampshire triumph, set the gears in motion for
Huntsman to leave Beijing and return to the United States to helm
a campaign that had already been built for him. But from the day
of his announcement, when members of the media were provided

with credentials that spelled Huntsman's first name incorrectly, just about everything that could go wrong did. By early fall, Huntsman's once-promising prospects were already tumbling toward irrelevance, requiring him to dramatically scale down his ambitions. In late September, he packed up his national headquarters in Orlando and decamped to New Hampshire, where he planned to bank everything on winning the primary. McCain had twice provided a blueprint on how to pull this off, and with much of the party aligned against the front-runner, Mitt Romney, it appeared to be a gambit that had at least some chance of success. In short order, however, it became clear that Jon Huntsman was no John McCain.

What Huntsman offered the Republican electorate was a dose of sanity in a deeply unsettled Republican race that was replete with colorful characters of dubious viability. With Godfather's Pizza CEO Herman Cain and arch-conservative congresswoman Michele Bachmann of Minnesota taking their own unlikely turns at the front of the pack, the soundtrack for the 2012 race for the GOP presidential nomination might have been circus music. Yet Huntsman proved ill-equipped to take advantage of the madness. It wasn't just the extent to which he oddly sought to downplay his conservative record that made him look anemic, his inconsistent style of campaigning also held him back. One day, he would make it a point to emphasize that he was the adult in the room—the responsible leader who'd always take the substantive high ground in the race. The next, he was characterizing GOP front-runner Mitt Romney as a "perfectly lubricated weathervane" who "doesn't believe in putting his country first." Huntsman did have one powerful asset working in his favor: the media wanted a real race, and with a series of other long-shot Republican contenders rising and falling in quick succession, he looked like the candidate who was best positioned to give Romney a scare in New Hampshire.

As it turned out, Romney never had reason to be particularly concerned, even as he maintained a slightly improved version of the quirky style that he had exhibited during his 2008 run. When he was campaigning in New Hampshire, the hard-charging former

Massachusetts governor made it a point to return to his home in the Boston suburb of Belmont almost every night. After one stint on the trail, Romney told Susan Duprey, who served as chief of staff for his wife, Ann, about how much he was looking forward to getting back to Belmont. "As soon as I get home," Duprey recalled the multimillionaire candidate telling her, "I'm going to open my suitcase, and I'm going to separate my clothes into the dark pile and the light pile, and then I'm going to put them into the washer." It's an endearing tale in retrospect, and it'd be a stretch to say that Romney was more concerned about doing his own laundry properly than he was maximizing his time on the campaign trail in New Hampshire—but perhaps not much of one.

Huntsman, meanwhile, was gunning for second place in New Hampshire, and he was making some progress on that front. On the Sunday before Primary Day, I trailed the bomber-jacket-clad, Kennedy-handsome candidate around the state. After months of inconsistency and depressingly low turnout at his events, the energy that was suddenly surrounding Huntsman became palpable and contagious. And no one felt it more viscerally than the candidate. At a jam-packed coffee shop in Hempstead, he leaped onto the counter and beamed down at the crowd. "They say this state loves an underdog," Huntsman called out. "Ladies and gentlemen, here is your underdog!" His supporters roared. Later that night, he packed a crowd of over three hundred people—mammoth, by Huntsman's standards—into a town-hall meeting in the liberal college town of Keene. They were fired up there, too. Huntsman was clearly feeding off the energy, as he appeared to be peaking just at the right time. Would this go down as the latest installment in the long volume of soaring New Hampshire comeback stories? No, it would not. But the manner in which it all fizzled out would be memorable.

On Primary Night, the Huntsman campaign booked the Black Brimmer—a cramped and divey two-story bar and "night club" on the corner of Elm and Lowell Streets in Manchester. As inconclusive exit polling numbers and the requisite, anecdotal observations about turnout started coming in that afternoon, Huntsman's national spokesperson, Tim Miller, swung by the venue to talk through logistics with the members of the advance team, who were responsible for setting up the press risers, stage, and other basic elements of this low-budget celebration. One of these young advance staffers mentioned to Miller that he had procured a couple of confetti cannons to punctuate the occasion, in the event that there was reason to celebrate. Miller absorbed this information and then gave his directive: If Huntsman somehow finished in first place, it barely merited mentioning, they would not only douse the place in a thick coating of confetti, the campaign team might consider burning down the bar in celebration. If he got second place, Miller added, the young staffer should launch the confetti at will. It'd be a clear moral victory, and they wanted to project enthusiasm heading into South Carolina.

Third place? That was tricky. Huntsman had bet it all on New Hampshire, and it was difficult to see any realistic path forward for him if he couldn't place or show. Still, it had been a long, tough campaign, and the campaign might be eager to commemorate a moral victory, even if it was of questionable value. Miller decided that in the event of a third-place showing, the confetti launch decision would be contingent on what *kind* of bronze medal they'd earned. If Huntsman finished in a close third—one that could reasonably be deemed just about as good as a second-place showing, he would then seriously consider authorizing a confetti launch. But if it was a *distant* third-place finish, he told the young staffer, hold the confetti.

It turned out that the Huntsman party attracted a much bigger crowd than the campaign had expected—much of it members of the media. The venue was packed to the walls, and everyone's hopes seemed to get a little higher with each passing hour that the bar stayed open and the beer bottles piled up. Still, no one on hand appeared to be especially surprised or disappointed when Huntsman ended up finishing in a distant third place—twenty-two points behind Romney and six points behind the second-place finisher, Ron Paul. With no real operation or base of support to speak of in any of the states ahead, Jon Huntsman's campaign was over.

Back at his private suite, Huntsman powwowed with top aides and family members to decide whether he should continue on to South Carolina as planned. He decided that he at least wanted to let the dust settle overnight and keep his options open. There was no particular rush to get out of the race at that point and just enough uncertainty about the results to make "sleeping on it" a reasonable judgment, even if he was all but certain that there was no path forward. Because he wasn't going to bail out right away, it was clear that Huntsman needed to strike an optimistic tone when he spoke that night. "Maybe I'll stay in," after all, wasn't a reasonable message to convey to his supporters. He had to project enthusiasm.

When he took the stage at the Black Brimmer, Huntsman—like countless losing candidates before him—beamed with the fervor of someone who'd just won the Super Bowl, the Nobel Prize, and the World Cup all at once—not a presidential hopeful who had just lost his most important state to Ron Paul. "I'd say third place is a Ticket to Ride, ladies and gentleman!" Huntsman, the passionate classic rock fan, declared to the rowdy crowd, who might have re-plied, "Beep beep, beep beep, yeah!" had he added that the bar was staying open for another hour.

Then it happened. I was somewhere in the back of the room, and so I didn't see it right away. But I remember hearing a quick popping sound, and then the confetti started raining down from above. Unbeknownst to Miller, the young advance staffer had gone rogue. The campaign may have been over, but that confetti was not going to waste.

Within minutes, the Romney campaign began circulating a video clip of Huntsman's third-place confetti launch internally. The moment instantaneously became a running punch line for Romney's director of operations, Will Ritter. Every time Romney would go on to lose a primary or caucus state, Ritter would repeat the same warn-ing to his young staff: "Don't blast the cannons!"

In New Hampshire, not every runner-up can be a Comeback Kid.

CHAPTER 25

I WAS RETURNING TO THE Manchester Radisson from dinner
with my colleague Jon one night in early November 2015 when I
caught a glimpse of a familiar figure standing in the lobby. He
was alone, suitcase in hand, his dry-cleaning slung over his shoulder.
The early 2000s-style flip phone was the giveaway: it was Lindsey
Graham.

The senator offered each of us a customary fist bump. "Good to
see y'all," he said. "Where's the bar?" The only reason Graham didn't
already know where the hotel bar was located was that he wasn't
usually a Radisson man. The South Carolina senator typically stayed
at the Hilton Garden Inn down the street instead. But the HGI cost
$50 a night more than the Radisson during this particular week,
and the cash-strapped candidate, who was still polling deep within
margin-of-error territory, needed to save every penny he could.

Graham had traveled from DC to New Hampshire on his own,
his campaign unable to spring for a single aide to accompany him.
For just about anyone else, it would have been a sad scene. Here was

a sitting US senator, one with the most impressive foreign policy résumé of anyone in the GOP field, reduced to the ranks of a lonely guy on a business trip looking for someone to have a drink with. But Graham wasn't in the least bit unhappy. For him, it was all just part of the ride, and he was always eager to share a drink and a laugh.

We headed down the hallway to JD's Tavern. Moments after ordering his Bailey's on the rocks, Graham dove into his warmongering stand-up act: "Christie and I might be a good ticket," he said. "Because we both just want to kill people."

"People"—in this context, I should say, was shorthand for "terrorists." In public and in private, Graham talked a lot about killing terrorists. He viewed the world as an exceptionally dangerous place, ready to detonate at any moment. Still, he knew that many of his detractors saw him as a reckless jingoist who hadn't truly absorbed the lessons that had come from launching the Iraq fiasco in the first place. That's why he talked about killing "people" sometimes instead of killing "terrorists." Embracing the warmonger caricature was his way of deflecting it.

After he was finished talking about killing, Graham opened up the floor by asking us the overriding question that continued to nag at him: "How the hell am I losing to these people?" There was no good answer—not one, at least, that would ever satisfy him. The truth was that Donald Trump was a unique phenomenon who had managed to obliterate all of the normal rules of how you win a presidential nomination. On that front, Graham more or less agreed. When the conversation turned to his less reckless opponents, we told him that we were planning to spend the following day on Jeb Bush's campaign bus.

"Why do you think Jeb is running for president?" Graham asked.

"Because he feels like he's supposed to?" I replied.

"Bingo," he said.

"Now, why am I running for president?"

Jon and I answered in unison this time: "To kill people!"

Graham slapped the table and nodded pensively, as he hoisted his Bailey's. By any objective measure, the man had a zero-percent chance of being elected president, but as his drink slowly disappeared, he couldn't help but lay out for us his magical path to the nomination: exceed rock-bottom expectations in Iowa, finish in the top three in New Hampshire, win his home state of South Carolina, and then he'd be off to the races from there. It was never going to happen, and Graham must have known it. I couldn't help but think that he remained in the race mostly for the fun of it—the sheer joy of schlepping around New Hampshire to regale his audiences of a couple of dozen people in public and a couple of journalists in private. The boundless pleasure of needling his three top targets for ridicule—Ted Cruz, Rand Paul, and Donald Trump—was perhaps his very favorite thing of all.

"I'm fairly confident that if I went onto the Senate floor and murdered Ted Cruz, I could get a majority of Republican senators to testify that it was suicide," Graham told us. It was an exceptionally provocative thing for a sitting US senator to say, which made the remark especially hilarious and, I thought at the time, strictly private. Three months later, however, Graham repeated the very same joke at the Washington Press Club Foundation Congressional Dinner on stage in front of a live audience. I was surely among the most surprised when a few weeks after that, Graham *endorsed* Cruz's campaign, pegging the reviled Texas senator as the last best chance to stop Trump's march to the nomination. One thing about Lindsey Graham was that he always kept you on your toes.

After we ordered another round of drinks, Jon texted our two other HuffPost colleagues to let them know that they'd better get down to JD's, if they ever wanted to hear a US senator expound on how he could get away with murdering one of his colleagues. Within moments, they had joined us at the table. By that time, Graham had gotten his fill of Ted Cruz homicide jokes and had moved on to skewering Rand Paul. "I'd do anything to get on that debate stage with Rand," Graham, who'd been relegated to the undercard debates, said. "I just want to poke him a little bit." He stuck his index finger out and poked the air to illustrate.

As much as he salivated over the prospect of going toe-to-toe against Paul, Graham's dream scenario was to find a way to share a stage with Trump, the Republican competitor for whom he harbored his most visceral disgust. Someone at the table asked Graham what would be the first question he'd pose to the Republican front-runner in such a scenario. This was the first time all night that he turned serious. "What exactly did you mean when you said that John McCain was not really a war hero?" he said without hesitation. Graham added that although his own failure to break through in New Hampshire didn't really trouble him on a personal level, the thing that did hurt was the degree to which he knew that McCain wanted him to win. He hated the idea of letting his old buddy down.

When it was time to call it a night, the senator thanked us for taking care of his tab, and then we all poured out into the lobby. As he headed toward the elevator, we had to remind him about his dry-cleaning, which he'd left hanging under the staircase. This was what running for president of the United States was like for Lindsey Graham.

After spending a long, boring day on the trail with Jeb Bush, on the following night, my colleagues and I returned for a late dinner to JD's, one of the only places in town that served food after 9:00 p.m. on a weeknight. We had just sat down at our table when a familiar face entered the bar. He'd been out on the campaign trail, too. Once again, the senator from South Carolina was flying solo, and he didn't need to ask this time before pulling up a chair. When the waitress came, he first ordered a water but then thought better of it and asked for a glass of Riesling.

Graham was in an even spicier mood than he'd been the night before, as he in rapid succession wondered aloud how Bobby Jindal had convinced his wife to marry him, questioned the trustworthiness of people who don't drink, and talked quite a bit more about killing people. When I excused myself briefly to call my editor, Sam Stein, Graham took the phone from me and recorded a voice mail for Sam. "Scott's in jail," the senator deadpanned. I'd never enjoyed the company of a politician so thoroughly.

Although he hadn't made a dent in the polls, Graham was making his own kind of impression on New Hampshire. After he got up to use the restroom, our waitress came over to refresh everyone's drinks.

"Where'd Riesling guy go?" she asked.

I fidgeted in my seat. "Actually, he's a US senator," I said.

"Oh, Bailey's guy?" the waitress replied. "Yeah, I know Lindsey."

CHAPTER 26

I N DECEMBER, THE HUFFPOST video crew and I took up lodging at a five-bedroom house in the rural outpost of Chichester—a heavily forested jurisdiction just a few miles outside of Concord. As advertised on Airbnb, the place was indeed located in a "quiet, secluded spot" atop a hill and at the end of a dirt road not noteworthy enough to earn the attention of Google Maps. It suited our particular news coverage needs well, and it also would have been a great setting for a horror film. The old wooden floors creaked with every step, and complementing the wood-burning fireplace was a wide variety of what looked to be centuries-old furniture, including a cradle that appeared to be an ideal spot for a ghost baby to take a nap.

We left our spooky new home to drive up to the ski town of Waterville Valley to catch a Trump rally. We would have to be sneaky about it, because Trump's campaign was continuing its blackballing of the *Huffington Post*. This punishment, however, turned into a blessing, as it forced us to stray from the so-called press pen and enter all of Trump's events as members of the general public, where we were free to roam among the chest-thumping masses. Meanwhile, the reporters who identified themselves as such were confined like cattle, once Trump took the stage. This accommodation, which all of the major networks had agreed to abide by, was emblematic of the utterly shameful capitulation that the TV news industry had been making to the Trump campaign for months. As long as he remained a ratings bonanza, Trump was more or less allowed to dictate terms to the networks that often carried his speeches live, and would remain uninterrupted by anyone holding him to account for the near-constant stream of half-truths and lies that he spewed. There were a lot of good reporters covering Trump aggressively on the ground. But to many of their bosses, it was far more important to be on good terms with Hope Hicks and future paid CNN contributor Corey Lewandowski—the operatives who made the decisions about who "Mr. Trump" would grant exclusive interviews to—than it was to hold a mendacious demagogue to account.

Thanks to El Niño and in stark contrast to the record-breaking snowfall of the previous winter, it had been unusually mild in New Hampshire, with temperatures regularly above freezing. On this particular evening, snow would have been preferable to the cold and driving rain inundating the area. When we arrived at the indoor soccer field at the White Mountain Athletic Club, about half of the 1,000 or so chairs that had been set up were empty. I began to wonder if the weather would keep the crowds away this time. As volunteers passed out "Trump For President" signs, there was a distinct lack of spark in the air. I took a seat near the front and soon noticed that the college-aged kid sitting next to me was using Tinder, the mobile dating app. As I watched him swipe left more often than right, rejecting photo after photo, it occurred to me that the Republican primary fight in New Hampshire had become a real-life version of the popular app. GOP voters in New Hampshire, for the time being at least, weren't shy about their lack of interest in personal qualities like experience and judgment. Instead, they wanted to be hit in the head with the goods, even if they hated themselves a bit for it. Donald Trump was the perfect candidate for the Tinder generation, unskillfully spray-tanned and self-obsessed. He would probably end up being a disappointment in the end, but hey, at least he wouldn't be boring.

As it turned out, Trump's speech that night was—by his standards, at least—rather tame. He sounded more like a traditional candidate than he usually did, pandering when it came to New Hampshire's role in the process ("There is something beautiful about tradition."), and was particularly unimaginative in his attacks on his rivals ("Jeb Bush loves Common Core. How do you love Common Core? You can't love Common Core."). There were none of the usual outbursts about Obama's Muslim/Kenyan/anti-American leanings. Trump even included an offbeat and extensive anti-alcohol harangue at the end of his speech that drew nothing but silence from the crowd, and he seemed to be running through the motions when he came to the part in which he expounded on the virtues of his border wall.

"Someday you know what it's going to be called, right? The Trump Wall," he said of the fabulous barrier that would one day protect the nation's southern border and maybe cure cancer, too. "We have to make it beautiful. We have to make it beautiful. We have to make it beautiful." The lameness of this particular event belied Trump's comfortable first-place standing in New Hampshire. You couldn't argue with the success the guy was having, even at times when his shtick seemed to be wearing thin. The story remained Trump versus everyone else, and everyone else was losing big league, as the front-runner might say.

For the Democrats, the state of the race was more complicated. Although Clinton led Sanders by large margins just about everywhere else in the country, she was still running behind him in New Hampshire. In spite of the obvious historic potential of her candidacy, Clinton was struggling mightily to inspire younger Democratic women to get excited about the possibility of the first female president—a deficiency that her campaign had made it a priority to address. I attended one particular Clinton event at Southern New Hampshire University where she spoke to a midday crowd about women's economic empowerment—a subject that could scarcely be any more squarely in her wheelhouse. The event took an uncomfortable turn, however, when the candidate received the following question from a college-age woman in the crowd: "Secretary Clinton, you recently came out to say that all rape victims should be believed. But would you say that Juanita Broaddrick, Kathleen Willey, and Paula Jones should be believed as well?"

Hearing the names of three women who had accused Bill Clinton of sexual misdeeds over the years probably caused a few Clinton staffers' blood pressure to spike dramatically, but the veteran performer didn't even flinch. "Well, I would say that everyone should be believed at first until they are disbelieved based on evidence," Clinton shot back with a confident smile. As much as she was struggling to generate a lot of enthusiasm among the voters who should have been in her wheelhouse, Clinton knew how to rise to the occasion in moments when less experienced political hands might easily have faltered.

Although her core supporters were far less rabid than Sanders's young legions, Clinton also knew how to fire up a crowd. At an evening town-hall meeting in Amherst, near the Massachusetts border, the energy that emanated from 1,000 or so people who packed the elementary-school gym was electric from start to finish. In fighting form, Clinton seized the opportunity to rip into Trump for his "shameless and dangerous idea" of banning Muslims from traveling to the United States and deployed to great effect the truism that the simplest attack is often the most effective one when she noted that the Republican front-runner was "trafficking in paranoia." Just in case Trump ended up fading from the scene, as many people were still expecting him to do, Clinton wasn't shy about making a case of guilt by association. "We're not only dealing with one inflammatory demagogue," Clinton said. "We're dealing with a party in danger of losing its way." Clinton said nary a word about her Democratic opponent, but Sanders was becoming more difficult for her to ignore with each passing day.

The following week, I arranged to spend the day trailing the Vermont senator as he campaigned across the seacoast region. My first impression upon spending time up close with him was that I'd never met a candidate who had less tolerance for anything that slowed him down. New Hampshire voters often have a tendency to get a bit long-winded when there's a microphone put in front of them, and for the most part, candidates indulge their non sequiturs and extended soliloquys. Not Sanders. He seemed incapable of even trying to pretend to have patience for anyone who was wasting his time. "Good. Good," he'd say in the middle of each New Hampshire voter's long-winded question. The subtext was, "I get it. I know exactly what you're going to say next, and I'm not going to pretend I don't already have a canned answer lined up here to answer you. I'm in a hurry, and I'm feeling crabby, so come on. Let's get this over with and move on. Good. Good."

Sanders's aversion to wasting time with voters' endless digressions paled in comparison to his searing abhorrence for reporters' questions about political process. A tried-and-true ideologue, he wanted to talk about policy and nothing else, and every moment he spent on process was a moment lost to a discussion about the disappearing middle class and the millionaires and billionaires who were ruining everything for everyone else. And God help you if he was ready to go and you weren't, as I would soon find out.

The Sanders campaign had blocked out twenty minutes for my interview with him at The Friendly Toast—a whimsically decorated and mouthwatering breakfast spot in downtown Portsmouth. My crew and I arrived there more than an hour early, in order to make sure we had plenty of time to set up. As we were doing so, the campaign let me know that Sanders would be making an unscheduled appearance at Portsmouth Book and Bar, a hip little coffee and beer-serving bookshop just a short walk from the Friendly Toast. So I headed there with Jon, where we watched Sanders address a small crowd of fired-up supporters. We left a couple of minutes early to finish setting up for our interview at The Friendly Toast, which was scheduled for 1:45 p.m. The problem, as it turned out, was that Sanders was running ahead of schedule, and unlike us, he was driving to the event, not walking—and he was in no mood to wait around.

At the moment I stepped back into the restaurant, I received a two-word text message from my colleague Marielle: "He's here." Uh-oh. I made my way as quickly as I could to the back of the restaurant and saw that though we did have one camera set up on a tripod, our second cameraman and our audio technician had not yet arrived back on site. I approached Sanders's New Hampshire press secretary, Karthik Ganapathy, who was chatting nervously with Julia Barnes, the campaign's state director. I could make out just one snippet of their conversation, and it wasn't especially reassuring: "Oh, he's not going to like this."

I tapped Karthik on the shoulder. "You said 1:45!"

"I know," he replied apologetically. "But we're running early."

"Well, we need some time to set—"

Before the words had finished leaving my mouth, the door to the men's room swung open, and a hunched-over septuagenarian with professorial glasses and an untamed coil of white hair emerged at a pace that suggested he was running late for his office hours. "OK," Sanders said. "Let's get going."

With the implicit understanding that asking him to wait for a few more minutes was out of the question, I said hello and pointed vaguely in the direction of where we wanted him to sit. Sanders lumbered over to the booth in front of our one camera that was already set up, as the other two members of our crew scrambled to get into place. Fortunately, the persnickety candidate was unhappy with the booth. "I don't like this," he said. "It's too low." He didn't add, "What's the deal with booths these days, anyway? Most are too low, like this one. But then some are so high, my feet barely even touch the ground. How hard is it to get a booth that's the right height?" I was fairly certain that was what he was thinking.

I knew enough about the man's sources of irritation at this point not to waste any time trying to kill any initial awkwardness by warming over the conversation with small talk. Fortunately, the video crew somehow managed to get everything set up speedily. As Sanders settled into a chair of agreeable height, I dove right into the interview. In a campaign where perceived authenticity appeared to be the single-most-important quality that a candidate could have, Sanders's utter lack of guile was what stood out most, but he also left no doubt that he'd been around the block, too. When I asked him a fairly innocuous question that I thought might reveal something interesting about the man ("Who is your favorite Republican in Congress?"), Sanders not only refused to take the bait. He scolded the fisherman.

"You want me to destroy somebody's good reputation," he told me in a lecturing voice that was so earnest, I at first thought he was joking. "You want me to have a situation where his opponent will be running thirty-second ads against him. You know what? For that reason, I'm not going to give you the answer."

"Oh, man," was all I could muster in response.

"No, I mean, that's the reality," Sanders continued. "I have friends who I have worked with and who I like, but if I say that, that becomes then a thirty-second ad against that person. That's the reality. So I'll spare that person." I couldn't argue the point. He was right, and that was sad. Sanders had absolutely no interest in trying to become the proverbial "Guy You Want to Have a Beer With," it was safe to say, which was exactly why his young devotees appreciated him so much on a personal level: he wasn't trying to make you like him. Instead, he was just going to level with you.

The biggest news hook out of the interview came when I asked Sanders whether he had begun to think about what it would actually be like to become president of the United States. "Have I started writing my inauguration speech, as opposed to the speech I have to give tomorrow?" he responded. I waited for him to scold me for asking such a preposterous question. Instead, he took his answer in a far different direction than what I'd expected from his setup. "Look. The answer is yes. It is a very sobering thing to be thinking about oneself as president of the United States and the enormous responsibilities that go with that."

If Hillary Clinton had said something like that, it would have been considered a significant gaffe—presumptuous and disrespectful to her opponent. Coming from Sanders, though, it sounded more endearing than arrogant. Aw, he actually thinks he can win! After our interview concluded, Sanders shook hands with several people who were eating in the restaurant—a rare example of a bit of old-school retail campaigning for a man who was regularly drawing thousands of people at his rallies but had little use for glad-handing.

"You have great, smiling eyes," one woman who was sitting at the bar told the candidate, whose eyes might more accurately have been described as glowering, if you'd asked me.

"Wow," Sanders replied. "That's the first time somebody has said that." He agreed to stop for a selfie and then was quickly out the door, still running ahead of schedule.

One candidate who was never in that kind of a hurry was Lindsey Graham. On a Saturday morning in mid-December, I arrived at Spare Time bowling in Manchester to meet him. It was one of those modern joints with strobe lights, music, and a distinct lack of the cigarette odor that permeated the candlepin bowling alleys of my own youth. I was coming from an event across town and arrived fifteen minutes late. Lindsey Graham was right on time, of course, and when I walked in, he was standing patiently beside one of the lanes with a couple of aides, eager to bowl but not in the least bit irritated about my tardiness. I greeted him with a fist bump and paid for our lane, embarrassed enough about making a senator wait around for me that I didn't notice when the woman who was operating our scoreboard listed Graham as "Senator Grant."

"Story of my life," Graham deadpanned. "The most poetic thing about this campaign!"

Eager to get past this rough start, I made a beeline for the bar and ordered myself a beer and Graham a Riesling. There aren't a lot of US senators who would allow a reporter to document them drinking a foreign white wine at a bowling alley, but Graham would never even think to pretend to be a Bud Lite bottle kind of guy. We laced up our shoes, and from his very first shot, he was clearly having a blast. In between knocking down pins, Graham began taking gratuitous potshots at some of his enemies, including Donald Trump, Ted Cruz, and the world's most feared international terrorist organization. "This is the grand plan for ISIL, just mow 'em down," he said just after picking up a spare.

Graham beat me pretty easily in our first game. The man who'd grown up in a bar had played this game before, it was clear, and he was a lot better than me. Regardless, after I finished my first beer, my confidence was up, so I challenged him to a bet for the second game. If he won, I'd buy him a steak dinner. If I won, he'd agree to crash a Trump rally. Graham agreed to my terms immediately and enthusiastically.

After falling behind early, I managed to eke out a narrow victory. We shook hands, and as I saw the roguish smile creep across the senator's face, I wondered whether he'd thrown the game intentionally, just so he'd have an excuse to mess with Trump one last time. Unfortunately, I never had the opportunity to collect my winnings. After failing to generate even the slightest bit of false hope, and no longer able to fund his shoestring campaign, Lindsey Graham dropped out of the race on December 21. Through his final days on the trail, he gobbled up every last crumb of the experience that is campaigning for president in New Hampshire.

CHAPTER 27

As TRUMP CONTINUED TO coast with the holidays approaching, one Republican candidate who looked like he might stumble upon a late surge into contention was Marco Rubio. As a young, eloquent Hispanic first-term senator who also happened to represent the biggest swing state in the Senate, Rubio was in several ways every GOP consultant's dream candidate. His campaign had largely succeeded in its efforts to keep expectations low, and compared to most of his Republican competitors, he hadn't spent much time on the ground in New Hampshire. With the countdown to Primary Day now being measured in weeks rather than months, the Rubio campaign was ready to make its move.

The fundamental problem for Rubio, however, was that though he was many New Hampshire voters' second choice, he had trouble standing out in a field filled with more compelling options. His top selling point was his electability, but even that perceived strength was flimsy when you realized that it was mostly cosmetic. Yes, Rubio could throw a tight spiral and recite Tupac lyrics, but polls consistently showed that he had minimal appeal to younger voters, who vastly preferred the seventy-four-year-old Bernie Sanders because they agreed with him on policy. Rubio's views on almost every major issue made him just another boilerplate Republican, albeit one with fewer wrinkles on his face than most. He was against a woman's right to have an abortion even in cases of rape and incest, and he had folded to the pressures of political expediency when his push for comprehensive immigration reform went awry, coming out in opposition to his own proposals. I got a kick out of Rubio's stock answer to whether he believed man-made climate change was real. Time and again, the Florida senator would glibly point out that the "government can't control the weather." His audiences of deeply conservative, older voters ate it up, but for people who planned to spend another half century or more on the planet, it wasn't an especially convincing line and made Rubio look like the unambiguous opportunist that he was.

Rubio was precisely the kind of mechanical, always-on-message candidate that New Hampshire primary voters had tended to reject over the years more times than not. In the most egregious example of an attempt to position himself as a culture warrior à la Pat Buchanan or Ted Cruz, he released a TV ad in which the gangsta-rap-loving candidate lamented that he and many of his fellow Americans had come to "feel out of place in our own country." Right.

One discerning New Hampshirite who wasn't having it was Erik Eisele, a reporter for the *Conway Daily Sun*, which had a circulation of about 17,000. The decline in influence of local New Hampshire newspapers had never been more apparent than it was in the 2016 campaign. Few of them had the resources to cover many—if any—campaign events, and the coverage was typically superficial at best. Every so often, however, the small-town papers could still cut through on something meaningful, especially when they had a writer as skilled as Eisele.

In a December column, Eisele recounted a recent visit by Rubio to the *Conway Daily Sun*'s newsroom, when the candidate spent about twenty minutes making his case for why he should be president. Eisele, suffice it to say, was unimpressed. "In that time he talked about ISIS, the economy, his political record and his background," he wrote of Rubio's visit. "But it was like watching a computer algorithm designed to cover talking points. He said a lot, but at the same time said nothing. It was like someone wound him up, pointed him towards the doors and pushed play. If there was a human side to the senator, a soul, it didn't come across."

In addition to his devastating assessment of Rubio as a "a man so stuck on script it doesn't even matter when the cameras are off," Eisele's column also elaborated on New Hampshire voters' responsibility to everyone else. "Living in a political environment where only the script makes sense, where the race is about the television audience rather than the general electorate, why deviate?" he wrote of Rubio's strategy of playing it safe. "Those willing to risk off-message interaction also risk alienating. It's too great a risk, and retail politics drops by the wayside as voters are courted only by the millions, not one-by-one. New Hampshire sits as the bulwark against that world." It was a persuasive case for New Hampshire's continued relevance—a special status that was being challenged by the 2016 paradigm, in which the debates and national media coverage were defining the race. New Hampshire still had an opportunity to stand up for itself in the face of this new paradigm. Eisele's piece was a call to arms.

The only problem was that almost no one read it at first. The *Conway Daily Sun* didn't put all of its articles online right away, and this one remained in analog form for a couple of days after it had first appeared in the newspaper. But then, later in the week, a staffer from a rival campaign happened upon a print copy of the Rubio takedown and sent a digital copy of Eisele's piece my way. I immediately posted it on Twitter, along with some accompanying praise, and the collective reaction proved to be in keeping with my own assessment of the column. A lot of observers who'd been following Rubio closely thought it hit the target. On a debate stage in Manchester a little more than a month later, Rubio would demonstrate just how prescient Eisele's biting assessment of him had been.

I remained in New Hampshire pretty much full time until Primary Day on February 9. As the campaign entered the stretch run, it was already clear that just about everyone who had made a prediction had been wrong. On the Democratic side, Bernie Sanders had gone from Dennis Kucinich with a worse haircut to the clear-cut New Hampshire front-runner, and the trajectory had been even more volatile in the GOP race, as potential challengers to Trump continued to flail. As for the ill-tempered Orange Creamsicle himself, Trump seemed scarcely able to believe what was happening, as he pointed out that he could probably stand "in the middle of Fifth Avenue and shoot somebody" without losing any of his support.

My first Trump rally of the new year was at a high school gym in Claremont—a western New Hampshire town of 13,000 people in sparsely populated Sullivan County. I arrived an hour early, and there was already a line out the door of over 1,000 people. It was especially cold—no more than 6°F or 7°F outside, but there they waited without complaint, as if queuing for the bus on a nice spring afternoon. As I continued to be a card-carrying employee of the Huffington Puffington Post, there was no way I was getting a media credential for the event. Still, I made my way to the media entrance, where I was greeted by a friendly campaign volunteer who, wouldn't you know it, couldn't seem to find my name on the list. I began to issue a rather mild protest, when a blonde woman from the Trump campaign stepped in. She seemed to have more authority and was eager to use it.

"If you're not on the list, you can't get in," she told me with a disdainful scowl.

"I'm a credentialed reporter," I said, not letting on that the term was essentially meaningless in this particular context. "Can't I just sign in now, and you can let me in?"

"That's not how it works," she replied.

It wasn't going well, and I wasn't helping matters. "Well, that's how it works with every other campaign, except for this one. Doesn't that strike you as odd?"

We didn't seem to be coming any closer to a resolution, and each of us was appreciating the other a little less by the second. I stepped aside to consider my next half-baked attempt to get in, as a local reporter who was being similarly excluded from the event began to issue his own protest. With nothing to lose, I decided to start shooting video on my iPhone of the confrontation between the Trump staffer and the irritated local reporter who was now being denied access. The Trump aide wasn't especially thrilled. She immediately covered her face with her hands and darted off to the side, as if I had taken aim at her with an Uzi.

"There's no shooting video in here!" she shouted.

"That's not how it works," I replied calmly, pleased with myself.

The Trump staffer turned to the female Secret Service agent standing behind her. "Tell him to stop shooting in here," she demanded.

The Secret Service agent folded her arms across her chest. "It's a public space," she said dispassionately. "He's a journalist, and he has a right to shoot video, if he wants to."

The Trump aide stormed off, and then the Secret Service agent waved me into the event, with the slightest hint of a smile crossing her lips.

On this particular night, Trump brought his A game from the moment he took the stage. He began the festivities by complaining about his microphone, whining that if he continued to be unhappy with the sound mix, he wouldn't pay the vendor who provided the audio equipment. Then, like the old political pro he was, Trump seamlessly transitioned into mocking his supporters who were still waiting outside the venue in the cold. "We've got a lot of people standing out there," he told the crowd who'd made it into the venue. "Should we wait for them? No!" Next, Trump held aloft his big, beautiful numbers from the latest Reuters poll, scribbled out on a piece of scrap paper. He talked about building the big, beautiful wall with the big, beautiful door, and during the call-and-response segment of the sermon when Trump asked who was going to pay for it, the crowd screamed out in unison, "Mexico!"

When Trump got to the part of his act where he began talking about how "politicians are incompetent people," a man standing right

behind me screamed, directly into my ear, "You're right!" His name,
I learned when I spoke with him after the rally, was Daniel, and
he was a volunteer for the Trump campaign. Well over six feet tall
and dressed memorably in a bright-yellow tie, dark green checkered
shirt, and brown sport coat, Daniel had salt-and-pepper hair and an
exceptionally loud voice. And he truly adored Donald Trump.

"Yaay! Yaaay! Yaaaay!" Daniel kept shouting, as Trump hurled
more insults and added to his list of promises. Daniel laughed at all
the right moments, too, like when Trump alluded to the remoteness
of his current venue: "How many people come here when it's not me?
Like nobody."

"You're a winner!" was Daniel's response to that one.

Daniel had jokes, too. When a protester was taken out of the
arena, the exuberant Trump volunteer shouted, "It's Hillary!"

Trump liked that one. "Oh, it's Hillary," the candidate replied
from the stage to much laughter. In response to this brief moment of
direct interaction with his favorite candidate, Daniel began giggling
maniacally. It was at this point that I noticed he was carrying a copy
of *The Art of the Deal* tucked underneath his arm.

For his next act, Trump took a direct turn into minimally coher-
ent conspiracy theory territory, and Daniel was right there with him.
"There is anger in our country because the people are smart," Trump
told the crowd. "The people that are representing them are either dis-
honest, not smart, incompetent, or they have some other agenda that
we don't even know about. And some of these things, you'd think
they have another agenda because you would say things they do, deals
that they make, like the Iran deal. Who would make this deal?"

"A Muslim!" Daniel shouted, again directly into my ear, and
loud enough for just about everyone in the gym to hear.

Trump chuckled.

"What did you say?" the delighted candidate asked, putting his
finger to his ear in feigned confusion. "I didn't hear him."

"A Muslim!" Daniel again screamed gleefully.

"OK, I didn't say it," Trump shot back, extending his tiny hands
as far to his sides as they would stretch. "I didn't say it. I refuse to

get in—oh, I'm supposed to reprimand the man. Who is the man that said that?" Daniel beamed like a third-grader who'd just been singled out for acclaim by the teacher. He waved at Trump.

"I have to reprimand him," Trump deadpanned to Daniel's delight. "How dare you. OK. I've reprimanded him. Now the press can't be angry."

Trump continued his speech with a couple more direct interruptions from Daniel, who now had all the validation he needed to interject at will.

"You're brilliant!" Daniel shouted at one point toward the end of Trump's remarks.

"He says I'm brilliant," Trump replied, just in case anyone hadn't heard, all but waving his ring to be kissed.

After Trump concluded his latest self-deification session, Daniel pushed his way to the front of the crowd that had lined up to try to shake the candidate's hand. Leaning over the rope line, he managed to get close enough to exchange a series of pleasantries with the candidate, who dutifully signed his copy of *The Art of the Deal*. Daniel raised the book in triumph.

As he prepared to stream out of the gym with the last few dozen rally-goers, I tapped Daniel on the shoulder and introduced myself as a reporter. He happily agreed to be interviewed.

I started by asking him why he had shouted about Obama being a Muslim. "I don't know if I should say this," was how Daniel began his response. The humane thing for me to do might have been to cut him off right there and say, "You shouldn't, actually." I let him continue.

"There was a big issue with Iran, and what's happening with our president," Daniel said. "And Obama has talked about his Muslim faith."

"No, he hasn't," I might have said then, "Because he's a Christian." In general, I think it's important for reporters to speak up when someone says something that is factually inaccurate. But this was a taped interview to which I'd be able to add context and correct the record. And so I continued to listen without interjecting.

"And so, Trump has made allusions to whether or not the expansion of Islam has anything to do with our administration right now in the country, in the world," Daniel said. "I mean, I think we can believe in any God we want to believe in."

The thing about it all was that Daniel actually seemed like a nice enough guy—a painfully obsequious and grossly misinformed nice guy, but a nice guy nonetheless. Still, he was the personal embodiment of why Trump was so dangerous. This was a presidential candidate who was extremely skilled at playing on people's ignorance and igniting their worst instincts. He was winning by an especially wide margin in New Hampshire, and people were still underestimating him. It really was scary.

After my interview with Daniel, I pulled up a stool at the Salt Hill Pub in nearby Newport. My expectations were modest, but when I arrived, I was pleasantly surprised to find a cozy brick tavern on the second floor of a historic building. The bartender was even willing to put on the college basketball game that I wanted to watch. I ordered a burger and a pint and turned my attention toward the game. Within seconds, though, my ears were assaulted by the loud rants of a moderately intoxicated young woman. Her extended anti-Trump diatribe was ostensibly for the benefit of her boyfriend and the heavily tattooed firefighter who was sitting on her other side. But it was delivered so loudly and without interruption that there could be no doubt the diatribe was intended to ensure that all eight of us in the pub knew exactly where she stood on the matter. Her commentary was so unrelenting that it would take an additional book to fully do justice to it, but here is a heavily condensed list of her grievances against the Republican front-runner.

- Donald Trump is such an idiot.
- How can anyone deal with Donald Trump?
- Donald Trump is a racist.
- Donald Trump had a cameo in *Home Alone 2*.
- Now she knows what it must've been like during the rise of Hitler.

- Donald Trump sucks.
- You're an idiot if you like Donald Trump.

I was almost finished with my burger by the time the bartender, also a young woman, brought over to the anti-Trump evangelist another drink. Then she dropped the bomb. "I gotta admit it," the bartender said during one of the rare five-second intervals when it was possible for anyone to get a word in. "I'm voting for Trump."

You'd expect that a fight might have followed, or at least a bit of painfully awkward tension. Two people with diametrically opposed views on the most controversial presidential candidate in modern history had been set against one another in a place where a lot of alcohol was being consumed. Instead, something more interesting happened. The young woman who'd been railing against Trump with rare gusto backed down immediately and sought reconciliation.

"Oh, it's not about his supporters," the anti-Trump evangelist assured her pro-Trump bartender. "I'm voting for Bernie, but you do *you*." Meaning the bartender should feel absolutely free to do her own thing without judgment.

The thoroughness of her capitulation was what struck me. Here was an obviously idealistic young woman who disdained everything Trump stood for and wasn't afraid to say so, as long as she wasn't offending anyone. Mere seconds before the bartender made her own views known, she had been comparing Trump to Hitler. Yet when pressed in the mildest way, she was entirely unwilling to stand up for her beliefs. As much as the majority of voters continued to oppose Trump—many of them passionately—the act of supporting him had become normalized. It was nothing to get into an argument over, at least. "You do *you*." With a big assist from a compliant TV news media, Donald Trump had become socially acceptable.

"Yeah, I don't even like Trump," the bartender added, continuing the theme. "I just can't support anyone else that's running."

I stayed for another beer, but as I tried to refocus on the basketball game, I noticed that the two women's conversation had veered completely away from politics. They had moved on to discussing

Titanic, and whether they'd cried the first time they saw it. Politics was just an entertaining diversion—something to take up a few minutes of time on a boring night in a boring town.

A few days later, the *Union Leader* announced that it had been dumped from its partnership with ABC News to host the Republican debate that was scheduled to take place three days before the primary. The Trump campaign had been complaining about the *Union Leader*'s participation in the debate, noting that the paper had been critical of Trump on its editorial page. It was a scurrilous argument, but ratings were on the line, so the Trump campaign got what it wanted.

Via his Twitter account, Trump immediately took credit for having the *Union Leader* "removed" from the debate, as if he had been a bouncer who had escorted off the premises an unruly patron. Newspaper editorial boards had been criticizing candidates for decades without their news divisions suffering repercussions from campaigns, but Trump had all the leverage now. It was another feckless capitulation by a network news division that fully confirmed where the power between the Trump campaign and major journalistic institutions rested. There were a few murmurs of protest in the broader media over ABC's decision, but nothing significant. Everyone just moved on and started talking about something else.

CHAPTER 28

TED CRUZ HADN'T BEEN in New Hampshire much, choosing instead to focus his early state campaign strategy on evangelical-rich Iowa. But as he began to slip past Trump in the Iowa polls, every US senator's least favorite colleague returned to New Hampshire for a mid-January push that—if even modestly successful—might have cemented his status as the full-throated conservative who could win. Cruz was few mainline Republicans' idea of a savior. He may have been a deeply unlikable obstructionist with little chance of winning a general election, but at least he was a conservative who had read books with bigger words than the ones contained within the pages of *The Art of the Deal*. And most important, Cruz might turn out to be the last man standing in the way of the party of Lincoln handing over its reins to a man who believed in charity for none, malice toward all.

New Hampshire Republicans may not have been nearly as religious as their Iowa counterparts, but their devotion to their firearms was at least as intense, and so, a "Second Amendment Rally" outside the Granite State Indoor Range and Gun Shop in Hudson was an appropriate venue for Cruz's return to New Hampshire. It was an icy January afternoon, but the rough-and-tumble Ivy League debate-team champion wanted to show that he wasn't afraid of a little cold weather. Immediately upon arriving at the event, my attention fixated on a guy in a camouflage jacket who was standing directly in front of the press riser. He was packing a black pistol that was holstered out-side his belt at the right hip, clear as the sky above us. Once I saw his gun, it was hard to look away, which—I assume—was precisely the point. Ted Cruz didn't have Secret Service protection, and I had no doubt that this gentleman was ready to spring into action on the off chance that one of the America-hating Communist journalists on the press riser deigned to try something funny. It was a little unsettling.

To begin the program, the resplendently mustachioed former congressman Bob Barr introduced Cruz, and then the gratingly fa-miliar chords of Aaron Tippin's "Where the Stars and Stripes and the Eagle Fly" signaled that it was time for "the next president of the United States" to take the stage. In a reprise of his inaugural New Hampshire visit almost a year earlier, it took Cruz a full minute to emerge. Stage timing was not really his thing. When the candidate finally did appear, something strange happened. Cruz was greeted on stage by a young man carrying a clipboard, who identified himself as belonging to a group called Arm America. Cruz appeared a bit con-fused at first but then allowed the mysterious individual to address the crowd, probably assuming that his staffers had failed to brief him properly on a local politician who was slated to introduce him. The Texas senator continued to stand there, holding his microphone at his chest, as the man with the clipboard addressed the audience.

"What made everyone so weird and sad that they had to come out here?" the unknown man asked.

It was, I had to admit, a fair question. Still, I was as confused about what was happening as Cruz appeared to be.

"Why is everyone so excited about guns?" the man continued. This was definitely not a part of the program. I eyed the guy in the camouflage jacket nervously.

"Sir, who are you?" Cruz asked the man in his best impression of an exceedingly polite and physically ill-equipped law-enforcement officer. He put his hand on the man's shoulder. "Sir, who are you, and what are you doing here?"

There was some laughter in the audience at this point. People must have thought it was some kind of comedy routine from the hokey impression-loving Texan.

"Are you a little bit confused?" Cruz continued, for the first time looking around to see who might help him address the situation. "You're welcome to be in the crowd, but you're not part of this group."

With still no sign of any official security intervention in sight, the man was finally ushered off the stage by someone in Cruz's entourage. Someone shouted something in the crowd. "That's a very good point, I think he did go to Yale," the Princeton and Harvard alumnus Cruz shouted back incongruously. Then, the candidate did what he does best: he turned the situation into an opportunity to delivery a histrionic monologue, fit more for Shakespearean theater than a serious presidential campaign. "It's almost like did he not get the memo, Live Free or Die?" Cruz bellowed. "Now, am I right? That is, in fact, New Hampshire. It's not 'live coddled by a bunch of nanny state liberals, who control every aspect of your life, or die.' It's not 'trust Hillary Clinton and her village to raise your kids and strip them of their liberties or die.'"

This was Ted Cruz the mediocre improv actor, ever unflustered and always looking for the next opportunity to attack the nefarious progressives. But the situation still wasn't in check. Suddenly, another young man with a clipboard jumped up onto the stage and approached Cruz. Again, I looked over at the guy in the camouflage jacket with no little trepidation. I was pretty sure I could see him stretching his trigger finger.

"Oh, we've got another young man who's very confused," Cruz said, walking right over to this interloper. At this point, behind the stage, whatever assortment there was of aides constituting the event's security team, including a lone local police officer, began to scramble into what might generously be referred to as "action." Cruz, for his part, continued to act as if he were unfazed. "Boy," the candidate said, as the second young man was ushered away. "It's almost like the Bernie Sanders guys are scared! The Bernistas are out in force!"

Except for the security scare, Cruz's rally was unremarkable, as the candidate was every bit as robotic as Rubio on the trail. About the most memorable thing that happened once the gate-crashers were cleared was Cruz's attempt to flex his atrophied comedy muscles. It happened suddenly and without warning when he launched into an impression of Ted Kennedy that—as my colleague Will Tooke dutifully noted at the time—sounded more like the Child Catcher from *Chitty Chitty Bang Bang*.

That night, Cruz appeared at a rally at Londonderry High School. It didn't help my frayed nerves that the introductory speaker was none other than Jack Kimball of Facebook conspiracy-spreading fame. When I entered the event, Kimball was shrieking into the microphone. Truly, I couldn't stand being in the room any longer, and so I left.

In fact, I left the state for a few days. The Republican candidates were slated to debate in North Charleston, South Carolina, on January 14, so I boarded a southbound plane to cover the festivities, which were being hosted by Fox Business Network where my wife, Jo, was a correspondent. The night before the debate, Jo and I had dinner at Husk—one of downtown Charleston's excellent restaurants with dishes such as crispy pig's ears and cornmeal-dusted catfish on the menu. We were just about to dig into our southern-fried chicken skins and wood-fired oysters when I heard a familiar voice and then noticed a tuft of feathery blond hair out of the corner of my eye. It was none other than Lindsey Graham.

Graham and his dining companion were seated at the table next to us, and true to form, he moved quickly to turn the white-tablecloth restaurant into a raucous BBQ. The now former presidential candidate regaled us with stories about everything from his New Hampshire travails ("I just had so much fun!") to the time that a dance party broke out when he was endorsed in his first Senate bid by the delightfully incongruous trio of Strom Thurmond, Bob Dole, and the Godfather of Soul, James Brown. I hesitated to bring it up, but I had to ask him about Ted Cruz, who was still looking like a plausible victor in Iowa, even though he'd dipped in the polls there recently, as a result of Trump's ridiculous but relentless questioning of the Canadian-born Cruz's qualification to run for president under the Constitution.

"Iowa?" Graham deadpanned. "All I can say is that Ted better win New Hampshire. That's a home game for him. He's from right next door!"

Just before ordering the table a couple of Bailey's on the rocks, I asked Graham if he was planning to endorse. All he would tell me was to stay tuned. Based on our previous conversations, I thought that he might go with Christie. As it turned out, Graham was willing to overlook his concerns about Jeb Bush's toughness, which he'd previously conveyed to me, and lent the Floridian his official backing the day after the Republican debate on January 15. Graham may have underwhelmed as a candidate, but maybe he could still make an impact in a role that was a far more natural fit for him on the presidential campaign trail: the good-natured sidekick.

Less than a week later, I was back in New Hampshire at the Puritan Backroom in Manchester, where Bush and Graham were doing some meeting and greeting. The two former rivals formed quite a visually striking pair, as they made their way around the main dining room, shaking hands with chicken-tender-chomping lunchtime regulars. At six foot four and five foot seven, respectively, Jeb and Lindsey carried themselves a bit like the center and point guard for a JV basketball team. A couple of happy-go-lucky goofballs who weren't quite ready for the big time but were enjoying the ride, even if they never made the varsity cut. For his part, Bush shook just about every hand in the room before he got to mine.

"Hi, governor," I said, as I extended my arm toward him. The former governor of Florida gave me a look that I can only describe as impish. He gripped my hand. In the split second in which our thumbs were entwined in the customary masculine greeting, he stuck out his index finger and wiggled it into my palm. "Secret handshake," Bush said. And then he walked away. No explanation. Just a secret handshake that Jeb Bush developed on the spot and tried out on a reporter he barely knew. Yes, he was a member of America's most famous political dynasty, but now he had Lindsey Graham as a cohort, and things were going to get a little weird.

Before leaving the Puritan Backroom, I interviewed the two of them briefly, finishing with an open-ended question about the importance of New Hampshire. Unsurprisingly, Graham was roughly 1,000 times more eloquent on the subject than Bush was. For all of his faults as a candidate, the man could talk a dog off a meat wagon. At the end of his soliloquy, I asked him if I could get in one more question: "How do you think Ted Cruz will do in New Hampshire?"

Lindsey's expression lit up. "Well, let's put it this way," he said. "If Ted doesn't win here, he's lost a home game because he's from Canada, right next door."

On cue, he laughed at his own joke in the same manner that he had when he first told it to me in South Carolina. "You can throw a rock and hit Canada from here," Graham continued, turning directly to the camera that was trained on him. "Ted, you better win!" And with that, America's newest, and shortest-lived, political odd couple stepped out the back door of the Puritan Backroom, on their way to try to win over another few dozen voters at yet another town-hall meeting. They didn't know how to do it any other way.

CHAPTER 29

T HE NEXT DAY, I was eating lunch alone at The Bridge Café on Elm Street in Manchester with plans to attend a Bernie Sanders event at Southern New Hampshire University that afternoon when three guys in their twenties took the table next to me. With their button-down shirts and nervous energy, they had the smell of campaign people. And sure enough, as soon as they sat down, they began jabbering to each other about things like "low-intensity supporters" and "GOTV." But they only spent a brief amount of time talking about their work in New Hampshire, as the conversation quickly shifted to a discussion about whether it was fair that Per Se—the jackets-required midtown Manhattan haunt deemed the third-most-expensive restaurant in the world—had recently received a negative review in the *New York Times*. Yes, these low-level political operatives knew their way around a $900 restaurant tab, and it soon became clear, they were working for Hillary Clinton.

When the conversation shifted back to the campaign, they talked about it dispassionately, as if they were neutral observers rather than participants. "Did you see the new Bernie ad?" one of them asked, referring to his Simon and Garfunkel–sound-tracked "America" spot, which had launched that morning.

"No," one of them responded. "Any good?"

"It's a feel-good thing. People really like it."

And then the conversation turned back to New York City restaurants. In my New Hampshire travels, I'd met my share of Hillary supporters who were just as enthusiastic as the most passionate Bernie backers. But not as many of them, I had to say. Like a lot of the people working the ground for Clinton, these particular young organizers didn't have any real skin in the game—no emotional investment in the race. They were a type: well-off strivers, to be exact—kids whose families probably had money and who probably lived in New York or Washington. They had an interest in politics as a career and had gone to work for the person they'd calculated was most likely to become the next president. I hadn't encountered anyone in the state who fit that familiar archetype and was working for Bernie Sanders.

When I arrived at Southern New Hampshire University later that day, the second-floor dining hall banquet room where the event was being held was so packed that Bernie's advance staffers finally relented and opened up the sliding doors that they'd previously kept closed. I spotted a Sanders aide I'd been badgering for another interview with the candidate and began nagging him again. "I'm gonna level with you and tell you something I probably shouldn't," he replied to my appeal. "We're really cautious right now about doing any interviews or setting up anything that could in any way mess up what we've got going."

From a strategic standpoint, Sanders had become the careful candidate, but he was anything but restrained in addressing the crowd. He drew some of the biggest cheers of the event with his call for free college tuition—one of the proposals that he cheekily deemed to be the kind of "radical idea" that was actually common sense, and the thrust of which would subsequently be adopted by Hillary Clinton.

"I will invest in more jobs and education for our young people, rather than more arrests and incarceration," he said, as the fired-up crowd of college kids roared their approval. "And we need major, major reform in our criminal justice system."

Sanders spoke extensively about campaign-finance reform, which had been a signature issue of his campaign from Day One. He'd proven all of his skeptics wrong by raising gobs of money with more individual contributors in the history of American politics, all without an aligned super PAC. His platform included overturning Citizens United through a constitutional amendment, requiring large contributors to fully disclose where their money was going in every circumstance, and getting big money out of politics in general by moving toward a publicly financed system. I knew that many of the people from the nominally nonpartisan New Hampshire Rebellion had gone on to become avid Sanders backers. Although none of the Republicans in the race had been able to harness the issue in the way that John McCain had in 2000, at least he had taken up the charge with full force on the Democratic side and was being rewarded for his efforts.

Sanders wasn't charming, and he wasn't trying to be. Instead, he was passionate, he was authentic, and he had his audience hanging on his every word. Jobs, education, social justice, equal rights—he was hitting on all of the issues that mattered most to the young people on hand who didn't want to hear about incrementalism and compromise and were more interested in paying off their loans than they were in ascending their next rung up the career ladder. The senator from Vermont, it was clear by this point, was almost definitely going to win the New Hampshire primary.

I followed Sanders back to Iowa for the final stretch leading up to the February 1 caucuses. The Bernie rally at the University of Iowa that I attended that Saturday night was one of the most electric events I'd experienced in covering three presidential cycles. There were 3,500 people packed inside the gym, most of them students, and they were loud. Vampire Weekend played. Bernie sang. The atmosphere felt very much like the lead-up to Obama's Iowa victory that had launched him to the presidency eight years earlier.

The next morning, I stayed in Iowa City for a Ted Cruz rally at the muddy Johnson County Fairgrounds. It would have been impossible to dream up a political event more diametrically opposite to the optimistic, youth-propelled Sanders rally. Almost everyone in the audience at the Cruz event had gray hair. Instead of Vampire Weekend, Phil Robertson of *Duck Dynasty* fame spoke. So did Glenn Beck, for about forty-five minutes, in fact. It felt like 2009 all over again, and the only thing missing was the infamous chalkboard that had helped to launch Beck to fame during the height of his Tea Party–era paranoia. He rambled on topics ranging from George Washington's military strategy to how, Beck believed, there's only one way to deal with a "bad Muslim." "An Islamist needs to be killed," he said in a straightforward manner, as if it should have been obvious to everyone. A man in the back of the room who'd been quiet throughout the proceedings to that point took this cue as an opportunity to insert himself into the proceedings. "Allah does not exist!" the man shouted. "Islam is a cult!"

This was what the race in Iowa had boiled down to. Unlike almost everywhere else in the country, where Trump had them in his pocket, Ted Cruz had secured the rabid right-winger vote. On the heels of his unrivaled ground game—an advantage that is typically far more important in a caucus environment than it is in a primary—Cruz ended up winning a surprising three-point victory over Trump, who'd been favored going into Caucus Day. Sanders and Clinton finished in a dead heat, with Clinton barely edging the Vermonter out by less than half a percentage point for some rather dubious bragging rights heading into New Hampshire, to which I returned on February 2.

The final sprint between the Iowa caucuses and the New Hampshire primary has earned a reputation as the most exciting few days in politics. The national media have long treated it as such, with every big-name anchor parachuting into downtown Manchester. For journalists who'd actually spent a lot of time in New Hampshire beforehand, this quadrennial ritual breeds some inevitable resentment directed toward the know-nothing newcomers. The best way that I'd learned to handle the situation was to dial back my own intensity level somewhat, just as everyone around me was dialing up theirs. And what better way to bring down the blood pressure, I thought, than to attend a Jeb Bush event?

The Margate Hotel in Laconia was an hour's drive from the Manchester media beehive and looked to be just about a half century past its prime. By the time I arrived at the hotel's clammy basement conference room, Bush had already begun speaking. Dressed in his beige half-zip sweater, which he wore almost every day on the trail, he was in the middle of running through what passed as his "stump speech"—a meandering laundry list of policy proposals and general observations that he still hadn't managed to tighten up into a compelling narrative after about a year of practice. The room was flat-out depressing. A New Hampshire–style barbecue—boxes of Dunkin' Donuts munchkins and coffee—sat untouched on a folding table off to the side of the folding chairs, where an array of unanimated senior citizens sat quietly. The carpeting was yellow with a floral pattern that looked like it came from the 1930s, and the wallpaper was funeral-home gray.

Just as I took my seat, Bush was saying something about "a servant's heart." I managed to stay awake until the end, when the now long-shot candidate went on a surprising little riff that made me sit up in my chair. "I trust you entirely," he told the crowd. "I totally trust you. The pundits have already written the story. They're already saying it's over. They're talking about this in the past tense. That's not true. You all have a chance to decide next Tuesday how you want our country to look." He then "humbly" asked for their support before saying something that was objectively a bit nutty: "I honestly believe you're looking at the next president of the United States."

Politicians project unwarranted optimism about their own dim chances all the time. In Bush's case, however, I believed that he believed it. And that was remarkable. He was a smart guy. By what objective measure could he possibly think that he was going to win this thing? After the event, I drove back to Concord with my friend Tim, Bush's communications director, and asked him this very question. He didn't answer me.

"I'm in a bad place," Tim said instead. I knew that like everyone who worked for Jeb, Tim genuinely liked and respected the guy. And so this slow, painful death of his candidacy was particularly hard to deal with, even as he put on a brave face. Making the situation even more painful for the Bush camp was the recent rise of Rubio, Bush's one-time protégé. "Marco has my goat," Tim told me. "My goat lives in Marco's bedroom."

The other thing that had Tim's goat was the media. Earlier in the day, reporters had jumped all over Bush after he'd asked the room to clap for him. How pathetic! But what the short video clip that was making the rounds on cable news that day didn't show were the members of the crowd at the event (a rarity for Bush) who *had* clapped for the candidate mere seconds before. Bush shouldn't have said, "Please clap"—there was no question about that. But if any other candidate had said the same thing, it wouldn't have been presented by the media as abject humiliation. With his poll numbers still anemic, the collective urge to highlight Bush's inadequacies as a candidate and to mock him for his ineptitude on the trail was too much for the press to resist. The media loved to pile on against the guy who was supposed to win it all but hadn't managed to get off the ground. Trump, meanwhile, was getting away with rhetorical murder on a daily basis.

So, to a lesser extent, was Rubio. That very night, the Florida senator had complained that he was sick and tired of President Obama always "pitting people against each other," citing the president's recent decision to speak at a mosque in Maryland as an example of the divisiveness that he just couldn't stand. "Look at today," Rubio said. "He gave a speech at a mosque. Oh, you know, basically implying that America is discriminating against Muslims."

The charge, of course, was entirely nonsensical. How was Obama's outreach to a religious minority an attempt to pit people *against* each other? Yet Rubio was paying no political price for spewing such nonsense.

After another forty-five minutes or so of venting from Tim, we finally made it to the Barley House in downtown Concord. In the dining room, Bush's top strategist, Dave Kochel, was already seated at a table with Trent Wisecup, who was leading the campaign's debate prep team. After Wisecup ordered a Bud Lite, I asked him how preparation for the final debate was going and posed him a question I'd been wondering about for some time. "What if Jeb went right at Trump, as hard as he can?" I asked.

Although the first couple of debates had featured some memorable confrontations between Trump and Bush, the latter candidate had in more recent face-offs sought to lay off the front-runner, in an attempt to remain above the fray. It hadn't been working at all, so I was curious about why he wouldn't just throw a Hail Mary and at least try to stick a needle in his tormenter's eye on his way out the door.

"That's what I think he should do," Tim said. "Present Trump as a loser who sits around in Trump Tower and tweets insults all day."

Wisecup said that he agreed, and that this was indeed the plan. It was just a matter of whether Jeb could execute it.

"I have an idea," Kochel chimed in. "If Jeb were to punch Trump in the face and get arrested, I'm pretty sure he would win the New Hampshire primary."

I'm not sure he was wrong. Alas, we never got to find out.

The next night, I checked out a Rubio town hall at the Fisk Elementary cafeteria in Salem. There were easily three hundred people there, and from the moment Rubio started speaking, I was surprised by how good he was. He still exhibited his machine-gun-fire, too-many-cups-of-coffee style, but in this setting it was more controlled—and far more effective than I'd seen in his previous New Hampshire events. Rubio played all the hits without sounding quite as rehearsed as he once had, and the crowd loved it. He still wasn't better at this than Christie was, but the New Jersey governor had by this time faded into near obscurity, thanks in no small part to Rubio's super PAC, which had been taking a shovel to Christie's record since his early December rise and had scarcely let up since. With Trump threatening to destroy the GOP as we knew it, Rubio's closing message, which had previously seemed uninspiring, now sounded on point. "No one running for president in the Republican Party can unify this party faster or better than I can," he said. "And I will."

With just five days to go until the primary, I was now convinced that this argument would resonate with GOP voters who wanted a variety of things from their ideal candidate but were united by their mutual desire to find someone who could actually win the thing. No, Rubio wasn't going to win over many of the apolitical waitresses and taxi drivers who'd never voted in a primary before and were going to come out in droves for Trump. But he didn't have to. Second place would probably be good enough to consolidate the anti-Trump forces heading into South Carolina and beyond.

For Christie, the dynamic couldn't have been more dissimilar. It'd been a couple of weeks since I'd seen him on the stump, during which time he had continued to fade into near irrelevance. The last I'd spoken to him was in Hooksett at Robie's Country Store—one of the iconic retail campaign stops in New Hampshire, with walls filled floor to ceiling with presidential primary paraphernalia. My impression of him during our interview there was that I was speaking to a defeated man. Christie was still saying the right words: he had every confidence in the people of New Hampshire, no one had been working the retail circuit harder than he had been, he was going to surprise some people on Primary Day. All of that stuff. But unlike the Pollyannaish Bush, Christie's demeanor was that of a man who knew he was going to lose badly. What I didn't know at the time was that he was planning to bring someone else down with him.

The final New Hampshire debate began inauspiciously with a botched candidate introduction that memorably featured a baffled Ben Carson-in-headlights declining to walk to his podium when instructed to do so. But the debate would end up joining the annals of New Hampshire primary history for a different reason when moderator David Muir asked Rubio to defend his readiness to ascend to the presidency, given charges from his opponents that he was an unaccomplished first-term senator. After Rubio delivered a meandering initial response, Christie cut in to challenge his younger opponent's leadership credentials directly before the Florida senator twice reverted to his canned talking point about how "Barack Obama knows exactly what he's doing." When Christie calmly pointed out that Rubio was reverting to a "memorized twenty-five-second speech" to make his point, Rubio repeatedly failed to pivot, in the end asking his audience five separate times to dispel with the notion that Barack Obama didn't know what he was doing. Through it all, Christie took apart his younger opponent with devastating, prosecutorial precision, noting that Rubio's reliance on his canned line was just the kind of crutch he was able to use on the Senate floor, whereas real leaders had to actually govern. When Rubio tried desperately to push back one more time, Christie offered one final putdown for his flustered opponent. "It gets very unruly when he gets off his talking points," the authoritative New Jerseyan said. Even at the time, it was pretty clear that this moment wasn't going to be enough to boost Christie's candidacy toward a strong finish in New Hampshire, but it was quite enough to mortally wound Rubio's entire candidacy.

The Florida senator would go on to finish in fifth place in New Hampshire three days later, just barely falling short of Jeb Bush's fourth-place finish but besting his tormenter. Christie, I found out later, was especially pleased with his own performance, telling a group of aides in private that if he couldn't save his own candidacy, at least he'd single-handedly taken down a pretender who—in his view—was woefully unprepared to be president. As we would all see later that month via his irresponsible, embarrassingly fawning, and legacy-defining endorsement of Donald Trump, there might also have been a part of Christie that knew he'd just accomplished something else that might breathe new life into his political career: helping to secure Trump's path to the GOP nomination.

The day before the primary, it snowed. If the storm had come just a few hours later, it just might have depressed turnout a bit, boosting the slim possibility of a surprising result. But really, it probably wouldn't have made any difference—not in hard-bitten New Hampshire, and especially not in a year when the collective level of interest in the campaign was as high as it ever was. From public polling and the posturing of both Democratic campaigns it was clear that Bernie Sanders was going to win big. The only question was how big. On the Republican side, it appeared almost equally certain that Trump would triumph with a lot of room to spare. Then again, his numbers heading into the Iowa caucuses had turned out to be inflated. Maybe there really was some kind of Trump bubble that would at least make things a little more interesting. The last remaining hope that sanity might prevail (and it was a big stretch to use the word "hope" in this case) was John Kasich, who had surged into second place in most of the final New Hampshire polls.

I caught my last pre-primary glimpse of Kasich at the Searles School and Chapel in Windham. On my way there, I drove past two spun-out cars and wondered whether anyone would really turn out in these conditions just to see the long-winded governor of Ohio one more time. When I arrived at the venue, my question was answered. The place was so jam-packed that I couldn't even get inside. I spotted a Kasich advance staffer heading toward a back room and followed him in. Several other aides were mulling around there, waiting for the candidate to finish the event so that he could shoot an interview with MSNBC. Among them were former New Hampshire GOP chairman Fergus Cullen, longtime operative Tom Rath, and John Weaver, Kasich's top strategist. Staring at his smartphone intently, Weaver wanted to know what I was hearing.

"Probably nothing that you're not hearing," I replied truthfully.

He told me that they were feeling "very good" about second place and that it wasn't entirely crazy to think that Kasich could even knock off Trump for first. To me, that did sound entirely crazy, in fact. But I didn't say that. These guys knew they were in for a big day, and I saw no particular reason to diminish the sugar high of a long-shot campaign that had little chance at long-term success but was on the cusp of perhaps its one shining moment.

After wrapping up the town-hall meeting and sitting down for his interview with MSNBC, I asked Kasich's press secretary, Chris Schrimpf, if I could get in a couple of quick questions before they headed out. Chris was fine with it, and the typically moody Kasich—who happened to be especially cheerful on this anticipation-filled afternoon—was happy to oblige. First, I asked him about the midnight vote in Dixville Notch that would take place in just a few hours. He had been the only candidate to hold an event there this cycle and had talked to all nine Republican voters there. Did the tradition still matter?

"Yeah, they all came in," Kasich said. "It was a snowstorm, and I was on my way to go to my daughter's sixteenth birthday. It took me seven hours to get from Dixville in the snowstorm all the way to Columbus, Ohio, so I could have dinner on my daughter's sixteenth birthday. I'll never forget it."

I was recording his words, but I wasn't really listening to them. What struck me was not what Kasich was saying but rather how impossibly relaxed he seemed. I'd been covering him for months and had never seen a politician who was more consistently comfortable in his own skin; but still, this was next-level Zen. The primary was just hours away, and the man who had bet his entire campaign on New Hampshire was just shooting the breeze with me without a care in the world. When I asked him how he was capable of being so relaxed, given the circumstances, Kasich seemed taken aback by my question.

"Well, look, this is not like your life ends," he said, showing off his penchant for taking a mundane political question into an existential place. "I mean, life is just beginning. No, it's true. You can see it. I'm having so much fun. Everybody is."

But, really, I reminded him again. The *New Hampshire primary* was tomorrow. You know, the thing that he'd spent hundreds of hours of that life trying to win? Remember? This was a big deal. Wasn't it?

"Hey, you know what, when you're happy, when you're a uniter, when you cut through with a positive message, I love to think it'll pay off," he said. "And I guess the reason I'm relaxed is I know what this ground game is all about. And look, I feel good about everything. It's been a great experience. I have no regrets. None."

I was floored by the sanity of it all. There was a lot not to like about John Kasich as a candidate, a reality to which he himself would sometimes allude. Still, here was a man who was truly at peace—the walking, talking antithesis of Trump's score-settling, ego-inflating approach to life and campaigning. For all of Kasich's faults, his attitude about the journey was profoundly refreshing. But would the Republican primary voters of New Hampshire see that way? Well, 15.8 percent of them did—good enough for a distant second-place finish. Kasich's showing amounted to a mere blip in the historic record amid Donald Trump's first victory on his once unthinkable march to the 2016 Republican presidential nomination. Once again, New Hampshire proved ultimately to be an accurate indicator of the national mood, which was fed up with political norms and ready to try something dramatically different. National politics had become detached from rank-and-file voters' emotional realities until the 2016 New Hampshire primary came around and rocked the system to its core.

CHAPTER 30

━━━━━━

ROM THE MOMENT I arrived just before the festivities began,
nothing about Jeb Bush's primary night party at Manchester
Community College on February 9, 2016, was tense. There
was a cash bar, some political reporters tweeting about early returns
in bellwether towns, and a bunch of Bush supporters trying their
hardest to care about whether their candidate would finish in third,
fourth, or fifth place. For Jeb, it was over, as it had been for a long
time. It all felt like a formality—a Tuesday-night awards banquet
for the lone senior graduating from the high school volleyball team.
There would be speeches. There would be polite applause. There
would even be gag gifts—in this case, cheap paper fans that said,
"Jeb! Number One Fan." This was February in New Hampshire—no
one wanted a paper fan, but his supporters pretended that they did.
That's what people do when they're going through the motions.

On some level though, Jeb still believed. The man who had a
$100-million head start over every other candidate in the race had
underwhelmed to such an extent that "better than expected" now

meant anything above 10 percent in New Hampshire. But as long as he beat Rubio, he still had some hope to win his "lane" of becoming the establishment-friendly Republican in the race. The problem for Jeb, and everyone else not named Donald Trump, was that "lanes" didn't really exist—not in 2016, at least. It was just Trump versus Everyone Else, and Everyone Else couldn't get it together.

Unlike most states, which report election results by county, New Hampshire announces the vote totals in each of its 221 towns and thirteen cities. Sure enough, Trump was winning just about everywhere, and by big margins. Just a few minutes after I started poring through the numbers, I glanced up at the wall-mounted TV inside the multipurpose conference room and saw that CNN was already declaring victory for Trump. Bernie Sanders, meanwhile, was demolishing the expectations that had been set for a solid victory of his own. He would go on to defeat Hillary Clinton by twenty-two points. Though this result had not been unexpected, it was truly astonishing from the standpoint of where the Democratic race in New Hampshire had begun.

I was still slumped in my green chair, attempting to discern in what order the candidates would finish behind Trump, when Ryan Williams, a Republican operative whom I'd known for a long time, approached. A former aide to Mitt Romney in both of his presidential campaigns, Ryan had deep New Hampshire ties. He gave me a nod and reached for his phone, which he'd been charging in the outlet next to my chair. Then he read aloud the text message he'd just received from a prominent New Hampshire Republican figure, whose name I told Ryan I'd omit from this book, in order to protect the innocent.

Here, in its entirety, is what the text message said: "Fuck. Fuck. Fuck. Fuck."

That's when it really hit me. As expected as the Republican primary results had been, this was a truly historic moment for the country. Donald Trump had won the New Hampshire primary. He'd won easily, in fact, and so had Bernie Sanders—albeit with a far more uplifting posture. In tandem, their victories signaled a massive change in American politics. When it came to Trump, the

Republican "establishment"—whatever that meant at this point—had first laughed at him, then dismissed him, then opposed him, and then tried to figure out a way to deal with the plurality of GOP voters who had backed him. They'd failed in every effort. The traditional power brokers who had always maintained order within the GOP had proven themselves irrelevant. And on the Democratic side, even though his New Hampshire victory would mark the high point of Bernie Sanders's campaign, the ramifications of his win when it came to affecting the eventual nominee's ideological positioning and governing agenda were equally profound. New Hampshire was the first real sign of how weak a Democratic nominee Hillary Clinton would end up becoming.

Later that night, I caught up with the South Carolina senator Lindsey Graham backstage at Bush's event, where he greeted me, of course, with a fist bump. I reminded my favorite former candidate about something he'd said a few weeks earlier: that having to choose between Donald Trump and Ted Cruz (the surprisingly strong third-place finisher in New Hampshire) would be the equivalent of picking between being poisoned or shot. So which did he prefer now? Graham thought about it for a moment. "Well, you're still dead," he said, upon consideration. "I guess one is slow. One is quick. In my case, I'd rather just have it done."

Like pretty much all of his Senate colleagues, Graham loathed Cruz, but he detested Trump. Although he was always willing to talk, I could tell that Graham wasn't eager to continue this particular conversation, given the circumstances of the moment. He wanted to get back to talking to Jeb, who was—in his typically endearing manner—jumping up and down and waving at me from his position at the other end of the room backstage. So I said good-bye to Lindsey, offering one more parting fist bump. "It gets better for Jeb in South Carolina," Graham assured me. Uh-huh.

"This campaign is not dead," Bush declared from the stage a few minutes later, to cheers from his mostly ambivalent supporters. Actually, it was. Bush had, after all, convinced only about 11 percent of the New Hampshire Republican primary electorate to vote for him—31,310 people in all—not quite one-third of the votes that Trump had gotten. And the terrain was looking even worse on the horizon.

Trump's monumental win, executed with a message that was as brazenly mendacious and manipulative as anything in modern political history, had taken place in the state that was supposed to be the sober anecdote to Crazy Uncle Iowa. Had I just been suckered into spending all of this time venerating an American political institution that didn't deserve its high station? I felt sick. Then I started thinking back to the beginning.

It was then that I realized the broader context in which Trump's New Hampshire victory has to be considered. It wasn't an accident or a coincidence that two of the unlikeliest victors in the history of the New Hampshire primary—Trump and Bernie Sanders—pulled off their feats in the same year. Over the primary's history, New Hampshire voters have often sought to send a message that Washington was failing them. But in 2016, that message was delivered via bullhorn pressed directly against the party leadership's eardrums. Whenever I struck up conversations with people in New Hampshire in the weeks leading up to Primary Day and asked them whom they planned to vote for, one of the most common answers I received in response was this: "I'm not sure. Either Bernie or Trump." That a demagogue with some neo-fascist tendencies and a proud democratic socialist were often culling from the same crop of voters in New Hampshire should tell you everything you need to know about the level of people's frustration with the political system in 2016. Trump and Sanders may have been diametrically opposed when it came to their fundamental philosophies, but they were more or less the same when it came to their overriding message (the system is rigged against you) and delivery method (loud and aggressive old men who were skilled at making the case for radical change and weren't interested in making new friends).

"You're getting this wrong." This was the underlying message that the voters of New Hampshire sent to the people who controlled the levers of political power in 2016, and there is no doubt that it was received. On the Democratic side, Hillary Clinton began sounding more and more like Bernie Sanders with each passing week after the primary, emphasizing that she was right there with him on issues of systematic economic inequality, even if she continued to have some trouble playing this role authentically. Ultimately, she could never make the case as persuasively as he had.

In 2016, New Hampshire voters did what they've been doing for the last century. As usual, they turned out in large numbers (a record-breaking 287,653 people voted in the Republican primary and 254,780 in the Democratic primary) and with the earnestness with which they have always approached the task. On the GOP side, 35 percent of them voted for a man I consider to be a disgrace. But Trump's 2016 success doesn't invalidate the underlying principles that have made the New Hampshire primary work for a century. Trump may not have campaigned "the New Hampshire way." He didn't pretend to care about looking into people's eyes and answering all their questions in their living rooms. But as New Hampshire radio host Arnie Arnesen pointed out to me, he'd already gone one stage further: he'd been in their living rooms for years, by way of their TV sets. Trump was a unique candidate and thankfully, we're unlikely to see another quite like him. In marking his ascent as someone who could actually win the presidency, New Hampshire once again proved itself as a belwether of the national mood.

Is New Hampshire a good way of beginning the process of picking presidents? Yes, I think that it is. At the very least, to paraphrase Winston Churchill, it's the worst method, except for all of the others. A national primary would be more purely democratic, but there is no doubt that this method would make it even easier for well-funded front-runners to triumph without giving the proverbial "little guy" (i.e., Bernie Sanders) any shot at all. As the last half century of presidential campaigns have demonstrated time and again, money is important for running successfully in New Hampshire, but it's not nearly as central to victory as it is in bigger states with more expensive media markets. And that's why the idea of implementing a rotating system for determining states' positions on the calendar each cycle also falls short of what we have now.

As we've seen with the introduction of new early voting states, such as Nevada, where only a tiny slice of the electorate bothers to show up on Caucus Day, there is something to be said for the accumulated expertise and habit that New Hampshire has developed in going first for so long. New Hampshire voters really do take their roles in the process more seriously than voters do just about anywhere else. They pay attention. And perhaps far more important, they make the candidates pay attention. As Steve Duprey put it to me, "It's good for them to be humbled, and New Hampshire does it."

There is a sense of community in New Hampshire that doesn't exist anymore in a lot of places in the United States, and during primary season, that community centers around politics. New Hampshire voters have real conversations with each other about the candidates, and not just on Facebook and Twitter. John H. Sununu describes the dynamic as "social media without the electronics." It's still that way in the second decade of the twenty-first century.

Will the New Hampshire primary survive? There are some powerful forces lined up against it. Bill Gardner won't be secretary of state forever, prominent national leaders from both parties have spoken out against it, and state law isn't bulletproof in the face of national outrage drummed up effectively. When I asked him before the 2016 primary whether he feared that New Hampshire might one day lose its cherished first-in-the-nation status, Gardner didn't feign certainty. "I'm always concerned about it," he said. But the primary *should* survive. The 2016 campaign confirmed its worth.

CHAPTER 31

I

T'S PROBABLY A FOOL'S errand to attempt to highlight just one
particular moment in the primary's history as being emblematic of its very essence. But on one weekend in mid-November
2007, everything came to a head for the quintessential New Hampshire candidate. The setting was befitting of a nineteenth-century
Russian novel or perhaps a castle in the forest in a Grimm brothers
fairy tale—an ideal venue for John McCain. Since he had become a
fixture in the state more than eight years earlier, the Arizona senator
had favored the isolated New Hampshire locales that fed his romantic spirit, so the Balsams Grand Resort Hotel was right up his alley.

Darkness had long since fallen over Dixville Notch, as the season's first snowflakes descended upon the late-fall landscape. Inside
the great hotel's dining room, not all that much had changed since
the place opened in 1875. As a small group of reporters sat around
the banquet table with the candidate for a three-course meal, bow-
tied waiters filled and refilled wine glasses to try to keep up with
the flowing conversation. As was usually the case with McCain, the

dinner was entirely on the record. It was an almost unheard-of allowance to the fourth estate, especially with alcohol on the table, at
a time when the fast-acting virtual quicksand then known as "the
blogosphere" had ensured that any ill-conceived, off-the-cuff remark
from a presidential hopeful would become national news within
hours. McCain wasn't worried about any of that. He was a candidate
with nothing to lose—he had been acting like one, at least.

After the wine-infused members of the press had, once again,
run out of questions to ask him, the candidate retreated to the historic
Ballot Room, where the traditional midnight vote was held. Neil Tillotson, who had regaled McCain with his story of meeting Teddy
Roosevelt eight years earlier, had since passed away. But all current
seventeen Dixville Notch voters were there to see the former fighter
pilot make his case for the 2008 primary. And that's exactly what
he did, with the focus and intensity of someone speaking to 17,000
people instead of seventeen, taking every one of the voters' questions.
That night, the candidate rested easily with the knowledge that he'd
won over another handful of New Hampshire primary voters.

With the Thanksgiving holiday approaching and the fresh
snowfall making travel difficult, McCain and his staff decided to
stay an extra day at the Balsams, at the end of which McCain pre-
sided over a more intimate dinner in a quiet corner of the grand dining room with a small group of New Hampshire aides, influential
supporters, and close friends. Everyone at the table was buoyed by
the momentum that McCain had started to generate, yet most of
them saw one major problem that would continue to hold him back:
Iraq. For months, he had been promoting and defending President
Bush's troop surge—a last-ditch effort to turn the tide of the war
against the insurgency. The plan was extremely unpopular with the
American public at the time, about two-thirds disapproving Bush's
handling of the war. But McCain was unequivocally on board with
the surge. Two months earlier, when the cash-strapped candidate
had launched his "No Surrender" bus tour, *The Daily Show*'s Jon
Stewart suggested that a more appropriate moniker might be "John
McCain's Traveling House of Stubbornness."

The No Surrender tour had garnered some desperately needed media attention but not much movement in the polls. The act of supporting anything having to do with Bush and Iraq remained a toxic posture, even for many Republican voters who were growing tired of a war that appeared to be increasingly unwinnable. At some of his town-hall events around the state, McCain attracted more protesters than he did participants.

Some of the candidate's confidants at the dinner weren't much more optimistic about the surge's prospects than the general public was. As the snow continued to fall outside the Balsams, Steve Duprey and former New Hampshire congressman Chuck Douglas led the charge to try to get McCain to reconsider his position on the surge. Not only were they concerned, like most of the country was, that Iraq was already lost. They also believed that even if the surge did work, the effects of any military success wouldn't be felt politically by the time the January primary rolled around. Everyone at the table was just looking out for his best interests, they explained. He had to at least stop talking about it so much. "People are sick and tired of Iraq," one of his advisers said, summing up the consensus view in the room.

McCain listened quietly until all the people present had added everything they intended to say. And then he took his turn to weigh in. "Look, I believe the surge is right," he said. "And if I can't convince the people of New Hampshire the surge is right, I shouldn't be president. I'd rather lose a campaign than lose a war."

They never attempted to change his mind again.

It was August in the desert, but on this particular Thursday, the thermostat was expected to top off at a merciful 97°F—practically New Hampshire–like conditions compared to the highs of 107°F and 108°F that were in the Phoenix-area forecast for later in the week. Shortly before 10:00 a.m., I joined about two hundred Humana Pharmacy employees who were seated in neat rows inside a sterile conference room at their company headquarters in Glendale. Moments before the guest of honor was to arrive, a company representative stood at the front of the room and asked the younger-skewing crowd to stand and clap when he entered—a somewhat desperate plea that you'd rarely if ever see at a New Hampshire political event but one that was not out of place in the context of the low-octane Arizona primary. Although the employees obeyed the decree, there were few signs of sincere enthusiasm when John McCain entered the room, dressed in a crisp suit and tie. The candidate, who was seeking his sixth Senate term, nonetheless appeared in good spirits just a couple of weeks shy of his eightieth birthday.

"After I ran for president, I slept like a baby," McCain said by way of warming up the staid, heavily air-conditioned room. "Slept two hours, woke up, cried."

The line killed, as it always did. It was vintage McCain: wry, self-deprecating, a little bit dark, and considerably well worn. After making one of his patented off-key Betty Ford Clinic jokes, McCain next tried out the one about how he'd begun his career all the way back in the Coolidge administration before segueing into the yarn about the Irish twins who got so drunk together at a bar in Boston that they failed to recognize each other. Then there was the one about the two prisoners in Illinois. "One says, 'The food was better in here when you were governor.'" The crowd now on his side, the jokes kept coming, as McCain offered a memorably lighthearted response to a man who thanked him for his military service in Vietnam. "By the way, it doesn't take a lot of talent to get shot down," he said. "I'm one of those for whom the number of landings doesn't match the number of takeoffs."

It was McCain's distinct way of disarming in the most charming way imaginable Donald Trump's witless criticism of his war record in Vietnam. As I sat in the back corner, the only print reporter in the room, I was impressed by the performance. The man was still giving it his all. In a sense, he had to. McCain's 2016 bid was not exactly going seamlessly. His November faceoff against Democratic congresswoman Ann Kirkpatrick was still almost three months away. By necessity, McCain remained focused for the time being on fending off a less serious but still menacing GOP primary challenge from Kelli Ward, a former state senator and avowed Donald Trump acolyte, who dabbled in wondering open speculation about the chances that the soon-to-be octogenarian senator might die in office. For McCain's part, fending off Ward while preparing to face Kirkpatrick meant walking a shaky political tightrope. On the one hand, he'd have to try to find a way to maintain the maverick image that had been central to his identity and recognize the extent to which Hispanics—a critical voting bloc in Arizona—would rally against Trump in a year when the Democratic presidential nominee was vying seriously to win the state for the first time in two decades. Meanwhile, McCain needed to avoid turning off the rank-and-file Republican voters who supported the unlikely 2016 GOP presidential nominee. It was perhaps the most difficult balancing act of McCain's political career. True to form, the candidate made clear that he was in on the joke. "If there's anyone here who can predict this election, please raise your hand because I sure as hell can't," McCain said. Then his voice lowered into a barely distinguishable mutter, as he looked down at his feet. "I just know we're going to make America great again, and it's going to be huge," he mumbled.

He was being sarcastic, of course, but his frustration over Trump's successful takeover of the party that the Arizona senator himself had led eight years earlier was palpable. I took it as a given that McCain harbored abject contempt for Trump. And yet, he was still supporting him, albeit as halfheartedly as humanly possible. In so doing, however, McCain risked openly abandoning his reputation for being a man of unbending principle, no matter the political cost. It was an aura that had been solidified during his two New Hampshire primary campaigns, even as it was rightly challenged in other contexts. Why, I wondered, would he want to jeopardize the esteemed status that he had worked so hard to build for the sake of winning the dubious prize of getting to spend another six years in Washington?

Here in Arizona, he still had an audience, both for his jokes and for his speeches that lambasted President Obama over health-care reform and foreign policy, but there was very little of the give-and-take that he loved so much about campaigning in New Hampshire. After opening up the floor "to any questions or comments or insults you might have," McCain took just two questions from the crowd—a measly allowance that would have been an inconceivable slight during either of his New Hampshire primary campaigns. But it wasn't that *he* wanted to cut the event short. It was just that only two people had raised their hands to query the candidate. This was Glendale, after all, not Goffstown, and this particular audience had to get back to work. Their bosses, no doubt, had little desire for them to waste the afternoon engaging in any kind of prolonged political discussion.

Back in New York the following week, I received a call one morning from McCain, who was traveling between campaign events in Arizona. His disdainful rendering of how Trump was going to "make America great again" was still fresh in my mind. Even if Trump didn't win in November, I asked, did McCain fear that Trump had effectively killed the New Hampshire primary? By winning the primary and using that victory as a springboard to the nomination, had this nakedly opportunistic purveyor of grievance and nutty conspiracy theories proven that New Hampshire isn't really so special after all? No, McCain answered right away, explaining that he viewed the 2016 Republican New Hampshire primary results as an aberration, laying the blame squarely at the feet of the people who once composed his base: the media—cable news commentators, in particular.

"Obviously, Trump turned the standard procedure of political campaigning on its head," McCain said. "I think you cannot overstate the importance of the media love-in with him. Many of them, like Morning Joe, who now have turned completely against him, gave him millions of dollars of free airtime. You couldn't purchase the airtime he got with sixteen or seventeen opponents, sucking all of the oxygen out of the room, while Morning Joe Scarborough and others slobbered all over him every single morning and every night. I just don't see that happening in the future. I think that in 2020, we will go back."

Even though he was at the moment in the middle of his tough campaign in Arizona, true to form, McCain was eager to reflect on his past triumphs in New Hampshire. I asked him if he believed there truly was something unique about the character of the Granite State voter. "I do," McCain said without hesitation. "I think it is a deep awareness of the importance of their individual vote that then leads them to view their decision with utmost seriousness."

"Stop me if you've heard this one before," he added quickly, as he went into the joke about Mo Udall campaigning in New Hampshire ("What do you think about Mo Udall for president?" "I don't know, I've only met him twice."). In spite of his directive, I didn't stop him. Neither did I stop him when he began to tell me the story about his visit to Dixville Notch during the 2000 campaign, when Neil Tillotson told him that a run-in with Teddy, not Franklin Roosevelt, had been his most memorable personal encounter with a presidential candidate. The sheer joy he got from retelling that one was more than enough to justify having to listen to the familiar yarn again. John McCain just could not get enough of talking about New Hampshire.

With just a few moments remaining before he had to get off the phone and head into his next event, I asked McCain one final question: What would he say to those who argued that the first-in-the-nation primary was outdated—a once-vibrant institution whose utility has faded in a new era of national politics? Did he think that the calls to change the nominating system had at least some merit?

No, he did not. "There are certain traditions in American politics that kind of define the American process, and New Hampshire plays that unique role," McCain said, his tone remaining wistful. "Without New Hampshire, it would change dramatically the whole face of American politics, and I think money would play a much greater role. And I'm not sure that's good for American politics."

ACKNOWLEDGMENTS

I'D LIKE TO THANK my parents, Lynn and Jim Conroy, whose stories about working on Capitol Hill as twenty-somethings triggered my own early interest in politics. I'm also grateful to my wife, Jo Ling Kent, who read and reviewed an early draft of the manuscript.

My agent, Alice Martell, once again provided indispensable guidance every step of the way, and my editor, Clive Priddle, pushed me to do better. Peter Osnos first invited me into the PublicAffairs family, and Carl Cannon, Tom Bevan, Arianna Huffington, and Sam Stein allowed me the bandwidth that I needed to spend so much time in New Hampshire leading up to Primary Day. I also appreciate the encouragement that my sister, Erin Conroy, and my mother and father-in-law, Janice and David Kent, provided me.

In the course of my own reporting on three presidential cycles in New Hampshire, countless Granite Staters have shared generously with me their stories and observations about the primary and its history.

Among the people who were most generous with their time during the course of my research for this book were Arnie Arnesen, John Broderick, Ray Buckley, Steve Chaggaris, Mike Dennehy, Mike Dunbar, Steve Duprey, Susan Duprey, Secretary of State Bill Gardner, Senator Lindsey Graham, Karen Hicks, Joe Keefe, Rich Killion, Neil Levesque, Senator John McCain, Jeff McClean, Jim Merrill, Tom Rath, Peter Robio, Scott Royce, Bill Shaheen, Terry Shumaker, Kathy Sullivan, former Governor John H. Sununu, John Weaver, Jeff Woodburn, and Paul Young.

I'd also like to thank Irmela and Robert Fitzgerald, as well as Ellen and Ed Bernard, for inviting me to stay in their beautiful New Hampshire homes at various stages of the research and writing process.

BIBLIOGRAPHY

Barnicle, Mike. "A Q. & A. About N.H." *Boston Globe*, January 11, 1984. Accessed by full-text search, for pre-1997.

———. "Truly a State to Laugh At." *Boston Globe*, November 30, 1983. Accessed by full-text search, for pre-1997.

———. "Vermont vs. New Hampshire." *Boston Globe*, September 29, 1994. Available at http://boulter.com/nh/barnicle.html.

———. "What a Sap, What a State!" *Boston Globe*, January 21, 1996. Accessed by full-text search, for pre-1997.

Bernstein, Carl, and Bob Woodward. "FBI Finds Nixon Aides Sabotaged Democrats." *Washington Post*, October 10, 1972. Accessed November 3, 2014, at http://www.washingtonpost.com/wp-srv/national/longterm /watergate/articles/101072-1.htm.

Brereton, Charles. *First in the Nation: New Hampshire and the Premier Presidential Primary*. Portsmouth, NH: P. E. Randall, 1987.

Broder, David. "The Story That Still Nags at Me." *Washington Monthly*, February 1, 1987. Available at http://www.thefreelibrary.com/The+story +that+still+nags+at+me.-a04696993.

Eisele, Erik. "All (Presidential) Politics Is Local." *Conway Daily Sun*, December 23, 2015. Available at http://www.conwaydailysun.com/opinion /columns/123862-erik-eisele-all-presidential-politics-is-local.

"George H. W. Bush Wins 1980 Iowa Caucus." *The Today Show*, NBC News, January 22, 1980.

"Mysteries Remain in Du Pont's Wake." *Boston Globe*, February 21, 1988.

Nagourney, Adam. "Democrats Propose Moving Up Nevada in Presidential Caucuses." *New York Times*, July 22, 2006. Accessed January 3, 2015, at http://www.nytimes.com/2006/07/23/washington/23dems.html.

"New Hampshire Population, 2013." May 20, 2013. Accessed September 26, 2014, at https://www.google.com/?gws_rd=ssl#q=New+Hampshire +Population%2C+2013.

"NH Growth Slows as Population Ages." WMUR, June 13, 2012. Accessed September 26, 2014, at http://www.wmur.com/special-reports /NH-growth-slows-as-population-ages/14804392.

"NH Leads Country in Primary Voter Turnout." WMUR, August 24, 2016. Available at http://www.wmur.com/politics/nh-leads-country -in-primary-voter-turnout/40248802.

"Nine Months After 'Snowtober' Storm, Nashua Hospital Sees Baby Boom." *Nashua Telegraph*, August 2, 2012. Accessed September 26, 2014, at http://www.nashuatelegraph.com/mobile/mnews/969970-264 /nine-months-after-snowtober-storm-nashua-hospital.html.

Robidoux, Carol. "Candidates Will Sign Paperwork on N.H. Presidential Primary History." *Boston Globe*, June 18, 2015. Accessed June 19, 2015, at https://www.bostonglobe.com/news/politics/2015/06/18 /candidates-will-sign-run-presidential-primary-history/KxJolU167ggb OOZWKQXOmK/story.html.

Santora, Marc. "On the Road: McCain Steers the Bus." *The Caucus* (blog), *New York Times*, December 18, 2007. Accessed November 8, 2014, at http://thecaucus.blogs.nytimes.com/2007/12/18/on-the-road -mccain-steers-the-bus/?_r=0.

Scala, Dante J. *Stormy Weather: The New Hampshire Primary and Presidential Politics*. New York: Palgrave Macmillan, 2003.

Shirley, Craig. "Fast Times at Nashua High." *National Review Online*, October 19, 2009. Accessed March 3, 2015, at http://www.nationalreview .com/article/228434/fast-times-nashua-high-craig-shirley.

West, Paul. "Clinton Struggles to Regain Lead in N.H." *Baltimore Sun*, February 11, 1992. Accessed November 1, 2014, at http:// articles.baltimoresun.com/1992-02-11/news/1992042083_1_clinton -new-hampshire-electable-democrat.

INDEX

SCOTT CONROY is the co-creator and executive producer of "Embeds" on Verizon's Go90 platform. Previously, he worked with *Vice* to help launch its nightly news show on HBO. He is coauthor of *Sarah from Alaska* and created and directed *New Hampshire*—a seven-part *Huffington Post* original documentary series about life on the 2016 trail in the first-in-the-nation primary state. He was national political reporter for the *Huffington Post* and *RealClearPolitics* and a campaign embed reporter for CBS News.

PublicAffairs is a publishing house founded in 1997. It is a tribute to the standards, values, and flair of three persons who have served as mentors to countless reporters, writers, editors, and book people of all kinds, including me.

I. F. STONE, proprietor of *I. F. Stone's Weekly*, combined a commitment to the First Amendment with entrepreneurial zeal and reporting skill and became one of the great independent journalists in American history. At the age of eighty, Izzy published *The Trial of Socrates*, which was a national bestseller. He wrote the book after he taught himself ancient Greek.

BENJAMIN C. BRADLEE was for nearly thirty years the charismatic editorial leader of *The Washington Post*. It was Ben who gave the *Post* the range and courage to pursue such historic issues as Watergate. He supported his reporters with a tenacity that made them fearless and it is no accident that so many became authors of influential, best-selling books.

ROBERT L. BERNSTEIN, the chief executive of Random House for more than a quarter century, guided one of the nation's premier publishing houses. Bob was personally responsible for many books of political dissent and argument that challenged tyranny around the globe. He is also the founder and longtime chair of Human Rights Watch, one of the most respected human rights organizations in the world.

·   ·   ·

For fifty years, the banner of Public Affairs Press was carried by its owner Morris B. Schnapper, who published Gandhi, Nasser, Toynbee, Truman, and about 1,500 other authors. In 1983, Schnapper was described by *The Washington Post* as "a redoubtable gadfly." His legacy will endure in the books to come.

Peter Osnos, *Founder and Editor-at-Large*